Psycholinguistics

SECOND EDITION

Psycholinguistics

SECOND EDITION

DAN ISAAC SLOBIN
University of California, Berkeley

Scott, Foresman and Company

Glenview, Illinois   Dallas, Tex.   Oakland, N.J.
Palo Alto, Ca.   Tucker, Ga.   London

The first edition of this book was part of The Scott, Foresman Basic Psychological Concepts Series, Lyle E. Bourne, Jr., University of Colorado, Series Editor.

Library of Congress Cataloging in Publication Data

Slobin, Dan Isaac, 1939-
  Psycholinguistics.

  Includes bibliography and indexes.
  1. Psycholinguistics. I. Title.
BF455.S543 1979   401'.9   79-11436
ISBN 0-673-15140-9

  45678910-RRC-8584

Acknowledgments:

48–52 Excerpted from *Psychology and Language* by Herbert H. Clark and Eve V. Clark, © 1977 by Harcourt Brace Jovanovich, Inc. Reprinted by permission of the publisher.

52 From *Psychology and Language* by Herbert H. Clark and Eve V. Clark. Copyright 1977 by Harcourt Brace Jovanovich, Inc. Reprinted by permission of the publisher.

80 From *The Structure of Communication in Early Language Development* by P. M. Greenfield and J. H. Smith. Copyright 1976 by Academic Press, Inc. Reprinted by permission of the authors and the publisher.

89 From "Early Language Development: A Second Stage" by D. Parisi and F. Antinucci in *Problèmes Actuels en Psycholinguistique*. Copyright 1974 by Editions du Centre National de la Recherche Scientifique. Reprinted by permission.

116 From *On the Origins of Language: An Introduction to the Evolution of Human Speech* by P. Lieberman. Copyright 1975 by P. Lieberman. Reprinted by permission of Macmillan Publishing Co., Inc.

117 From *On the Origins of Language: An Introduction to the Evolution of Human Speech* by P. Lieberman. Copyright 1975 by P. Lieberman. Reprinted by permission of Macmillan Publishing Co., Inc.

119 From *The Cerebral Cortex of Man* by W. Penfield and T. Rasmussen. Copyright 1950 by Macmillan Publishing Co., Inc., renewed 1978 by T. Rasmussen. Reprinted by permission of Macmillan Publishing Co., Inc.

120 From "Motor Systems" by T. C. Ruch in *Handbook of Experimental Psychology,* edited by S. S. Stevens. Copyright 1951 by John Wiley & Sons, Inc. and Chapman & Hall, Ltd. Reprinted by permission.

127 Adapted from Figure 2-4 in *Psychology of Language* by D. S. Palermo. Copyright 1978 by Scott, Foresman & Co. Reprinted by permission.

137 From "Two-way Communication with an Infant Chimpanzee" by B. T. Gardner and R. A. Gardner in *Behavior of Nonhuman Primates,* edited by A. M. Schrier and F. Stollnitz. Copyright 1971 by Academic Press, Inc. Reprinted by permission of the authors and the publisher.

157–158 Jean-Paul Sarte, *Nausea,* translated by Lloyd Alexander. Copyright © 1964 by New Directions Publishing Corporation. Reprinted by permission of New Directions, Hamish Hamilton Ltd., and Editions Gallimard. All Rights Reserved.

168–169 From *Machine Age Maya: The Industrialization of a Guatemalan Community* by Manning Nash. Reprinted with permission of Macmillan Publishing Co., Inc. Copyright 1958 by The Free Press, a Corporation.

174–175, 180–181 From *Selected Writings of Edward Sapir in Language, Culture and Personality,* ed. D. G. Mandelbaum, pp. 157–159 and 162. Copyright 1949 by The Regents of the University of California. Reprinted by permission of the University of California Press.

183–185 From "The Function of Language Classifications in Behavior," by John B. Carroll and Joseph B. Casagrande in *Readings in Social Psychology, Third Edition,* edited by Eleanor E. Maccoby, Theodore M. Newcomb and Eugene L. Hartley. Copyright 1947, 1952, © 1958 by Holt, Rinehart and Winston, Inc. Reprinted by permission of Holt, Rinehart and Winston.

187 From "Burnt Norton" in *Four Quartets,* copyright, 1943, by T. S. Eliot; renewed, 1971, by Esme Valerie Eliot. Reprinted by permission of Harcourt Brace Jovanovich, Inc. and Faber and Faber Ltd.

PREFACE

Cratylus: Well, but surely, Hermogenes, you do not suppose that you can learn, or I can explain, any subject of importance all in a moment—at any rate, not such a subject as language, which is, perhaps, the very greatest of all.

—Plato,
Cratylus [c. 399–387 B.C.]
(1961, p. 462)

Not in a moment—and not in a long textbook—and certainly not in a short one. But language IS one of the greatest subjects. I wrote the Preface to the first edition of this book in May 1969—a little over nine years ago. What you have here is a thorough rewriting of that volume. The second edition is so different from the first because an increasingly large number of people have been devoting careful attention to many aspects of language. We have learned a lot in nine years. As a result, I have had to be very selective. In 1969 it was easy to weave a good story about psycholinguistics, because little had been done and much was promised. There was a dominant theory—transformational grammar—and a small number of devoted investigators. Now we have a multiplicity of theories and an overwhelming treasury of findings, produced by hundreds of researchers. The story is complex—both richer and more tentative than before. We know enough to have doubts of what we have learned. We also have techniques and man/womanpower to learn more than we have ever learned before. What I have tried to do in this second edition is to show you why, for some of us, this subject is "the very greatest of all"—because the study of language intersects with every aspect of the study of human thought, feeling, behavior, and development.

I have not been able to tell everything about psycholinguistics in this little book. Rather, I have followed the subfields which I know the best.

My colleagues will notice numerous lacks—most notable, perhaps, the omission of the area of the auditory-vocal system of language (phonetics, phonology, speech perception and production). The aim of the book, however, is to tell a story about the role of language in cognition, and to reflect the achievements of the child in decoding and constructing linguistic structures. I have tried to achieve this goal by focusing on the cognitive and semantic aspects of language, centered on the nature of grammar. Sociolinguistic colleagues will notice more about the pragmatics of language than in the first edition—but still less than they would desire. I have omitted a number of important grammatical models and experimental paradigms, because these details will change in the next few years, and I want the reader to have a GENERAL idea of what our endeavor is about. Longer textbooks and treatises, cited throughout the book, provide details for those who seek them. The chapters on linguistic universals (3 and 7) and biological foundations of language (5) are entirely new, and reflect important new developments in the field. We have begun to put human language into a universal framework—both in terms of the linguistic universals of the communication systems of our species, and in terms of the biological setting of our species-specific behavior.

Philosophically, there is an important difference between the stories of the first and second editions. In the first edition, fresh from the promises of the Harvard-M.I.T. breakthroughs in cognitive psychology and language of the early sixties, I promised that the study of language would yield insights into the nature of the human mind. I still believe this is true. But the second edition adds an answering voice from psychology: Psycholinguistic study of the mind promises to yield insights into the nature of human language. We psycholinguists are beginning to be able to pay back our debt to linguistics. What is emerging is a new field which studies language and cognition from many intersecting points of view. Hints of this new field can be perceived throughout this book.

There is an old tradition in Chinese scholarship that the writer of a treatise owes his readers an initial account of himself. This obligation was fulfilled in the form of an intellectual autobiography, serving as a preface to orient the reader to the sources of the viewpoint he was about to encounter. I would like to encourage the revival of this tradition in an age when we never cease encountering books by people we have never met.

My work in psycholinguistics reflects a lucky accident in my life: I spent the years of my graduate study, 1960–64, at the Center for Cognitive Studies at Harvard. There I was influenced by a remarkable group of teachers, whose work I am still attempting to unite in my own teaching and research. At that time, Noam Chomsky influenced us all with his new formulations of transformational grammar and its eventual psychological significance. George Miller took some of these ideas to the psychological laboratory, looking for reflections of grammar in memory and reaction time; and Roger Brown took them to nurseries and playrooms, listening for evidence that children were building grammars. The late Eric Lenneberg began the search for the biological underpinnings of the structured behavior which had captivated so many of us. And Jerome Bruner introduced us to Vygotsky and Piaget, putting our studies of language development in the appropriate broader settings of cognitive growth. The careful reader of this book will see that it is little more than an attempt to put together Chomsky, Miller, Brown, Lenneberg, and Bruner—and it is to them that I still owe my thanks. To them, and to the many students (some of them now colleagues) who have never stopped questioning, understanding, misunderstanding, and appreciating psycholinguistics. Teaching them, and learning with them, has made this second edition both necessary and possible.

As for my own work, I have been at Berkeley since 1964, gradually building a program of cross-linguistic study of language acquisition. This you will see reflected in Chapter 4. And this work also accounts for the proliferation of Turkish examples which you will find scattered throughout the book. I spent 1969–70 and 1972–73 in Turkey, learning Turkish and learning how small children learn Turkish. It is a rich and fascinating language and, as you will see, it provides me with contrasts to English and moves me towards thinking of linguistic universals.

Finally, some special thanks. This book has been made easier for you to read by some attentive and skillful pre-readers: Ayhan Aksu, Elizabeth Bates, Julie Gerhardt, Bambi Schieffelin, and Leah Shelleda. Discussions with many colleagues have enriched my understanding of psycholinguistics. In this book one can see most clearly the influences of Francesco Antinucci, Elizabeth Bates, Thomas Bever, Eve and Herbert Clark, Susan Ervin-Tripp, Judith Johnston, and Eleanor Rosch. James Romig, Executive Editor at Scott, Foresman, has treated me with more patience and generosity than a procrastinating professor deserves. Mimi Isler protected my writing time and kept fresh flowers on my desk. Julian White made it possible for me to work consistently on two keyboards. Nancy Rothenberg Tepperman typed the manuscript. My daughter, Heida, helped prepare the index. Marilyn Martin labored to transform the manuscript into a clear and consistent printed work. The James McKeen Cattell Fund gave me fellowship support during a 1977–78 sabbatical year, enabling me to complete writing of the book. And support through the years from the William T. Grant Foundation through the Institute of Human Learning, and NIMH through the Language-Behavior Research Laboratory, both at the University of California at Berkeley, has helped in more ways than I know—certainly in aiding the cross-linguistic perspective reflected in this book and in my own research.

As always, responsibilities for both the strengths and weaknesses of this book are mine.

Finally—a textbook author rarely gets to talk with his readers. So I invite you to send me questions and comments: Department of Psychology, University of California, Berkeley, CA 94720.

Dan Isaac Slobin
Berkeley, California
July 1978

CONTENTS

5 BIOLOGICAL FOUNDATIONS OF LANGUAGE 113

6 LANGUAGE AND COGNITION 143

7 RECAPITULATION: FORM AND FUNCTION IN LANGUAGE   *187*

to my linguistic informants:

> *my parents, Judith and Norval Slobin, who*
> *gave me both primary linguistic data and*
> *a love of language*

> *and*

> *my children, Heida and Shem, who fed that*
> *love as I listened to them construct*
> *English and Turkish*

I have tried to suggest that the study of language may very well, as was traditionally supposed, provide a remarkably favorable perspective for the study of human mental processes.

—Noam Chomsky
(1968, p. 84)

INTRODUCTION

This is a book about the human mind—the most accessible and the most inaccessible object of study. It is a book about language, which many have looked upon as "a window to the mind." For the past twenty-five years or so, investigators in the subfield of cognitive psychology called psycholinguistics have been trying to clean the panes of that window. The view is still dark, and the object may not be visible even when the window is clean, because the structures and processes which underlie language and thought are, by and large, unconscious. Perhaps a window is the wrong metaphor. The mind cannot be seen. It leaves its traces, like particles in a cloud chamber. There are many traces for the psycholinguist to ponder. We try to discern the workings of the mind from traces of speech, from the evanescent inner states which accompany speaking and understanding, from responses to speech, from the growth and malfunctioning of children and adults, from the nature of the human brain. In this book you will get a brief overview of what psycholinguists of the late '70s have learned about language behavior and its relation to mental events.

Psycholinguists are interested in the mental processes that are involved in using language and in learning to speak. In order to study these processes, one must bring together theoretical and empirical tools of both psychology and linguistics. The hybrid name for the field, PSYCHO-LINGUISTICS, thus reflects a truly interdisciplinary endeavor. Linguists are engaged in the formal description of an important segment of human knowledge—namely, the structure of language. This structure includes speech sounds and meanings, and the complex system of grammar, which relates sounds and meanings. Psychologists want to know how linguistic structures are acquired by children, and how they are used in the processes of speaking, understanding, and remembering.

In brief, then, psycholinguists are interested in the underlying knowledge and abilities which people must have in order to use language and to learn to use language in childhood. I say "UNDERLYING knowledge and abilities" because language, like all systems of human knowledge, can only be inferred from the careful study of overt behavior. We are concerned here with the overt behavior of speaking and understanding speech. Thus, the problem of the psycholinguist is the same as that of all social scientists who venture beyond description of behavior—namely, to postulate underlying structures and processes which may account for apparent orderliness in observed behavior.

It is important to grasp the distinction between overt behavior and underlying structure. In English and other languages, the distinction is expressed in the concepts of LANGUAGE and SPEECH: SPEECH has a corresponding verb form, whereas LANGUAGE does not. We say: "He speaks the English language." To speak is to produce meaningful sounds. These sounds have meaning because they are systematically related to something called "the English language." Speech is behavior. You can listen to speech; you can record it on magnetic tape. But you cannot tape-record the English language; you can only record English speech. Because we know the English language, we can understand each other's speech. The English language, then, is a body of knowledge represented in the brains of speakers of English. The description of such bodies of knowledge has been traditionally the province of linguistics, while psychology has traditionally defined itself as "the science of human behavior." It should become clear to you, however, that this border between disciplines cannot reasonably be drawn. We cannot study behavior without a theory of the structure of that behavior, and we cannot study the structure without being concerned with the behavior in which the structure is manifested.

What is the nature of verbal behavior? What are the central issues of psycholinguistics? The behavior of speaking goes from thoughts to words; the behavior of listening goes from words to thoughts. For the purposes of this brief book, we will not concern ourselves with the sounds of speech (PHONOLOGY), but rather with words and sentences (SYNTAX) and their meanings (SEMANTICS). To use the English language, you must know the GRAMMAR—that is, the phonology, syntax, and semantics of English. And you must know about the physical and social worlds in which English is spoken in order to carry on meaningful conversations. All this knowledge must be put to use, moment-to-moment, in the process of speaking and understanding. Knowledge is STORED in the brain. It does not come and go from moment to moment, the way spoken sentences do. Behavior is temporal—that is, it consists of a series of acts performed sequentially in time. A linguistic message must be processed in time. However, it must be related to some body of knowledge. Linguists and psychologists and anthropologists describe the knowledge structures that underlie messages: grammars, thought patterns, social conventions, and the like. These structures are ATEMPORAL. They are not realized in momentary time, but exist as enduring mental entities. The task of the psycholinguist is to construct models of processes that make moment-to-moment use of stored knowledge. That is to say, you must not only know the English language, but you must know how to use it. The relation between knowledge and use poses complex philosophical questions which have certainly not been resolved. Psycholinguistics represents an empirical attempt to characterize what one must know about language in order to use it.

Let us consider the problem of the relation between atemporal structures and temporal processes at the level of the individual sentence. Before you speak a sentence, you have some idea of what you are about to say, though you may not have translated the thought into a series of words. What is involved in going from thought to speech (or from thought to writing or to manual signing)? You must analyze and organize your thought into a time-ordered entity. This problem was long ago recognized by Wilhelm Wundt, who founded experimental psychology at Leipzig in Germany a little over a hundred years ago.

He characterized the sentence as "a transform of a simultaneous cognition into sequential structure." It was clear to Wundt (1912, pp. 242–43) that a sentence cannot be considered simply as a chain of words, because the words of a sentence are interrelated and represent a total mental configuration:

> When I construct a sentence, each individual idea does not spring into consciousness at the moment that I utter the appropriate word for that idea. . . . The sentence is not an image running with precision through consciousness, in which there is never more than a momentary word or sound, while what precedes and follows sinks away into nothingness. Rather, as long as it is being uttered, the sentence is present in consciousness as a whole entity. If this were not the case, we

would irretrievably lose the thread of speech. . . .

From a psychological point of view, the sentence is both a simultaneous and a sequential structure. It is simultaneous, because at each moment it is present to consciousness in its totality, even though individual subordinate elements may occasionally disappear. And it is sequential, because the conscious experience of the totality changes from moment to moment, as particular ideas move into and out of the focus of attention, one after another.[1]

Here we have a central problem for psycholinguists: the meaning of a sentence is not just a string of words, but an idea which gives birth to that string and determines its temporal sequence. This temporal sequence in itself does not give meaning to a sentence, but rather meaning comes from your knowledge of how rules of order are to be interpreted in your language. It is your knowledge of English which enables you to construct an image of a covered cat from the sentence *The mat is on the cat;* and only a knowledge of Turkish would allow you to arrive at the same image from the utterance *Kedinin üstünde halı var,* which, taken word for word, reads 'cat's on-top-of mat is'.[2] The image, or the idea, has no inherent order; the sentences do. The meanings of the sentences, however, come from a cognitive activity which involves both knowledge of word meanings and knowledge of particular linguistic conventions or rules—that is, the grammars of English and Turkish.

We will have much more to say about grammar as we go along. It should already be clear, however, that grammar is some sort of knowledge or set of mentally stored procedures, which make it possible for us to instill sequences of words with RELATIONAL meanings—both as speakers and listeners. Without relational meanings, we are left with just the mat and the cat. Knowing grammar, however, the relation of mat to cat in the above sentences is obvious. There are many kinds of grammars, but what they all have in common are rules for connecting sequences of separate meaningful elements with underlying, unified structures of relational meanings. Linguists and psycholinguists have made numerous attempts to characterize such rules.

Why is it necessary to speak of "rules," rather than simply listing the sentence patterns of a language, as we list the words in a dictionary? It is possible to learn the vocabulary of your language, but it is not possible to learn the sentences of your language. This is because knowledge of language is PRODUCTIVE. We are almost never called on to create new words, and most of the sentences we hear do not contain new words to be understood; but we are continually being called on to create and understand new sentences. This fact often comes as a surprise. Somehow it seems intuitively that the stock of sentences could not be so large. To convince yourself that the stock of possible sentences is, for all practical purposes, infinite, just try this exercise: take any book, read a sentence (say, this very sentence), and then see how far you have to read to find that sentence repeated again. Unless you have chosen a cliché, or a theme which is

1. For more detail on Wundt's ideas about language, and other aspects of the history of psycholinguistics, see Blumenthal (1970).
2. Linguistic examples are given in italics; meanings of examples are indicated by single quotes.

quoted again and again, I think you will find the job hopeless. Sentences are, by and large, novel events.

Noam Chomsky, who revolutionized linguistics in the late 1950s with his system of "transformational grammar," put this problem of productive knowledge at the center of attention (1964, p. 50):

> The central fact to which any significant linguistic theory must address itself is this: a mature speaker can produce a new sentence of his language on the appropriate occasion, and other speakers can understand it immediately, though it is equally new to them.

It is this fact that impels us to speak of the learning or formation of something which is psychologically equivalent to a system of RULES, whereby we can extend a limited amount of experience with a limited number of sentences and communicative situations to the capacity to produce and understand an unlimited number of linguistic messages. One of the central problems of psycholinguistics is to understand the nature and development of this capacity.

The use of the word RULE does not mean that psycholinguists believe people can state explicit rules of grammar, or that children learn such rules. None of us can state all the rules of English grammar; indeed, these rules have not yet all been explicitly worked out by even the most skillful linguists. The crucial (and perplexing) phrase in the paragraph above is "something which is PSYCHOLOGICALLY EQUIVALENT to a system of rules." As the Berkeley psycholinguist Susan Ervin-Tripp has put it: "To qualify as a native speaker . . . one must learn . . . rules . . . This is to say, of course, that one must learn to behave AS THOUGH ONE KNEW THE RULES" (my emphasis) (in Slobin, 1967, p. x). The problem of rules is discussed in greater detail in Chapter 4. The central point is that children learn much more than a list of specific word combinations. They acquire knowledge that makes it possible for them to go beyond the specific collection of sentences they have heard, speaking and comprehending an endless variety of new utterances.

Linguists, by and large, have provided STATIC models, or descriptions, of the structures of sentences and their underlying meanings. That is, a linguist provides an overall picture of a language system but does not explain how a language-user might use such a picture. We might compare the linguist to a geographer who provides us with detailed road maps of a terrain, but no instructions for their use. As psychologists we want to study how people use maps to plan and carry out trips. A linguistic model is a map of a language; a psycholinguistic model is a description of how maps are used. Such a model must take account of time, directionality, and purpose. Although Chomsky set the problem of productive knowledge in the center of psycholinguistic attention, grammarians do not seek to explain how static knowledge is used in ongoing processes of communication.

Psycholinguistic research has moved from early attempts to verify the existence of underlying grammatical structures to studies of how linguistic knowledge is used in the processes of speaking and understanding. To follow the map metaphor, early research attempted to show that people really know about distance, compass points, routes, and so on. Current research is more concerned with how people figure out how to take particular trips, under particular circumstances.

One cannot study the USE of maps without studying the FORM of maps as well, and it would be foolish to construct maps without knowing what they are used for. Because of the interdependence of the study of knowledge and use of knowledge, our concern in the following chapters will be to characterize both the simultaneous, or structural aspects of language, and the sequential, or behavioral aspects of language use. Both aspects of language—structure and use—are rule-governed, and a central problem is to relate structural rules and behavioral rules.

In order to understand this endeavor, it will be necessary to examine both the theoretical work of linguists (Chapter 1) and the experimental investigations of psychologists (Chapter 2), putting all of this work together in a functional view of language (Chapter 3). Furthermore, we will want to know how linguistic capacity develops in children (Chapter 4). Having established that systematic structures and processes underlie language use, and that linguistic capacity has a developmental history in the child, we will want to examine the extent to which this capacity is a biological endowment of our species (Chapter 5). In Chapter 6 we will be concerned with the ways in which language interacts with other aspects of cognition—thought, memory, and mental development. Finally, in Chapter 7, we will be in a position to show that considerations of the nature of mind and behavior can contribute to an understanding of human language itself, just as study of linguistic phenomena can cast light on the nature of mind and its development.

READING

Comprehensive and current reviews of psycholinguistics can be found in *Psychology and Language*, by Herbert and Eve Clark (1977), and *Psycholinguistics*, by Donald V. Foss and David T. Hakes (1978). A technical introduction from the viewpoint of transformational grammar is provided in *The Psychology of Language*, by Fodor, Bever, and Garrett (1974). Ongoing work is regularly summarized in *Language and Language Behavior Abstracts*, and psycholinguistics is periodically reviewed in the *Annual Review of Psychology*. Psycholinguistic research is reported most frequently in the following journals: *Child Development, Cognitive Psychology, Cognitive Science, Cognition, International Journal of Psycholinguistics, Journal of Child Language, Journal of Experimental Psychology, Journal of Psycholinguistic Research, Journal of Verbal Learning and Verbal Behavior, Language and Speech, Memory and Cognition, Monographs of the Society for Research in Child Development.*

1

Just as we induce a three-dimensional space underlying the two-dimensional pattern on the retina, so we must induce a syntactic structure underlying the linear string of sounds in a sentence. And just as the student of space perception must have a good understanding of projective geometry, so a student of psycholinguistics must have a good understanding of grammar.

—George A. Miller
(1962, p. 756)

THE LINGUISTIC STUDY OF GRAMMAR

WHAT IS GRAMMAR?

The study of grammar is something most people try to avoid after years of traumatic encounters with it in "grammar school" and in later schooling. Why should a psychologist care about such a dry and formalistic field? The kind of grammar that makes people shudder is PRESCRIPTIVE grammar—the rules of how educated people "ought to" speak and write. But there is another kind of grammar, a DESCRIPTIVE grammar, which attempts to describe the knowledge people must have in order to speak and understand language. It is this sort of grammar that has excited psychologists, because it promises to tell us something important about the nature of the human mind.

What sort of thing is this grammar? What does grammar do? One way to look at these questions is to take a collection of words and see some of the ways in which they can be arranged. Consider the following three strings of words:

(1) pie little blue mud make eye girl was
(2) the little pie with mud eyes was making a blue girl
(3) the little girl with blue eyes was making a mud pie

People would probably agree that the first string of words is not a sentence; this is one way of saying that it has no grammar. The second and third word strings are sentences, though one is extremely anomalous and the other is not. If you read these strings out loud and ask people to remember them, you will discover that they find (1) hardest to remember and (3) the easiest. It is interesting that people can remember the sentences, (2) and (3), better than the unstructured string, (1), even though the sentences have more words and parts of words (suffixes) than the unstructured string. What has been added to the collection of words to make it a grammatical entity?

The most obvious addition in strings (2) and (3), in comparison with (1), is order. Order not only makes the whole sequence more coherent, but it also gives other information: Order (in English) tells us about the subject-object relationship. For example, in (3) the sequence of *girl-making-mud pie* establishes who is doing what to what.

There is also the addition of "markers." There are two types of markers here: FUNCTION WORDS (*the, a, with*) and SUFFIXES (*-s, -ing*). The markers identify classes (for example, *the* identifies a noun), specify relations (*with* relates *girl* to *eyes*), signal meanings (*-ing* signals ongoing activity, *-s* signals plurality), and so on.

All of these things together—order and various forms of markers—make up grammar and convert a disconnected string of words into a sentence. Grammar lies between the speech sounds you hear or say and the meanings you connect with them. You can only make sense of the strings of words you hear if you "know" (in some unconscious sense) the grammar of your language. You can only communicate with another person if both of you have the same underlying knowledge of the language.

In the broadest terms, we can characterize grammar as THAT WHICH MUST BE KNOWN BEYOND INDIVIDUAL WORD MEANINGS IN ORDER TO INTERPRET A SENTENCE. Grammar encodes relational concepts which hold between words—concepts of agency, location, causality, temporal sequence, and the like. In *The mat is on the cat*, the preposition *on* encodes the nature of the spatial relationship between the two objects; the word order tells us which object is on which. This sentence is fairly straightforward— that is, much of the information seems to be present on the surface, in the individual words and their order. Deeper examination of sentences and their meanings, however, reveals that vast amounts of information must be added to what is apparently evident on the surface. Even with this simple sentence, a comparison with its Turkish equivalent, given in the Introduction, demonstrates that there is no obvious relation between the surface order of elements and the underlying meaning. In other words, you can't always tell the meaning from the order, because different languages order sentence elements in different ways. What you must know are the ordering conventions of the particular language.

There are further problems which go beyond word order alone, because sentences with similar word orders can have different meanings. Linguists are fond of finding such examples, which clearly reveal the existence of deeper levels of structure. For example, consider a pair of sentences which has become famous in linguistic and psycholinguistic literature:

(4) John is eager to please.
(5) John is easy to please.

These sentences seem to be identical, except for the third word. Yet you know that they are quite different: (4) means that it is John who pleases someone; (5) means that someone pleases John. The relationship between underlying ideas and elements of utterances is not a simple mapping of one to one.

WHAT IS GRAMMAR FOR?

What would language be like if all of meaning had to be made explicit? (4) would have to be expressed as something like:

(4') There is someone named John, and he is eager to do something which pleases someone else.

And (5) would become something like:

(5') There is someone named John, and it is easy for someone else to do something that pleases him.

It would obviously take a long time for us to express our ideas if we had to be this explicit. Grammar makes it possible to leave much of the meaning of a message implicit. Since speaker and listener share the grammar, the basic structural notions need not be communicated directly. They are part of the background knowledge of language users. The existence of implicit knowledge is an exciting and difficult problem for cognitive psychologists— a problem which is dramatically highlighted by linguistic analysis.

This theme is worth dwelling on. One of the main reasons human languages have complex grammars is that time constraints make it impossible to express everything explicitly in the give-and-take of ongoing communication. Communication relies on shared knowledge—knowledge of the language and also knowledge of the world. It is not always easy to pull these aspects of language apart.

Let us begin with an apparently simple sentence and examine its underlying complexity. In the next few pages, I will try to race with you through the thickets of linguistic analysis, showing you the extent to which full linguistic understanding requires many levels of analysis and many sorts of knowledge. Then, in the remainder of the chapter we will examine some of the ways in which linguists have tried to account for such elaborately complex knowledge.

To begin with, consider the apparently simple sentence:

(6) Heat the coffee.

We recognize this sentence as an imperative, though the agent (*you*) is not mentioned. For that matter, the speaker is also implicit, though we know that it must be *I*. And *I* am telling *you* to do something. At its very least, (6) means something like:

(6′) I, who am speaking, command you, whom I am addressing, to do something to make the coffee hot.

On the "surface" of the sentence we have a single word, *heat*, which is a sort of compressed summary of several meaning components. It has, within it, notions of causality and change of state. The word *heat* is a conventional English abbreviation for 'DO something to CAUSE the coffee to BECOME hot'. The elements in capital letters, DO, CAUSE, and BECOME, are abstract meaning elements, assumed to be present in all languages. In other English verbs, like *tighten*, a suffix, *-en*, encodes the causal part of the meaning, while the stem, *tight*, encodes the end state. In some languages, such causative particles are always required for any verb with a causal meaning. In English this is only occasionally true. But, in any case, the surface elements hardly spell out the whole underlying meaning.

In fact, this underlying portion of the meaning is even more complex than I have indicated thus far. A whole network of separate meaningful statements, or "propositions," implicitly underlies this and every other utterance. For example, sentence (6) works as an appropriate imperative utterance only if certain PRESUPPOSITIONS are met. The definite article, *the*, indicates that specific coffee is referred to, thus presupposing—that is, taking for granted—that the listener knows which coffee is to be heated. It is also presupposed that the coffee is not, at the time of utterance, as hot as coffee is normally preferred in our culture. In addition, the speaker presupposes that the listener is able to change the temperature of the coffee. At the very least, then, sentence (6) means something like:

(6″) I, who am speaking, command you, whom I am addressing, to do something which will cause the particular coffee, of which you are aware, and which is not at present in a state of appropriately high temperature for coffee, to become in that state.

Without the shortcuts made possible by grammar and shared world knowledge, it would be impossible to carry on human verbal interaction, given the short-term memory constraints, boredom, and impatience of our species.

In delving deeply into the meaning of *Heat the coffee*, we must consider several different layers of linguistic structure. In speaking broadly of grammar, up to this point, I have been introducing examples from two parts of grammar: syntax and semantics. These layers of language overlap and intersect, and much of recent work in linguistics has been devoted to clarifying both the interaction and the separateness of syntax and semantics. Roughly, syntax deals with the organization of words in sentences, and semantics deals with meanings. The rules of word order which allowed you to interpret *The mat is on the cat* are syntactic rules; the components of DO, and CAUSE, and BECOME, and STATE which underlie the meaning of *heat* are semantic. But the boundaries are not clear. Furthermore, semantics shades off into world knowledge when we speak of such notions as the proper temperature for coffee in our culture.

We need grammar—the sets of rules that relate ordered sound sequences to meanings—in order to communicate underlying propositions compactly and efficiently. But we must also communicate socially appropriate messages. *Heat the coffee* means more than the paraphrase offered in (6″). Utterances perform PRAGMATIC functions—that is to say, they not only convey semantic propositions, but they are used in interpersonal settings to fulfill various social functions. Up to this point, I have argued that language is complex because we do not have time to express underlying meanings in fully elaborated syntactic form. But language is many times more complex becuase we are not content to have a single form to communicate each underlying set of meaningful propositions. *Heat the coffee* is not only an imperative, but it is a certain kind of imperative, with its own shades of interpersonal meaning. A variety of surface constructions can communicate the meaning of (6″) while also communicating the attitude of speaker to listener:

(6a)   I wonder if you could heat the coffee.
(6b)   Can you heat the coffee?
(6c)   This coffee sure is cold!
(6d)   Don't you know I always expect you to heat the coffee?
(6e)   Cold again!

Notice that none of these is imperative in grammatical form, yet all of them communicate imperative intent. As English speakers we know that the following answers, although syntactically and semantically correct, are pragmatically inappropriate:

(6a′)   So do I.
(6b′)   Yes.
(6c′)   So it is.
(6d′)   Yes, I do.
(6e′)   Uh-huh.

Because we are able to use language appropriately in social interactions—as well as grammatically and meaningfully—our knowledge of language must also include pragmatic rules. Many types of knowledge interact in the use of language.

In addition to interpersonal nuances, there are other types of implications that sentences can have—beyond the meanings they express directly and the meanings they presuppose. Sentences can also have unexpressed implications. For example,

(7) The professor remembered to grade the papers

PRESUPPOSES (i.e., takes for granted) that grading papers is something the professor should do. At the same time, (7) also IMPLIES that the professor did, in fact, carry out this responsibility. Contrast (7) with the following sentence:

(8) The professor forgot to grade the papers.

The presupposition is the same: the professor is supposed to grade the papers. But note that the implication is in the opposite direction. The more we probe sentences, the more aspects of unexpressed meaning seem to surface.

The presuppositions and implications of (7) and (8) are implicit in the underlying meanings of the words *remember* and *forget*. However, consider:

(9) I wanted to read the book at the library but it wasn't open yesterday.

In reading this sentence you knew automatically that *it* refers to 'the library' and not 'the book'. To interpret *it* as a book that is opened and closed on official schedule would be GRAMMATICALLY correct but CULTURALLY implausible. World knowledge allows potentially ambiguous sentences such as (9) to pass without notice (except in the case of jokes), avoiding the fuller grammatical elaboration which would otherwise be necessary, as in:

(9′) I wanted to read the book at the library but the library wasn't open yesterday.

COMPETENCE AND PERFORMANCE

In every case we have considered thus far, it has been necessary to assume that the language user has implicit structural knowledge. It is the goal of linguistics to characterize such knowledge, or LINGUISTIC COMPETENCE, in explicit and formal terms. There are many current grammatical models, of which we will review only a few general types. Their importance to psychology is that they are the most detailed available models of a segment of human knowledge. However, a full PSYCHOlinguistic theory must also specify how such knowledge is put to use in LINGUISTIC PERFORMANCE. The relations between knowledge and action, or between competence and performance, still elude successful description. In actual communication, as we have seen, many types of knowledge interact—knowledge of phonology, syntax, semantics, pragmatics, social conventions, the physical world, personality, and so on. Furthermore, linguistic performance can be affected by a variety of noncognitive disturbing factors, such as fatigue, switching of attention, distractability, emotional excitement, drugs, and the like. Many linguists hope that these interacting systems can be separately described in their own terms. Linguistic descriptions contribute the main structural component to psycholinguistic theories. It is especially in descriptions of syntax and semantics that modern linguistics has had a significant impact on psychology. Therefore, we must look more closely at the kind of underlying knowledge we have of the structure of English, for it is just such knowledge which must be accounted for by psycholinguistic theory. (English-language examples are used here simply because we are English-speakers, but the general facts presented in this book undoubtedly hold for all human beings, regardless of the languages they speak.[1])

A psycholinguistic theory will have to account for the various things we language-users know implicitly about our language (competence) AND for the various ways we use this knowledge of language (performance). Each sort of linguistic theory, or model, has implications for the type of psychological theory into which such a model can be incorporated. One's view of the nature of the human being constrains one's conception of the nature of language.

LINGUISTIC THEORIES

How does a linguist do his or her work? The informal discussion of the last few pages gives you some idea of the endeavor. The linguist's main source of data is a particular kind of linguistic performance—namely, one's INTUITIONS about language. That is, the linguist or a native informant makes judgments about linguistic examples, relying on implicit knowledge of the language, and the results of such intuitive judgments are evaluated in relation to a particular theory. In considering the sentences offered as examples above, you have used various kinds of intuitions: (a) GRAMMATICALITY (in judging the acceptability of sentences 1–3), (b) ANOMALY (in rejecting sentence 2 as meaningless), (c) AMBIGUITY (in realizing the alternate meanings of sentence 9), (d) MEANING (in your ability to understand the examples), and (e) APPROPRIATENESS (in judging the social implications and possible responses to sentences 6a–e). Linguists try to account for such intuitions by building formal models—systems of rules in various notations, drawing on systems of mathematics, logic, and computer programming. The goal of such models is to systematize linguistic knowledge in a way which matches intuitions. For example, any adequate model would have to provide different structures for *John is eager to please* and *John is easy to please*, since we know that these two sentence types have different meanings.

A grammar is thus A THEORY OF A LANGUAGE. It is a theory which should be able to discriminate sentences from nonsentences, provide structural descriptions which relate meanings and sounds, account for the meanings of sentences and combinations of sentences, and so forth. The

1. For discussion of linguistic and psycholinguistic universals, see Bach and Harms (1968), Greenberg (1966, 1978), Slobin (1977), and the *Working Papers on Language Universals* published by the Language Universals Project, Department of Linguistics, Stanford University.

word "theory" is used here in the sense of any scientific theory. In your childhood you were able to figure out the underlying regularities of the language you heard spoken, and this knowledge enables you to produce and to interpret new utterances which conform to these regularities. You may not be able to explain what your theory is, but you can use it to reject some sentences and accept others, and to use language appropriately.

Over the past quarter century, linguistic theories have moved from surface to depth descriptions, beginning with sequences of words and becoming more and more concerned with underlying meanings and rules for the use of language in communicative settings. We will briefly review this movement from surface to depth and consider its implications for psychology.

One way to conceptualize the task is to look at the linguist's interest as an attempt to build a machine that can treat sentences in humanlike fashion. From this point of view, you could look on linguistic rules as instructions that you could give to a machine and see if the machine could in fact indicate if a sentence were grammatical, or if it were ambiguous, or if the machine could provide you with an interpretation or a likely verbal response, or even carry on a conversation. If you were interested in the production of language, you could program the machine to produce sentences according to your linguistic rules and determine if it could produce sentences which were grammatical or meaningful or appropriate in context—depending on the goals of your particular kind of linguistic theory. In other words, you would take the machine's performance as a criterion for deciding if you have properly modelled linguistic competence. The more you require the machine to act like a human being, the more psychological your linguistic model will become. If you want the machine to make only judgments of grammaticality, it can be programmed with less information than if you want it to carry on a conversation.

In fact, researchers in "artificial intelligence" have begun to carry out this task using computers, and we will consider their early products in the next chapter. But the main point of the example at this point is theoretical. If a machine can be programmed to perform in humanlike ways, it might be assumed that the rules underlying the machine's performance have some psychological equivalent in human beings. In writing computer programs, one must be completely precise and specific about every aspect of knowledge and processing involved in a task. Thus, writing programs is a way of making sure that one's rules are completely specified. In this way, the exercise of programming the machine serves to sharpen our notions of the sorts of knowledge people must have in order to demonstrate linguistic performance of the various sorts discussed above. If you think you have discovered what is involved, say, in analyzing and answering questions of a certain type, and on this basis you succeed in programming a computer to respond appropriately to such questions, then you can feel assured that your analysis has some practical reality. The success of a machine program based on a linguistic rule system would suggest that the knowledge of language reflected in that rule system is, in some sense, "psychologically real."

In considering the linguistic theories briefly outlined below, ask yourself what sorts of knowledge they assume the language user to possess. If a computer program were to be based on one of these theories, what sorts of linguistic tasks could the computer carry out? Or, in other words, if a given linguistic model were taken to be psychologically real, what sorts of linguistic performance would it make possible? In Chapter 2 we will review techniques developed by psychologists that greatly expand the data base beyond linguistic intuitions and judgments about sentences. First, however, we must find out what kinds of models have been proposed by linguists.

Chain Models

Nobody believes in chain models of language anymore, but it is useful to review this chapter in the history of psycholinguistics—both to gain some appreciation of the complexity of linguistic competence and to understand the close relationship between theory in psychology and in linguistics. Behaviorist, or stimulus-response (S-R) psychology held that the structures which underlie behavior consist of connections between stimuli and responses. The simplest way to account for sequential acts was to propose that each response becomes, in turn, a stimulus for the following response. This approach to psychology is explicitly noncognitive. That is, the organism has little inner structure and its actions are guided by external events. Behaviorists do not talk about "knowledge" and "mind," but about "actions" and "controlling stimuli." They see development as a process of environmental shaping, rather than a process in which the growing organism constructs inner structures on the basis of interaction with the environment. This approach is the opposite of that taken in this book, which expresses the structuralist, constructivist, and interactionist position of contemporary cognitive psychology. Let us see what language would have to be like to fit a behaviorist theory.

The model of grammar which has most appealed to traditional behaviorist psychology is a left-to-right probabilistic model, or "Markov process," in which the occurrence of each word is determined by the immediately preceding word or series of words. This model, of course, is consonant with a more general associative chain theory of behavior, in which each response serves as a stimulus for the next response. In 1951, the noted neuropsychologist Karl Lashley published an important paper entitled "The Problem of Serial Order in Behavior," in which he presented strong arguments against associative chain theories. It is noteworthy that he based much of his argument on linguistic evidence, anticipating later developments in linguistics. It was clear to him, as it had been to Wundt a half-century earlier, that the temporal sequence of words must be determined by an underlying structure of greater depth and generality than could be found in the series of verbal responses alone. Let us consider this significant argument from the point of view of psycholinguistics.

Lashley points out, first of all, that there is no intrinsic order to words in themselves. Depending on what is said, a given word can be followed by a variety of words. He gives as an example the word pronounced *rite*, which has four spellings, many meanings, and can serve as noun, adjective, adverb, and verb. He says (1951, p. 116):

> In such a sentence as "The mill-wright on my right thinks it right that some conventional rite should symbolize the right of every man to write as he pleases," word arrangement is obviously not due to any direct association of the word "right" itself with other words, but to meanings which are determined by some broader relations.

Lashley concludes that there must be an underlying intention to say something, a "determining tendency," and that a "schema of order" is responsible for the serial order of words in the resulting utterance. He finds evidence for these notions in slips of the tongue and errors in typewriting. The most frequent errors are those of anticipation—using a word or letter sooner than it is required in the flow of speech or typing. Thus there must be an underlying level at which elements larger than words are being readied for production. He speaks of syntax as "not inherent in the words employed or in the idea to be expressed," but rather as "a generalized pattern imposed upon the specific acts as they occur."

Further, he notes that word-to-word associations cannot account for the comprehension of speech any more than they can account for the production of speech. As an example, he offers the following sentence (which you should imagine as spoken rather than written): *Rapid righting with his uninjured hand saved from loss the contents of the capsized canoe.* When one is listening to this sentence, the meaning of *righting* is not determined until several seconds AFTER it has been heard. It is a frequent phenomenon in language that the selection or understanding of words early in a sentence is determined by words coming later in the sentence. This phenomenon seems to have no place in an associative chain model of language.

These are several of the incisive arguments offered by Lashley in his now classic paper. Several years later, Noam Chomsky began a revolution in linguistics, placing questions of structured knowledge in the center of linguistic attention. Lashley's discussion anticipates Chomsky's arguments against probabilistic models of grammar presented in 1957 in his pioneering book, *Syntactic Structures.* There Chomsky points out that the transitional probabilities between words in a string of words (i.e., the probability with which one word may follow another) have no relation to whether that string of words is a grammatical sentence. He offers the word string: *Colorless green ideas sleep furiously.* The transitional probabilities between these words are nil; that is, you have probably never heard sequences such as *colorless green, ideas sleep,* etc. Yet, most people would probably agree that this word string is a grammatical though bizarre sentence. On the other hand, if this sentence is read backwards (*Furiously sleep ideas green colorless*), it is no longer a sentence, though the transitional probabilities between the words remain insignificant.

What happens if we are careful to pick sequences of words which have a high probability of following one another? In the following string, the occurrence of each word is strongly determined by the preceding word: *Goes down here is not large feet are the happy days.* Clearly, there is no guarantee that a sentence will be generated if each word is picked on the basis of its probability of following the immediately preceding word. Thus, a probabilistic, left-to-right model is inadequate as a theory of grammar in that it fails to differentiate between sentences and nonsentences. The fact that a string of words is or is not a sentence is independent of the sequential probabilities between the words.

There is a deeper argument, however—and it is that a probabilistic, left-to-right model cannot possibly generate ALL the grammatical sentences of English, because we can embed sentences inside other sentences. Chomsky discussed this matter in *Syntactic Structures* (1957). He pointed out that there are several forms of English sentences into which other sentences can be inserted. Taking S as a symbol for "sentence," we have such constructions as:

(10) If S_1, then S_2.
(11) Either S_1 or S_2.
(12) The man who said that S is arriving today.

For example, take the sentence *The man who said S is here*, where S is another sentence. This sentence could be rewritten as: *The man who said Chomsky has very weak arguments is here.* In this example, the word *is* is dependent on *man*, which occurred much earlier. A Markov chain, in which each word is based on the immediately preceding word, cannot account for the transition between *arguments* and *is*, or for the fact that *is* is really related to *man.* Suppose we expanded the scope of our probabilistic chain, and allowed the choice of each successive word to be determined by the entire preceding chain, rather than just by the immediately preceding word. We would still have no basis for determining the occurrence of *is*, because this word is dependent on an element which appeared BEFORE the embedded sentence, and the probabilistic model has no way of recognizing this discontinuity. That is, it has no way of recognizing boundaries between phrases, clauses, or sentences.

The situation can get even more complicated—and not at all implausible—if we take the *if . . . then* construction and embed sentences within it. That is, an entire sentence can be placed between *if* and *then*: *IF the man who said that Chomsky has very weak arguments is here, THEN he should present his counterarguments. If* and *then* are discontinuous elements. They have a distinct linguistic connection, but the second element can only occur at a particular structural point in the sequence. This matter of discontinuous elements in sentences is a common grammatical device—probably used by all languages of the world. We find it not only in embedded sentences in English, but in *verb + particle* constructions (as in *she pickED the hat UP*), in various auxiliary constructions (as in *she IS walkING; she HAS walkED*), and elsewhere.

The general point is simply this: In language there are many cases in which the choice of an element is determined by an element which occurred much earlier in the sentence. Furthermore, the position of this element is determined by the structure of the sentence (e.g., *then* occurs after the completion of a clause; verbal particles like *up* appear after the direct object). Because of this overall structural dependency of elements within a sentence, it is not possible to explain sentence construction on the basis of a simple left-to-right model, in which each successive element is chosen on the basis of the immediately preceding element. It is necessary to REMEMBER what happened earlier in such sentences, and to keep track of these elements across gaps filled by intervening structures. This is Lashley's general argument about serial order in behavior, and why he introduced the notion of some underlying determining tendency. In our psycholinguistic framework, this underlying structure must include an adequate grammar of the language, reflected in procedures for identifying clause and sentence boundaries, and relating separate surface elements to common underlying structures.

There is another sort of argument against the attempt to account for the understanding of sentences simply on the basis of a knowledge of the ways in which words occur in sequence. This argument is based on the fact that words are grouped together STRUCTURALLY in sentences. For example, consider the sentence:

(13) They are visiting firemen.

This is an ambiguous sentence. It is ambiguous because you know something about its structure. What you know is that it really has two possible structures (in this case, two possible SURFACE structures). One way of indicating this is by bracketing the groups of words which go together as phrases:

(13a) (they) ([are] [visiting firemen])
(13b) (they) ([are visiting] [firemen])

In the first case, *visiting firemen* is a unit; in the second, *are visiting* is a unit. In terms of spelling or pronunciation, these sentences are alike. In terms of grammar and meaning, however, they are quite different. Your knowledge of the two possible grammatical structures tells you that they have two different meanings. This is part of what psycholinguists mean when they say that understanding a sentence is based on knowledge of its structure. One way of representing this structure is by means of bracketing, as in (13a) and (13b) above. Another way (much simplified here) is to draw a "tree" diagram. Note that the elements that are bracketed together branch from a common node: *visiting firemen* is a noun phrase in (13a); *are visiting* is a verb in (13b).

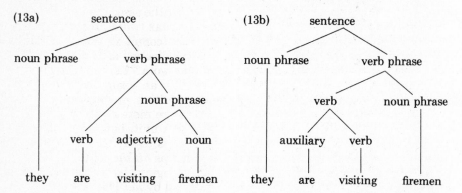

The tree diagram is a useful way of picturing sentences because it reveals that there is a hierarchy of LEVELS of structure within a sentence. Human languages are organized in hierarchies. There are many levels in language: from discourse, to sentence, to phrase, to subphrase, to word, to word part, to meaningless separate sounds, to distinctive features of sounds. Elements at each level are related to elements at other levels, and so it is impossible to speak of elements at any one level (say, words) as being determined in a serial chain. The position of an element at one level is determined by the simultaneous role it plays at other levels.

As we anticipated, therefore, chain theories are inadequate. They do not reveal the structure of language, and they do not adequately account for linguistic productivity. Any adequate linguistic model must be STRUC-TURAL, because a sentence is not just a sequence of words: it is a sequence of structures, of which words are parts.

Phrase Structure Grammar

At the very least, then, grammar must be organized in hierarchical levels. We can understand sentence (13) in two ways because it can be broken up into PHRASES in two different ways. It is the phrases which are bracketed differently in (13a) and (13b), and which are defined by the differing nodes of the two tree diagrams. Phrase structure grammars are familiar to you from your English courses. Such grammars "parse" sentences into constituent elements, called phrases. Most modern grammars structure sentences in terms of phrases. Where they differ is in terms of what else they consider to be important in addition to phrase structures.

What would our knowledge of language be like if the only thing we knew about sentences was that they could be parsed into constituent phrases? Phrase structure grammars allow for a degree of productivity, but they require only the relatively simple cognitive capacity of forming and arranging categories. In the history of psycholinguistics, such grammars were compatible with neobehaviorist theories which allowed for slightly more complexity than the simple behaviorist stimulus-response chains. According to such theories (e.g., Jenkins & Palermo, 1964), in addition to chains, higher order associations of elements are possible, mediated by common category membership. By grouping elements into categories, such theories allow for sequences of categories, as well as sequences of separate elements. But a phrase structure grammar and the associated psychological theories limit themselves to concerns with syntax (word arrangement) and morphology (word construction), thus ignoring complex issues of semantics (meaning) and pragmatics (social and communicative factors).

How does a phrase structure grammar work? Let us take a simple sentence which has been frequently used as an example (after Miller, 1962): *The boy hit the ball.* Your linguistic intuition, or whatever you want to call it, tells you that some pairs of words are more closely related than other pairs. *The ball,* for example, feels like a unit, but *hit the* does not. Another way to express this intuitive feeling is to say that *the ball* could easily be replaced by a single word—*it*—whereas *hit the* could not be easily replaced by another single word without changing the whole structure of the sentence. Likewise, *the boy* can be replaced by *he*. This is shown on the second line of the diagram. I think you will agree that *hit the ball* is a larger sort of unit, or constituent, which could be replaced by a more general word like *acted*, as you see on the bottom line of the box diagram.

The	boy	hit	the	ball
He		hit	it	
He		acted		

Linguists call this sort of process "constituent analysis." The segments of the sentences which can be treated as units are called its "constituents": *the ball* is a constituent, but *hit the* is not.

The procedure of constituent analysis is made more general by naming, or labelling, the different kinds of constituent units. For example, using this sentence again, *the* is an article (*T*) and *boy* is a noun (*N*); together they form a noun phrase (*NP*). *The ball* is thus also a noun phrase (*NP*). The verb *hit* is combined with this noun phrase to form a verb phrase (*VP*). At the highest level, the first noun phrase (*the boy*) combines with the verb phrase (*hit the ball*) to make a grammatical sentence. The names of the constituents can be introduced into the box diagram:

The	boy	hit	the	ball
T	*N*		*T*	*N*
		V	*NP*	
NP		*VP*		

Abstract structured patterns such as these underlie grammatical sentences. There are various ways of notating such structures—so far, you have seen bracketing, tree diagrams, and box diagrams. Another way to describe the constituent structure of a sentence is to use what is called a GENERATIVE GRAMMAR. This approach stems from ways of dealing with combinatorial systems in formal logic. The idea here is to start with a basic "axiom" (in our case, *S*, the symbol for "sentence") and apply rules of formation which allow for the rewriting of the axiom until a sentence is derived. The way to test the acceptability of the rules is to see if only grammatical sentences will be derived, or generated, in this way. Any sentence which cannot be derived from such rules will, on a formal basis, be considered ungrammatical. To make this concrete, let's see how a small segment of English grammar—that deals with the kind of sentence I've described above—might be expressed in this manner.

What you see below, greatly schematized and old-fashioned, is the essence of a phrase structure grammar. There is a set of symbols like those defined above (*T, N, V, NP, VP*), and a set of rules, such as $a \rightarrow b$, in which the arrow means "can be rewritten as."

Rules

1. S → NP + VP

2. NP → T + N

3. VP → V + NP

4. T → *the, a*

5. N → *boy, girl, ball*

6. V → *hit*

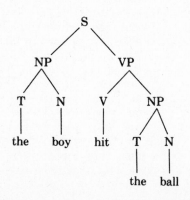

We start with the basic axiom, *S*. The rewriting rules 1-6 allow us to form the sentence *The boy hit the ball* in a sequence of steps. Beginning with Rule 1, *S* is rewritten as *NP* + *VP*. Rule 2 then allows *NP* to be rewritten as *T* + *N*; Rule 4 rewrites *T* as *the*; and Rule 5 rewrites *N* as *boy*. Since there is no rule available for rewriting *the boy* we must stop at this point: We have reached what is called a "terminal element." We go back to the next element which can be written: *VP*. Following Rule 3, this becomes *V* + *NP*. So at this point we have: *the boy* + *V* + *NP*. Rule 6 then allows us to rewrite *V* as *hit*, another terminal element. The only nonterminal element left now is *NP*, which, according to Rule 2 again, can be rewritten as *T* + *N*. Finally, using Rules 4 and 5 again, we can rewrite *T* + *N* as *the ball*, thus completing the possible application of rules in generating this sentence.

Note that we have two types of elements here. There are terminal elements (*the, a, boy, girl, ball, hit*), which means that there are no further rules for rewriting these elements. And there are nonterminal elements (*S, NP, VP, T, N, V*), which must be rewritten. We have formed a complete sentence when all of the elements are terminal.

Although this is a very simple example, it has that all-important attribute of productivity which is so central to human language. You can see that we could generate such other sentences as *the boy hit the girl, a girl hit a ball,* and so on.

A grammar of the sort I have just described—a phrase structure grammar—overcomes one of the chief weaknesses of the Markov process models: It can handle embedded sentences. Since the phrase structure trees are constructed from top to bottom, rather than from left to right, at any point in the tree we can insert the symbol *S* again, which means *sentence*. This allows us to work out an entire sentence and go on to rewrite other nonterminal symbols in the tree once the branchings under the embedded *S* have all ended in terminal symbols.

In formal terms, we can have rewrite rules of the following types:
$$S \rightarrow ab$$
$$S \rightarrow aSb$$
Thus, if *S* can be rewritten as *aSb*, we can rewrite further, since *S* is not a terminal symbol, and we can get structures such as *aabb*. This is a very powerful sort of rule system, because it can generate an infinite set of sentences. The rules can be applied again and again: they have the feature known in mathematics and linguistics as "recursiveness." A person who has learned this small, finite set of rules would have the capacity, in principle, to deal with an infinite set of outputs of these rules. Here we have formulated a most central psychological aspect of linguistic competence: the ability of a finite set of rules to generate an infinite set of sentences.

A phrase structure grammar can thus deal with matters beyond the scope of a Markov process, left-to-right model. It can deal with embedded sentences, and, as in the example of *They are visiting firemen*, it can deal with at least some ambiguous sentences by assigning different constituent structures to them. Such a grammar is also simpler from the point of view of the assumptions made about language development in childhood. In order to learn a grammar of the first type, a child would somehow have to compute the transitional probabilities between huge numbers of words. It has been estimated (Miller, Galanter, & Pribram, 1960) that human childhood is not long enough for such calculations to be carried out. In order to learn a phrase structure grammar, however, the child has to learn a vocabulary organized into classes (such as the traditional "parts of speech") and a set of rules for combining these categories into sentences. This is certainly far easier than learning all of the sequential probabilities of English words.

It should be clear to you, however, that you know much more about English than the hierarchical, constituent nature of sentences. You know about meaning and language use. A realization of some of the inadequacies of phrase structure grammar as a total model of language led to Chomsky's elaboration of transformational grammar, set forth in 1957 in his short but revolutionary book, *Syntactic Structures*. (If you are beginning to get the feeling that each linguistic model has weaknesses which the next model attempts to correct, you are right.)

Transformational Grammar

Transformational grammar is concerned not only with the surface arrangement of words, but with the abstract structures that underlie sentences. In demonstrating the presence of structures below the surface, Chomsky posed serious problems to psychological learning theory. If all of the linguistic structure is not evident in the surface forms of utterances, how do children acquire such structures? We will see in Chapter 4 that this problem has reintroduced issues of nativism (inborn knowledge) and rationalism into psychology, beginning a continuing debate with the traditional empiricism of American psychology. We will return to these issues, but first we must understand why it is necessary to postulate underlying structures.

Phrase structure grammar is based on rules of formation which rewrite symbols into other symbols, like the rule: $S \rightarrow NP + VP$. The additional level which Chomsky and his followers have developed is based on rules of transformation, which are rules for rearranging elements. For example, consider our familiar sentence and a corresponding question:

(14) The boy hit the ball.
(15) What did the boy hit?

These two sentences are obviously related, but phrase structure grammar does not reveal the relationship. How is the question (15) related to the declarative (14)? The question word *what* asks a question about the object of the verb *hit*. In (14) the object of that verb is *the ball*, and it follows the verb. In (15) there is no object, and the question word appears at the beginning of the sentence. Apparently, *the ball* and *what* play similar roles in relation to the verb in the two sentences. In transformational terms a question of this sort is formed by replacing the object noun phrase by an appropriate question word and moving that question word to the front of the sentence. Note that the type of element which is rearranged, a noun phrase, is an element revealed by the constituent analysis procedures of phrase structure grammar. Thus it is clear that we will need two types of rules and two levels of description in a transformational grammar of a language: phrase structure rules generating deep structures and transformational rules converting deep structures into surface structures.

At a deep level, *ball* in sentence (14) and *what* in (15) correspond to the same underlying notion: 'the thing that the boy hit'. This deep structure *NP* has different realizations in the surface structures of the two sentences.

Let us trace the sequence of steps taken thus far in transforming the declarative (14) into the question (15), omitting many fine details. (For simplification, I will act as if it is words which are being manipulated; actually, grammatical rules operate on abstract symbols, such as NOUN, NP, AUXILIARY, PAST, PLURAL, and the like.) We have carried out the following operations: *The boy hit the ball* ⟹ *The boy hit what* ⟹ *What the boy hit?* This last sentence does not yet correspond to (15) (although it is the sort of question form typically uttered by two-year-olds at a certain stage of language development). There is yet more transformational work to be done. Sentence (15) has an additional word *did*. Where did this word come from? Consider the following pair of sentences:

(16) The boy had hit the ball.
(17) What had the boy hit?

How does this pair of sentences differ from the former? The order of elements in the two questions, (15) and (17), is the same: question word—past tense auxiliary—noun phrase—verb. In the case of the latter pair, the past tense auxiliary (*had*) is also present in the affirmative sentence. In this case, therefore, the sequence of steps is: *The boy had hit the ball* ⟹ *The boy had hit what* ⟹ *What the boy had hit* ⟹ *What had the boy hit?* We have an extra step here—a step which apparently was not present in the first case. After moving the question word to the front, it was necessary to invert the subject and auxiliary: *the boy had* ⟹ *had the boy*. Formation of the question thus requires at least three transformational operations: (1) replacement of object noun phrase by *what*, (2) preposing of *what*, (3) transposing of subject and auxiliary.

Now back to the problem of that word *did*, which popped up in (15). Two paragraphs back we were left stranded with the childish *What the boy hit?* The next instruction is to transpose subject and auxiliary—but there is no auxiliary. In this case, therefore, we have to introduce an auxiliary, the "dummy" auxiliary *do*. This auxiliary is placed in its appropriate position before the subject, and it also takes on the past tense of the verb, resulting in sentence (15).

This may sound complicated, but it is, in fact, a great simplification of the actual transformational process. Note that we have accounted for the puzzling intrusion of *did* in the first question. Can you explain the presence of forms of *do* in other sentences related to sentence (14), such as the following?

(18) The boy didn't hit the ball.
(19) What didn't the boy hit?
(20) Did the boy hit the ball?
(21) Didn't the boy hit the ball?
(22) The boy DID hit the ball.

An explanation of these sentences (which we will not undertake here) reveals several important aspects of grammatical transformations: A transformation is an operation which converts one phrase structure into another. This is accomplished by such simple operations as SUBSTITUTION (*what* for *the ball*), DISPLACEMENT (preposing of *what*), PERMUTATION (of subject and auxiliary), and a few others. Such operations are linguistic universals, characteristic of all known human languages.

Another important aspect of transformational grammar is revealed in sentence (14). Although that sentence has no apparent auxiliary, it must have some abstract auxiliary in its underlying structure, since the auxiliary appears in the corresponding interrogative and negative sentences. Thus, as pointed out earlier, not everything we know about a sentence is revealed in the superficial string of words which are uttered aloud. This distinction between underlying and superficial linguistic structure, or "deep" and "surface" structure, is one of the major contributions of transformational grammar—both to linguistics and to psychology. Some additional examples may help clarify this important distinction.

An obvious example of the capacity to interpret sentences is your ability to discover the logical propositions underlying utterances: in simple terms, who is doing what to whom? The active sentence *Police club demonstrators* has the same meaning as its corresponding passive *Demonstrators are clubbed by police*. In each case you are able to discern who is subject and who is object of the verb, though the word order is changed. Within phrase structure grammar, however, there is no way to determine the fact that these two sentences, although differing in surface structure, have the same underlying meaning.

Phrase structure grammar is also inadequate when faced with sentences like:

(23) Visiting relatives can be a nuisance.

This sentence is ambiguous, but the ambiguity cannot be resolved on the surface. The sentence can be related to two other sentences, in which the ambiguous *can be* is realized in two different ways:

(23a) Visiting relatives are a nuisance.
(23b) Visiting relatives is a nuisance.

In sentences like (23), or similar examples (e.g., *The shooting of the hunters was terrible*), there is no basis for assigning two different immediate constituent analyses nor is there any word in the sentence which can be said to have two different meanings. Again, one must look to deep structural differences.

The difference between deep and surface structure is revealed in many other ways. As a final example, consider the sentence:

(24) Mary Sue was looking the word up.

There must be some way of indicating that *look up* is a unit—that these two words are part of the verb, though they do not occur contiguously in the surface structure, and that *was* and *-ing* likewise go together. It would take a tangled tree diagram to express these relationships!

There are many, many such examples. Linguists are very good at finding them, and their writings are full of clever and intriguing tidbits of this sort. But, most importantly, facts like these have led Chomsky to say (1968, p. 32):

It is clear, in short, that the surface structure is often misleading and uninformative and that our knowledge of language involves properties of a much more abstract nature, not indicated directly in the surface structure. Furthermore, even such artificially simple examples as these show how hopeless it would be to try to account for linguistic competence in terms of "habits," "dispositions," "knowing how," and other concepts associated with the study of behavior, as this study has been circumscribed, quite without warrant, in recent years.

The sort of linguistic competence referred to here is a system of rules which relates semantic interpretations of sentences to their acoustic phonetic representations. That is to say, syntax is a device which relates sounds and meanings. Such a model has important psychological implications. If the meanings of utterances are not directly expressed in the sounds we hear, then psychologists must develop a rich cognitive theory of the inner mental structures which make it possible to utter and comprehend sentences. This theory cannot deal with observable "stimuli" and "responses" alone, because all the information for the processing of speech is not present in observable behavior. And developmental psychologists cannot speak of language acquisition by children in terms of such variables as "imitation" and "reinforcement" alone; what the child learns is not a set of utterances, but a set of rules for processing utterances. (These issues are considered in greater detail in Chapter 4.)

Case Grammar

I have just said that the important contribution of transformational grammar to psychology was to point out that not everything we know about a sentence is revealed in the superficial string of words which are uttered aloud. Since the first formulation of transformational grammar, linguists have given more and more depth to this statement, expanding the catalog of implicit structure and meaning, as I pointed out at the beginning of the chapter. Transformational grammar itself has gone through a number of revisions (see, for example, Akmajian & Heny, 1975; Bresnan, 1978; Chomsky, 1965, 1970, 1972, 1977; Katz & Postal, 1964; Jackendoff, 1972). Furthermore, grammatical models have been extended to include more and more facts of meaning and communicative use of language.

One of the first attempts to accommodate additional dimensions of meaning within transformational grammar was Charles Fillmore's (1968) proposal of "case grammar." Fillmore pointed out that there are consistent meaning relations in the underlying structures of sentences which are not revealed by transformational grammar. To begin with, take the familiar example of active and passive sentences:

(25) Charles opened the case.
(26) The case was opened by Charles.

On the surface, *Charles* is subject of sentence (25) and object of the preposition *by* in (26). Following transformational grammar, *Charles* is the underlying subject in both sentences. *Case* is surface object of (25) and surface subject of (26), but deep object of both. So far so good. The same statements also apply to the following sentences:

(27) Charles opened the case with a key.
(28) The case was opened by Charles with a key.

Here we have added another word, *key*, which functions as the object of another preposition, *with*. But what of the following?

(29) The key opened the case.

Following linguistic intuitions, this sentence should be related to (27) and (28). But now there is no mention of *Charles* at all; *the key* has become both surface and deep subject. Furthermore, we can omit mention of both *Charles* and *the key*, saying:

(30) The case opened.

Here *case* has become surface and deep subject.

What do we have in deep structure? *Charles* and *key* and *case* can all be subject; *case* can be subject or object; *key* can be object of a preposition or subject. Following the linguist's practice of searching for general principles to account for intuitions, something seems to be missing in this description. Sentences (25–30) refer to the same situation and have a common underlying meaning. Fillmore argued that they should also have a common underlying syntactic structure. In order to make this possible, it was necessary to introduce some SEMANTIC notions into deep structure. Instead of talking about subjects and objects, which are purely syntactic terms, we can note certain underlying SEMANTIC ROLES in this collection of sentences. Fillmore called them "cases," using a traditional grammatical term. In the sentences above, *Charles* always performs the case role of AGENT; *key* is always INSTRUMENT; and *case* is always PATIENT. Fillmore (1968, p. 24) proposed a small set of such notions (including also EXPERIENCER, LOCATION, GOAL, and several others), suggesting:

> The case notions comprise a set of universal, presumably innate, concepts which identify certain types of judgments human beings are capable of making about the events that are going on around them, judgments about such matters as who did it, who it happened to, and what got changed.

If deep structure includes such case notions, special sorts of transformations are necessary to account for surface structures. Case grammar is organized around verbs and the cases which can occur with given verbs. For example, *open* can occur with PATIENT (e.g., *case, door*), and/or AGENT (e.g., *Charles, woman*), and/or INSTRUMENT (e.g., *key, crowbar*). Grammatical rules specify the ways in which underlying configurations of cases are expressed as surface sentences. If PATIENT is the only case role expressed on the surface, it will be the surface subject, as in (30). If PATIENT and INSTRUMENT are expressed, then PATIENT must become surface object, and INSTRUMENT surface subject, as in (29). If

AGENT is expressed, it is normally surface subject, as in (25) and (27); PATIENT is surface object; and INSTRUMENT is expressed as object of the preposition *with*. The passive sentences of (26) and (28) have the same underlying structures as their corresponding actives in (25) and (27), but with a difference in focus.

Case grammar excited the attention of psychologists, because notions like agent, patient, and instrument seem more "idea-like" than notions like noun phrase and verb phrase. By including general semantic categories in linguistic deep structures, one feels that the gap between thought and language has somehow been partially bridged. In child language studies, especially, case grammar was seized on as a means for describing what children might be intending to say in their first, primitive utterances. The complexities of syntax remain, but it may be possible to trace them back to the underlying mental configurations which concerned Wundt and Lashley.

Generative Semantics

Linguists in the late '60s and '70s continued their search into the intricacies below the surface structures of sentences. New scholarly camps arose, and the jousting between contending factions has made linguistics lively to its participants and confusing (and sometimes amusing) to its spectators. For the purposes of an introduction to psycholinguistics, we must avoid the arcane details and try to find general implications for an understanding of mental structures. Linguists agree that their descriptive systems are GENERATIVE—that is, they allow for the production and interpretation of novel sentences. But they disagree on what to take as basic and what to take as derived. To state the issue in highly oversimplified terms, transformational grammarians have taken syntax as central, while more recent schools of thought have put semantics in the foreground. You have already gotten a taste of this change in the discussion of case grammar. A number of linguistic models have attempted to generate sentences from more complex underlying semantic structures than those of case grammar. This approach, developed by George Lakoff, James McCawley, and others, has come to be known as "generative semantics." (For a readable and elementary introduction, see Parisi and Antinucci, 1976.) Because generative semantics breaks sentences down into underlying propositions and primitive meaning components, it has become a useful tool for cognitive psychologists and investigators of child language development. I will present a schematized overview, generalizing across several different but related approaches (Dowty, 1972; Lakoff, 1970; McCawley, 1971; Parisi & Antinucci, 1976).

Fillmore analyzed sentences into clusters of verbs with their related case categories. In terms of generative semantics, each verb and its associated nouns constitutes a PROPOSITION. For example, the proposition underlying

(25) Charles opened the case

would be represented by the verb *open* and the corresponding case categories of AGENT and PATIENT. We can go further and ask what kinds of propositions occur in human languages.

To carry out this task, generative semanticists often use a PREDICATE-ARGUMENT notation borrowed from logic. A predicate is a sort of verbal notion which has "arguments" associated with it, much as the relation of verb and case categories. Now, however, our interest will be in types of predicate-argument structures. The simplest predicate is one which takes only one argument. For example, we can express

(31) The case is open

as a one-place predicate, using PRED as an abbreviation for predicate and ARG for argument:

(31′)

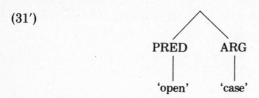

PRED ARG

'open' 'case'

This structure describes a simple, unchanging state of affairs. It is a STATIVE predicate with one argument, meaning something like 'the case is in a STATE of being open'. The elements at the bottom of the tree, 'open' and 'case', are given in single quotes to note that they are not English words (or words of any language), but meaning elements which will be realized as words on the surface after various English transformations have been applied. One appeal of this kind of analysis is that, at its deepest levels, it attempts to be free of the conventions of any particular language. The structure represented in (31′) (ignoring additional specifications as to tense, definiteness, etc.) could just as well be realized as *Der Kasten ist offen* in German, or *Kutu açık* in Turkish. Cognitive psychologists (e.g., Norman et al., 1975), computer scientists (e.g., Schank, 1972, 1973), and child language researchers (e.g., Antinucci & Parisi, 1973, 1975; Wells, 1974) have used such structures to represent thought patterns which underlie speech and comprehension.

What can one show with such structures? So far we have only stative predicates, like (31). States can change, as in (30), which I present here again as:

(32) The case opened.

Change of state can be represented by embedding one predicate-argument structure in another:

(32′)

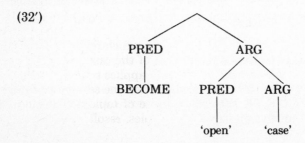

PRED ARG

BECOME PRED ARG

'open' 'case'

The "higher" predicate, BECOME, is given in capitals here. Following George Lakoff (1970), this is a "primitive verb"—a basic underlying semantic notion which is present in all sentences about changes of state. Literally, the structure in (32′) says something like: 'The case became open'. Or: 'Something came into being: namely, that a case was in a state of openness'.

Any change of state can be represented in these terms. For example, all of the following sentences about a change in color reflect the same underlying semantic structure:

(33a) The sky reddened.
(33b) The sky became red.
(33c) The sky turned red.
(33d) The sky turned to red.

(33′)

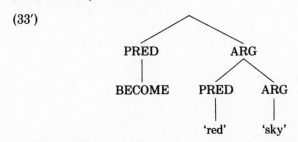

A change of state can also be CAUSED by an agent, as in (25) and (26), which can be reintroduced as:

(34a) Charles opened the case.
(34b) The case was opened by Charles.

Both of these sentences state that Charles DID something which CAUSED the case to BECOME open. Schematically:

(34′)

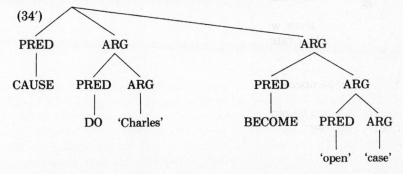

Here we have an even higher predicate, CAUSE, which relates two propositions: Charles' action and the change in state of the case.

The schematic underlying structure of (34′) applies to both the active and passive versions of (34), depending on whether one selects *Charles* as topic (34a) or *the case* as topic (34b). The choice of topic determines the application of particular English grammatical rules, resulting in an active or passive surface structure.

Just as transformational grammar revealed underlying SYNTACTIC elements not present on the surface (e.g., forms of the auxiliary *do*), generative semantics reveals underlying SEMANTIC elements, such as CAUSE, DO, and BECOME. Again, we are faced with the psychological problem of accounting for the origin and use of abstract knowledge that is required in order to use a system productively. You will remember the argument about sentences (4) and (5): *John is easy/eager to please.* These two sentences do not differ on the surface, but it can be argued that they have different underlying syntactic structures. A similar argument can be made about the following two sentences, which seem to have the same syntactic structures:

(35) Mary kissed John.
(36) Mary embarrassed John.

Both can be schematically described as:

(35–36′)

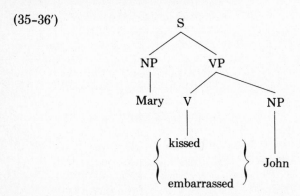

For both sentences, we know that *Mary* is the subject and *John* the object; in case terms, we know that *Mary* is AGENT and *John* PATIENT. But we also know that there is more to these sentences than these grammatical facts. We know that (35a) is not an acceptable paraphrase of (35), while (36a) is an acceptable paraphrase of (36):

(35a) What Mary did made John kissed.
(36a) What Mary did made John embarrassed.

This is because *kiss* does not imply a change of state; it is a simple action. What Mary does in (36), however, is bring about a change of state in John. (That is, more realistically, (35) does not tell us what effect Mary's kiss had on John, while (36), silent as to Mary's particular deed, tells us John's resultant state.) In generative semantic terms, these two apparently similar sentences have different underlying predicate-argument structures:

(35′)

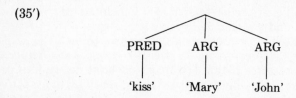

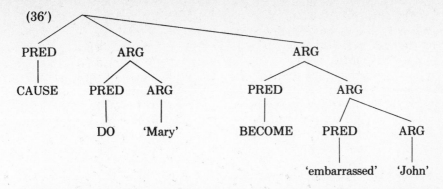

(36')

Here you see a fuller flowering of what I anticipated at the beginning of the chapter in discussing *Heat the coffee*. Grammar makes it possible to leave much of the meaning of a message implicit. In (36) the single word *embarrassed* encodes the underlying predicates CAUSE, DO, and BE-COME. On this level of underlying analysis, we are no longer dealing with the words of language, but with the ideas which get amalgamated into words in various fashions, depending on the particular language and the particular communicative focus of an utterance. As Wundt said, the cognition underlying a sentence is not a series of passing words, but a whole cognitive configuration.

I will not burden you with further rapid summaries of linguistic models. My aim has rather been to demonstrate the psychological issues posed by such models. Any current introductory linguistics text (e.g., Bolinger, 1975; Fromkin & Rodman, 1978; and as-yet-unpublished books) or introductory linguistics course will show you newer models and their attendant difficulties. All the deeper linguistic descriptions of the past twenty years—syntactic deep structures, case frames, generative semantic predicate-argument structures, and others—all these are partial and tentative attempts to map out part of the cognitive configurations underlying verbal behavior. Regardless of how one chooses to represent underlying form, it is always richer, more detailed than surface form. And this is the most important point to remember from this chapter—because my presentation of linguistic models has been almost inexcusably sketchy, and because all such models are superseded, revised, or replaced at an astonishingly rapid rate.

2

The most exciting idea in contemporary psychology is that it may at last be possible to begin to construct an experimental mentalism: a psychology which does justice to the richness and complexity of the mental processes that cause behavior but is nevertheless empirically disciplined in the ways a science ought to be.

—Jerry A. Fodor, Thomas G. Bever,
and Merrill F. Garrett
(1974, p. xi)

THE PSYCHOLINGUISTIC STUDY OF GRAMMAR

Psycholinguistic experiments have two sorts of goals: (1) to find evidence in language behavior for the sorts of STRUCTURES proposed in linguistic and psycholinguistic theory, and (2) to reveal the PROCESSES involved in the use of language. Stimulated by Chomsky's work, early psycholinguistic research in the 1960s attempted to take transformational grammar as a model of both structure and process.[1] In retrospect, much of this program was misguided, but the endeavor produced a refined collection of psycholinguistic research techniques and the beginnings of a theory of the use of language based as much on psychology as linguistics.

A basic concern of the early research was to find performance measures of linguistic complexity, as measured in terms of transformational rules. Some experiments demonstrated that sentences that are more complex linguistically take more time to understand; they tend to be simplified in memory; and so forth. It soon became evident, however, that linguistic complexity is only one of several interacting variables that affect ease of sentence processing. Sentences are also produced and responded to on the basis of such factors as meaningfulness, plausibility, appropriateness in context, and the like. Rule-counting has given way to the search for a wide range of factors that may influence language behavior.

Underlying the search for performance measures of complexity was the belief that transformational grammar may itself be a model of how people use language, although Chomsky repeatedly warned that he was not attempting to construct such a model. In general, experiments concerned with psychological reflections of linguistic structures have found behavioral evidence for many categories and levels of linguistic analysis, as proposed by various linguistic theories. Linguists, however, do not explain how structures are put to use in producing, perceiving, comprehending, and remembering speech. A major goal of psycholinguistic research has been to integrate structural descriptions into accounts of language processing. In this brief introductory book I will not bore you with the details of how psycholinguists have unsuccessfully tried to demonstrate in the experimental laboratory that one or another linguistic theory is THE "psychologically real" grammar which people carry in their heads. Rather, my concern will be to map out what little we know about the use of language on the basis of experimental research, showing you part of the considerable range of psycholinguistic research techniques.

HOW PSYCHOLINGUISTS STUDY GRAMMAR

Why do psychologists do experiments? One reason is to convince themselves, according to certain standards of evidence, that some mental or behavioral phenomenon is "really real." To the layman such research often seems like demonstrating the obvious—but the problem is that we cannot always be sure that the obvious is true. Psychological research is often most interesting—and most controversial—when it demonstrates something that goes against common sense.

The psycholinguist's relation to the linguist is rather like the psychologist's relation to the layman. Psycholinguists often take what is obvious to

1. For reviews of this phase of psycholinguistics see Cairns and Cairns (1976), Fodor, Bever, and Garrett (1974), and Slobin (1974).

the linguist and try to demonstrate it in a controlled setting. For example, they are not content to be told, on good linguistic evidence, that passive sentences are more complex than actives, or that certain sentences have given underlying presuppositions or implications. They want to see traces of linguistic entities for themselves, as in a cloud chamber in which one can measure reaction times, learning curves, memory errors, autonomic nervous system responses, and the like. This stance might be called "ideological," or perhaps "temperamental." Psychologists generally don't want to believe "obvious things" until they can make them happen themselves in their own laboratories and subject them to the standards of evidence they have come to accept. Maybe this reflects psychologists' needs for manipulation and control; or maybe psychologists have to "learn by doing"; or maybe psychologists only accept facts presented in a certain framework of terminology and methodology; or maybe (as many of them would like to believe), psychologists have "higher" or "more valid" criteria for truth. Often the scientific ideology of psychology has blinded its practitioners to important issues and important sources of evidence. Perhaps much of the research in psycholinguistics serves merely to "soothe the scientific conscience," as Chomsky has put it (1964, p. 81). Certainly the laboratory is a limited and artificial place to study behavior as rich and as social as language, and interest is growing in the systematic study of cognition in natural settings. But I will leave it to you to interpret and assess our needs and motives, and the value of our experimental results. At any rate, you may find some of the experiments engaging in their own right—and maybe that's why we spend our time doing them.

In addition to verifying models in the laboratory (whether they be derived from common sense, grammatical theory, or psychological theorizing), psychological experimentation is also aimed at bringing to light what is not obvious because it cannot be seen without laboratory techniques. We can introspect on language and thought, and we can build linguistic and psycholinguistic models on the basis of introspective evidence, but we cannot introspect on the lightning-fast processes of speech perception, or the subtle losses and alterations in memory over time, or the moment-by-moment processes involved in speaking. Nor is it obvious to the mind, or the theory-builder, how a large number of variables will interact—in real time, in real people of various types, in settings of various sorts. For purposes of more accurate DESCRIPTION of language behavior, it is necessary to study it in carefully controlled situations. Much of psycholinguistic research is not aimed at confirming or disconfirming theories but at providing more detailed descriptions of behavior, descriptions which must then figure in any theoretical work, both linguistic and psychological. However, the line between description and explanation is not easy to draw.

How can one systematically tap the processes underlying language use? One can record speech in various settings, studying the structure of natural communication. Many insights can be gained from naturalistic data; indeed, for some questions of child language and sociolinguistics, such data provide the main source of information. For more systematic study, one can control the setting in which speech or comprehension occurs. The most controlled setting is the psychological laboratory, where one can elicit speech and other responses to specific verbal or nonverbal stimuli. A weakness of laboratory control is the artificiality of the communicative setting, but only under laboratory conditions can one measure response time to speech and monitor ongoing nonlinguistic processes, such as pupil dilation, galvanic skin response, simultaneous perception of linguistic and nonlinguistic stimuli, and the like. In addition to studying ongoing verbal processes, one can study memory for written or spoken input, checking either RECOGNITION or RECALL of specific materials. One of the encouraging results of the large body of recent psycholinguistic research literature is the convergence of basic findings using a number of different methods. The availability of a variety of measures of psycholinguistic processes and structures makes theoretical models more susceptible to experimental support or disconfirmation, and some linguists are beginning to call on psycholinguistic evidence in the construction and justification of their theories. In the next chapter I discuss ways in which psycholinguistic findings may account for universal aspects of linguistic structure. But first I want to briefly review several main areas of psycholinguistic research, sampling from the experimental literature of the past ten years or so.

The greater part of this literature deals with the reception and storage of speech. There are three overlapping problems to consider: (1) PERCEPTION: What happens to sentences while you are listening to them? (2) COMPREHENSION: How do you determine what a sentence means? (3) MEMORY: How do you store the information you receive through speech? Researchers have paid more attention to the listener than the speaker for a simple reason: it is easier to control linguistic input and measure perception, comprehension, and memory than it is to systematically elicit speech from subjects. In the case of speech production, the initial stimulus is the speaker's INTENTION to say something, and intentions can only be indirectly manipulated. In reception, on the other hand, the initial stimulus can easily be brought under experimental control. However, to the extent that we have been able to study production, there is evidence for similar psycholinguistic structures in both the production and reception of speech. (See Clark & Clark, 1977, pp. 223–94; Fodor, Bever, & Garrett, 1974, pp. 373–434; Garrett, 1975; Osgood, 1971; Osgood & Bock, 1977. A volume on research and theory in sentence production has been edited by Rosenberg, 1977.)

What is the listener's task? He must rapidly convert a flowing sequence of sounds into an interpretable message. Most of the experimental evidence suggests that the listener carries out an ongoing clause-by-clause analysis of speech input, dropping exact wording from memory almost as soon as meaning is retrieved. What remains in the listener's memory is something like a set of underlying propositions, along with some idea of what effect the speaker intended to produce by the transmission of those propositions. At every step the listener is actively CONSTRUCTING an internal representation of the input, from the phonological level to the level of meaningful elements to the level of combination of meaningful elements resulting in interpretation of the message. Psycholinguists are interested in every step of the process and have proposed various models to account for the achievements of the listener. Let us consider research on what goes on while a person is listening to speech, and what remains in memory after the individual has analyzed and understood linguistic messages. First, we will concern ourselves with the rapid analysis of speech into linguistic units during ongoing perception. We will then ask how the listener, having segmented the input, succeeds in understanding its content. And then we will ask what remains of the linguistic message in longer-term storage, after short-term, ongoing processing has run its course. Thus, we will examine two major phases of psycholinguistic activity: ONGOING SPEECH PROCESSING (segmentation and comprehension) and REMEMBERING LINGUISTIC MESSAGES. Finally, having reviewed experimental work on processing and memory, we will consider problems of the nature of grammar from a psycholinguistic point of view.

SEGMENTATION OF SPEECH INPUT

Reception

When you listen to speech in your own language, it seems evident that there are strings of separate sounds that clump into words and sequences of words that clump into phrases and sentences. Yet, when you listen to speech in a language which you do not know, it seems like an undivided stream of sounds. The mappings between sounds and meanings are complex and indirect. There is nothing in the acoustic signal *per se* which reveals the existence of separate speech sounds and separate words, just as there is nothing in the string of words *per se* which reveals the underlying combinatorial meanings of sentences. Stored knowledge is necessary for segmentation of utterances and for interpretation of speech. Comprehension cannot take place unless speaker and listener know the same language. First, we will consider some of the ways the listener uses linguistic knowledge to identify speech sounds, and then we will consider ways in which sequences of sounds are perceived as meaningful messages. At every level of processing, from the acoustic to the semantic, the listener is involved in the construction of meaningful units from meaningless sounds. The single important point of this entire discussion is that SPEECH COMPREHENSION IS AN ACTIVE, KNOWLEDGE-GUIDED PROCESS.

Phonological Perception

Let us begin at the level of the word. Imagine you have a strip of tape-recorded speech that you want to cut into words. (Of course, you will have to know the language in order to do this.) What will these taped segments sound like? Pollock and Pickett (1964) carried out such an experiment. They played back single words cut out of a tape-recorded conversation and asked listeners to identify the words. Surprisingly, people were able to make correct identifications only about half of the time. Yet all of the words were quite intelligible if listeners were allowed to hear longer stretches of recorded discourse. This finding reinforces some of George Miller's pioneering work on speech perception. In 1951, Miller, Heise, and Lichten asked people to identify speech which was masked by white noise (a sort of hissing sound). In some cases people heard isolated words, while in other cases they heard sentences. It was far easier to identify words in sentences than separate words. Apparently we do more than process acoustic signals in listening. We try to make sense of what we hear, and this attempt actually modifies acoustic perception.

Warren and Warren (1970) have demonstrated that listeners even imagine sounds they have not heard, if such sounds are plausible in context. They had people listen to sentences in which one sound of a word was removed and replaced by a cough, as indicated by an asterisk in the sentence below:

It was found that the *eel was on the axle.

Listeners heard the segment **eel* as *wheel,* and were unable to tell just where the cough had occurred. Yet if the same sentence ended with *orange,* instead of *axle,* **eel* was heard as *peel.* Note that it is not until the end of the sentence that the sound masked by the cough can be guessed at, yet listeners imagine they have heard it accurately. Speech perception does not proceed bit by bit but is an integrative process, as discussed by Lashley.

But surely individual speech sounds must have a clear acoustic basis. Yet this apparently obvious claim is not supported by experimental evidence. Suppose you snip out a segment of tape-recorded speech containing the sound *pee* and, further, cut out just the consonant. Now splice this *p* onto a segment of tape with the vowel *a,* as in *papa.* You should hear *pa,* but it sounds clearly like *ka*! It turns out that the way we pronounce *p* is influenced by the following vowel. The noise we hear as *p* preceding a high vowel like *ee* is heard as *k* when preceding a low vowel like *a.* Sounds do not exist in isolation, because the tongue and lips and teeth are constantly moving from one sound to another, and so each sound is influenced by the entire syllable in which it occurs, just as the meaning of each word is influenced by the entire sentence in which it occurs. One cannot interpret speech on one level without simultaneous knowledge of other levels.

I will not attempt to summarize the wondrously complex psychological phenomena involved in the construction of meaningful units from meaningless sounds. Suffice it to say that there is no simple and direct mapping from acoustic entities onto linguistic entities. (For more detailed introductory discussion, see Clark & Clark, 1977, pp. 175-221; Fodor, Bever, & Garrett, 1974, pp. 297-313.) For the remainder of the discussion of speech reception, we will assume that the listener is able to segment the flow of speech into words and meaningful parts of words ("morphemes").

Ongoing Constituent Analysis

Effects of Constituent Boundaries on Sentence Processing   A basic assumption of linguistics, as noted in Chapter 1, is that sentences are not merely strings of words, but STRUCTURED strings of words consisting of hierarchies of units. This notion of constituent structure of sentences was first brought into the psychological laboratory by Fodor, Bever, and Garrett at M.I.T. (Fodor & Bever, 1965; Garrett, Bever, & Fodor, 1966). These researchers devised a technique for revealing the presence of phrase boundaries in the perception of sentences. The technique is based on the Gestalt assumption that a perceptual unit tends "to preserve its integrity by resisting interruptions" (Fodor & Bever, 1965, p. 415). In the experiment of Fodor and Bever, subjects listened to a sentence during which a click occurred; immediately afterward, they were required to write down the sentence and indicate where they heard the click. If a phrase is a perceptual unit, subjects should tend to hear a click which occurred during a phrase as having occurred between phrases.

One of the sentences was: *That he was happy was evident from the way he smiled.* This sentence has a major constituent break between *happy* and *was*. A click was placed at various positions in this sentence, as indicated by the asterisks below:

(1) That he was happy was evident from the way he smiled.
       * * * * * * ** *

Each subject heard the sentence with only one click in it.

Fodor and Bever found that subjects were most accurate in locating the click which occurred between the two major phrases of the sentence—that is, between *happy* and *was* in the above example. Clicks occurring before this break tended to be displaced towards the right (i.e., into the break), and those occurring after the break towards the left (i.e., again into the break). Fodor and Bever conclude that their findings "appear to demonstrate that the major syntactic break plays an important role in determining the subjective location of noises perceived during speech," thus supporting the hypothesis that "the unit of speech perception corresponds to the constituent." In most of this research, the relevant constituent phrase is the CLAUSE, that is, a phrase which corresponds to an underlying proposition.

One might call these results into question on the suspicion that the major syntactic break is signalled by some acoustic means, such as pause. In additional research, however, Garrett, Bever, and Fodor (1966) demonstrated that there are no clear acoustic cues which mark the breaks between clauses. The most dramatic evidence of this surprising fact comes from an experiment comparing pairs of sentences such as:

(2) As a result of their invention's *influence the company was given an award.*
                                             *   *
(3) The chairman whose methods still *influence the company was given an award.*
                                                   *   *

When subjects were asked where they hear the longest pause in these sentences, they report—as one might expect—that they hear a pause in (2) between *influence* and *the*, and in (3) between *company* and *was*. The perceived pause thus corresponds to the major constituent boundaries in the two sentences.

The ingenious part of the experiment comes next. The two sentences were recorded on tape, and the identical recording was used for the two italicized segments (i.e., the last portions of both sentences). SUBJECTS' PERCEPTION OF PAUSE LOCATION, HOWEVER, WAS UNCHANGED. The same is true of click displacement. As indicated by asterisks in the two sentences above, a click occurred either during *company* or *was*. The perception of click location, however, was significantly different for the two sentences. The click in sentence (2) tended to be heard between *influence* and *the*, and in (3) between *company* and *was*. But remember: the sentences were acoustically identical! Thus it seems that a listener perceives a sentence on the basis of his analysis of its constituent structure, and not because of a special acoustic cue to segmentation.

This finding is extremely significant, and is reflected again and again in studies of speech perception (see Liberman et al., 1967). It seems that the hearer assigns a perceptual structure to speech sounds on the basis of knowing the rules of language. Once again we see the perceiver as an active interpreter of the acoustic speech signals that are received.

The click technique has been widely used and also debated (see Carroll & Bever, 1976; Olson & Clark, 1976). In general, the findings suggest that errors in click location cluster at key points in the internal analysis of speech, especially between clauses. People seem to make some preliminary decisions about the structure of a sentence while they are listening to it. If a click occurs before the listeners have completed an ongoing structural analysis of a sub-part of the sentence, they apparently postpone hearing the click until they have completed this part of the analysis. The underlying assumption is that click and sentence perception compete for temporally limited processing space, and that only one thing can be attended to at a time. Further, it is assumed that units of speech analysis directly affect attention to clicks occurring during speech perception. Thus, these studies support both (1) linguistic analyses of sentences into constituent phrases, and (2) psycholinguistic theories of ongoing speech processing.

Other types of studies have also demonstrated an ongoing analysis of speech into linguistic phrases. Abrams and Bever (1969) had subjects press a key when they heard a click in a sentence. They found that reaction time to clicks occurring just before clause boundaries was slower than reaction time to clicks occurring just after clause boundaries. This indicates that the listener completes his perceptual integration of a clause before attending to a click occurring during the end of that clause.

Apparently some points in the speech flow require more concentrated attention than others. These points reflect decisions about linguistic structure. Another technique, the "phoneme-monitoring task" developed by Foss (1969), supports this picture. In this task the subjects are instructed to press a button as soon as they hear a word which starts with a given sound. If processing is difficult at a certain point in a sentence, there should be a delay in responding to a target sound occurring at that point. For example, Hakes (1972) asked listeners to push a button as soon as they heard a word starting with d in two versions of the following sentence:

(4) Everyone who was at the party saw (that) Ann's date had made a complete fool of himself.

In one version, the complementizer *that* was deleted (indicated by parentheses above). Note that in this version the d occurs in what could be interpreted as the final word of a clause and a sentence:

(4a) Everyone who was at the party saw Ann's date . . .

Response time in monitoring d was longer in such versions, suggesting that the listeners are trying to close off clauses and sentences as they go along. In version (4a) the d occurs at a point of heavy processing load. In the full version, with *that*, it is clear that more will follow after the word *date*. The d in this version occurs at a point demanding less linguistic processing, and therefore it can be responded to more quickly. Again, we have a picture of moment-to-moment fluctuations in the degree of processing of speech, based on linguistic features of the input sentence.

The phoneme-monitoring technique can even pick up momentary problems listeners have in dealing with difficult or unusual words. Foss (1969) compared response times to a target sound occurring after words differing in familiarity or frequency of occurrence. For example, listeners were asked to respond to *b* in the following sentences:

(5) The traveling bassoon player found himself without funds in a strange town.
(6) The itinerant bassoon player found himself without funds in a strange town.

Response time to the first sound of *bassoon* was slower in sentence (6), since *itinerant* is a more unusual word than *traveling*. It is clear that phonological, lexical, and syntactic processing all proceed simultaneously during the course of speech perception.

It is also clear that some semantic processing is carried out at the same time—indeed, before an entire sentence has been perceived. In another study, Foss (1970) had listeners monitor for sounds in ambiguous and unambiguous sentences. For example, subjects were asked to monitor *b* in:

(7) The merchant put his straw beside the machine.
(8) The merchant put his hay beside the machine.

It took longer to respond to *beside* in (7) than in (8), suggesting that the listener is trying to interpret the meaning of the sentence as it passes, exerting some additional mental effort on encountering an ambiguous word like *straw*. A large body of research on ambiguous sentences supports this point (Clark & Clark, 1977, pp. 80-84).

In sum, the click location and phoneme monitoring experiments show that listeners are actively processing speech as it passes, attempting to determine constituent boundaries and possible interpretations before a sentence has reached its end.

Effects of Constituent Boundaries on Immediate Memory   Up to this point I have described listeners as people who are actively segmenting speech into clauses as it passes. They use syntactic and semantic cues to anticipate the end of a clause, and exert special mental effort to "wrap up" each clause as it comes to an end. What happens to each clause after the work of short-term memory has been completed—that is, after its structure and meaning have been determined? Psycholinguistic research suggests that once a clause has been decoded, its exact wording becomes less and less accessible to memory. For example, Caplan (1972) studied the ability of listeners to recognize whether or not a given word had been heard in a preceding sentence. The subject would hear sentences such as (9) and (10), in which the second line was an identical recording, spliced onto two different initial portions.

(9) When the sun warms the earth after the
    rain clouds soon disappear.
(10) When a high-pressure front approaches
    rain clouds soon disappear.

It was probably easier for you to read (10) than (9). This is because the two lines of (10) correspond to two linguistic clauses, while the word *rain* is really part of the first clause in (9). (This "mini-experiment" you have just performed is, in itself, further evidence that one tries to break linguistic input into clauses.) Caplan's subjects heard the word *rain* immediately after listening to (9) or (10), and had to push a key indicating whether or not that word had occurred in the sentence. Since *rain* is part of the last clause in (10) and is part of the first clause in (9), response time should be slower in recognizing that *rain* had occurred in (9) than in (10). This is what Caplan found. In both cases the word is the identical distance from the end of the sentence, and there are no intonation differences, since the acoustic speech segment is identical. The difference in memory accessibility of the word must result from the fact that listeners have little need for storing exact wording once a clause has been decoded.

There is further evidence that listeners begin "purging" memory of verbatim content after a SENTENCE has concluded. In the above example, Caplan showed that it takes more time to RECOGNIZE a word from the next-to-last clause of a sentence than from the last clause. Jarvella (1971) has found that verbatim RECALL is also sharply reduced for clauses occurring earlier than the immediately processed sentence. These studies, taken together, show both (1) that clauses and sentences are psychologically real linguistic entities, and (2) that they also play a role in psycholinguistic processes. Jarvella's subjects listened to a long discourse and, from time to time, were stopped and asked to write down verbatim as much as they could remember of the material just preceding the interruption. The interruption always came after a series of three clauses in which the middle clause formed a sentence with either the first or the last clause, such as:

(11) The document also blamed him for   [20%]
     having failed to disprove the charges.   [21%]
     Taylor was later fired by the President.   [84%]

(12) The tone of the document was threatening.   [12%]
     Having failed to disprove the charges,   [54%]
     Taylor was later fired by the President.   [86%]

If people retain verbatim content in immediate memory until they conclude the analysis of a sentence, the middle clause should be recalled better in (12) than in (11). The numbers in square brackets after each clause represent percentage of correct, verbatim recall. For both (11) and (12), the last clause is well recalled, while only one out of five subjects or less can retrieve the exact wording of the first clause. It is the middle clause which reveals an important difference between the two items. In (12), where the middle clause is part of the sentence which has just been processed, it is recalled verbatim more than twice as often as in (11), where it belongs to the previous sentence. But even in (12), as in Caplan's study, the next-to-last clause is less accessible (54 percent) than is the final clause (86 percent). Jarvella's study thus shows that memory drops somewhat after clause boundaries, and even more after sentence boundaries. It appears that both clauses and sentences function as psychologically real units in the segmentation of speech. As we will see later in more detail, exact wording is needed only during the momentary analysis and decoding of speech. Verbatim memory disappears rapidly sentence by sentence (unless the wording of a particular sentence is particularly striking or noteworthy).

This conclusion fits in well with the approach to language taken in Chapter 1. Surface forms reflect underlying meaning, but meaning actually resides in structures which are more abstract than the word-by-word sequences which we hear. Analysis into clauses and sentences serves as a momentary bridge between sound and meaning. Once the underlying meaning has been retrieved, the surface form is no longer necessary and can be cast off from memory.

Later we will return to the question of what happens to form and meaning in memory. For now it is important to remember that both the perception and the memory experiments show that clauses and sentences play a key role in the ongoing segmentation of speech into interpretable underlying structures. Let us look at the process of interpretation in more detail. It is not enough to segment speech. What strategies does a listener use to arrive at UNDERSTANDING of linguistic messages?

SPEECH COMPREHENSION

What cues does the listener use to construct constituents and determine their meanings? Grammars do not describe ongoing processing, although it is clear that grammatical units, such as clause, sentence, and others, are involved in such processing. The fields of computer science and information processing have contributed to psycholinguistic attempts to describe some of the strategies listeners may use in decoding speech. The basic assumption is that the listener has a set of "heuristics" or "operating principles" that he or she uses to construct the best guess of what an utterance means while listening to it. The strategies represent one's knowledge of how sentences are constructed and what sorts of things people are likely to talk about in one's speech community.

Sentence Processing Strategies: A Simple Example

One way to conceptualize the nature of such strategies is to imagine a very simple language and determine what one would need to know in order to process such a language. Rather than construct an artificial example, we can draw upon an actual one. Simple languages, called PIDGINS, grow up in situations where there is minimal but essential contact between two groups speaking different native languages. Such languages have been created repeatedly as master-servant relationships in colonial settings, as trade languages between disparate groups, and so forth. My favorite example of such a language is Russenorsk.[2] As you can guess from its name, it is based on Russian and Norwegian. This was a trade language used in the Arctic Ocean during the brief summer thaw periods when Norwegian fishermen traded fish for Russian agricultural products in the centuries before the

2. Information on Russenorsk can be found in Broch (1927a, 1927b, 1930), and Neumann (1965). For readings on pidgin and creole languages, see DeCamp and Hancock (1974) and Hymes (1971).

1917 Russian revolution. Here we have a language with a minimal grammar and vocabulary, used for a limited range of functions. The simple grammar which developed in this language clearly reveals the minimum core of devices a language must have in order to be processible. The language could not function simply by using unordered sequences of words in context. There must be a grammar, and it must provide the listener with cues for sentence interpretation. In order to understand Russenorsk, it is necessary to know something about WORD ORDER and about GRAMMATICAL MARKERS. These are the basic guides to meaning found in all languages, and these factors will figure in the discussion of strategies for processing English which follows.

The simplest sort of sentence is a noun with a verb, or two nouns with a verb, such as the Russenorsk equivalents of:

(13) Captain drink.
(14) Drink tea.
(15) Sailor hit captain.

Sentence (15) would be ambiguous without a simple order rule, which says that a sequence of noun-verb-noun is to be interpreted as subject-verb-object. (13) and (14) reflect parts of this structure: subject-verb and verb-object. So even for this basic language to function, a word order rule is necessary.

In order to apply the word order rule, however, one must be able to identify nouns and verbs. One cannot determine part of speech from sentence position: for example, the verb is the first word in (14) but the medial word in (13) and (15). Word meaning can often reveal which word is noun and which is verb, but some words can be ambiguous, like the English *drink* and *hit*, which can be either noun or verb. As if to guide the listener in identifying the verb, Russenorsk evolved a suffix, *-om*, which served no other function than to indicate that the suffixed word was a verb:

(13′) Captain drink-*om*.
(14′) Drink-*om* tea.
(15′) Sailor hit-*om* captain.

From the point of view of the listener, so far, we have to call several sorts of sentence processing strategies into play. One is a conceptually or semantically based strategy for identifying nouns. Somewhat inadequately, we can phrase it as:

(A) A word which refers to a person, place, thing, conceptual entity, etc., is a noun.

There is probably a similar semantic strategy for identifying verbs, but it is reinforced by a morphological strategy:

(B) A word which ends in *-om* is a verb.

Notice that it is necessary to make reference to linguistic part-of-speech categories in order to make sentence processing strategies work. This is because these categories play a role in the syntactic strategies which are needed to interpret combinations of words. The first syntactic strategy we have encountered is a basic word order strategy:

(C) The noun preceding a verb is the agent, and the noun following the verb is the patient of the action referred to by the verb.

These strategies are not enough, however, because some relations hold between sequences of two nouns in which no verb is involved, as in:

(16) Captain ship.

Without additional grammar, it is not clear whether (16) should be interpreted as a possessive relation ('captain's ship'), or a locative relation ('captain on ship'), or a goal relation ('captain to ship'), and so forth. In Russenorsk, (16) would be interpreted as a possessive, thus requiring another word order strategy:

(D) In a sequence of two nouns, the first noun is the possessor and the second is the thing possessed.

To distinguish possessive noun-noun relations from other types, Russenorsk used another kind of grammatical marker, the function word *po*, which functioned as a generalized preposition which could be interpreted as locational, directional, dative, and so forth, on the basis of the plausible semantic combination of the two nouns. For example, *captain* PO *ship* would be interpreted as 'the captain is *on* the ship', but *captain* PO *cabin* would mean 'the captain is *in* the cabin'. Here are some actual examples from Russenorsk (Broch, 1927), with content words translated into English. (In fact, the content words were drawn from both Russian and Norwegian.)

Little money PO *pocket.* 'Not much money *in* the pocket'.
Master PO *boat?* 'Is the master *on* the boat?'
What you business PO *this day?* 'What are you doing on this day [=today]?'
Po you wife? 'Is there *by* you a wife?' [Do you have a wife?]
Steer PO *shore.* 'Steer *to* shore'.
Speak PO *master.* 'Speak *to* the master'.
How-many day PO *sea you?* 'How many days were you *at* sea?'
How-much weight flour PO *one weight halibut?* 'What quantity of flour *in exchange for* what quantity of halibut?'

It is clear from these examples that *po* does not have a specific meaning; rather, from the point of view of sentence processing, it functions as a perceptual cue that the relation between two nouns is not a possessive one. A strategy for interpreting *po* might be something like:

(E) Interpret a sequence of noun-*po*-noun as any semantically and contextually plausible combination, excluding possession.

Finally, we need a few rules for determining the function of a sentence:

(F) A sequence of words with a rising intonation is a question which can be answered 'yes' or 'no'.

(G) A sequence of words beginning with a question word ('what', 'when', 'how many', etc.) is an informational question.

(H) A sequence of words ending with a falling intonation is a declaration.

This schematic overview of Russenorsk shows that in order for a language to function, at the very minimum, it needs word-order rules, one general verbal marker, one general preposition, some question words, and some means of indicating yes-no questions, informational questions, and statements. For Russenorsk it has been possible to speak of "grammatical rules" and "sentence processing strategies" interchangeably. Presumably *-om* and *po* and the ordering rules are there to enable the listener to arrive at the underlying meanings of word combination. We have been dealing only at the level of surface structure, and in every language, surface structure markers—prefixes, suffixes, grammatical particles, orderings, intonation contours—serve to guide the listener to the proper initial analysis of incoming speech. By contrast, the grammatical rules which describe UNDERLYING structures and their relations to the surface are more complex and may not play a direct role in the description of sentence processing strategies. But every language requires surface analysis as the first stage of reception, and some psycholinguists and computer scientists have tried to specify surface analysis in sufficient detail to make simple speech comprehension possible. And, indeed, it is already possible to program computers with sufficient processing strategies—both syntactic and semantic—to carry on simple conversations between man and machine (Winograd, 1972, 1973).

English Sentence Processing Strategies

Strategies for English comprehension are like the eight strategies I have suggested for Russenorsk but, of course, more detailed and more complex. Noun-noun combinations in English are more differentiated, signalled by possessive inflections (-'s), a wide range of prepositions (*in, at, to, by, from,* etc.), and noun-compounding rules. But the basic idea of attending to word order regularities and grammatical functors (inflections, prepositions, suffixes, etc.) is the same in English and Russenorsk, and all languages. The complexity of processing a full-fledged language comes from the wide range of linguistic structures that are used, especially those which involve putting several clauses together in one sentence (as in the sentences presented above from psycholinguistic experiments). Correct placement of clause boundaries is obviously an important factor in the comprehension of multi-clause sentences. Let us first consider strategies for identifying clause boundaries in English, and then go on to strategies for determining the underlying semantic and pragmatic meanings of sentences.

Identification of Constituent Boundaries   We have already determined that constituent boundaries play an important role in the perceptual segmentation of speech. But how can the listener tell where such boundaries occur, or are about to occur? Several preliminary attempts have been made to describe the cues which listeners may use in identifying clauses in English.

Bever (1970; Carroll & Bever, 1976) has proposed that something like Strategy C, which we considered in the Russenorsk example, plays an important role in English perception. The basic idea is that the listener assumes that an initial sequence of noun and verb will be subject and verb of the same clause, and that a following noun will be object of that clause. Following this strategy, sentences like (17) and (18) will be difficult to understand.

(17) The man sold the painting admired it.
(18) The bomb rolled past the tent exploded.

In (17) the initial sequence of noun-verb-noun is perceived as a full subject-verb-object sentence, and the remaining verb and noun force a reanalysis (*The man who was sold the painting admired it*). Similarly, in (18) *The bomb rolled past the tent* is heard as a full sentence.

Chapin, Smith, and Abrahamson (1972, pp. 171–72) have proposed a general strategy for the imposition of linguistic boundaries. They suggest that the listener is always trying to complete each level of ongoing analysis as quickly and simply as possible. In their words:

> In imposing an initial structural description on a sentence, the *S* [subject in the experiment] attempts at each successive point to close off a constituent of the highest possible level [i.e., in a hierarchical structure]. Thus, if a string of words CAN be a noun phrase, the *S* assumes that it IS a noun phrase and that the next element heard will be part of some subsequent constituent.

They consider a pair of difficult sentences studied by Bever (1970):

(19) The editor authors the newspapers hired liked laughed.
(20) The editor the authors the newspapers hired liked laughed.

Such doubly self-embedded sentences are rare and difficult to interpret; but, like the use of perceptual illusions in the study of visual processes, they reveal something about normal speech processing. It is almost impossible for subjects to interpret (19), because they tend to interpret *authors* as a verb, thus leading them to end the sentence after *newspapers*. In (20), however, the sequence *the authors* makes it clear that *authors* cannot be a verb, making it somewhat easier to interpret this sentence. Chapin et al. (p. 172) try to explain the relative difficulty of (19) as a particular instance of their general strategy:

> *The editor authors the newspapers* is a potential sentence of English, and a sentence is the highest possible level of constituency. Thus our

hypothesis correctly predicts that subjects will tend to establish a sentence boundary at the end of that portion of sentence [19].

What makes sentence (20) easier than (19)? The article, *the*, makes it clear that *the authors* is a noun, thus blocking the noun-verb-noun strategy which leads you astray in (19). The use of an article to indicate a noun is similar to the Russenorsk -*om* to indicate a verb. Languages use a variety of devices to cue the part of speech membership of words—prefixes, suffixes, grammatical particles, and so forth. Such markers are essential to the operation of sentence processing strategies. These markers will play a role in other strategies, which must work in concert with the word order strategy we have just reviewed.

Let us examine a few of the specific strategies which have been developed to account for the decoding of English sentences. For example, Clark and Clark (1977, p. 59), following Kimball (1973) have proposed a general strategy:

> Whenever you find a function word, begin a new constituent larger than one word.

Function words are such things as articles, prepositions, conjunctions, pronouns, and quantifiers. Interpretation of sentence (20) is facilitated by a specific instance of this general strategy, which Clark and Clark (p. 59) phrase as:

> Whenever you find a determiner (*a, an, the*) or quantifier (*some, all, many, two, six,* etc.), begin a new noun phrase.

Applying this strategy to sentence (20), we arrive at an initial sequence of two noun phrases (*the editor the authors*), thus blocking application of the noun-verb-noun strategy.

Other strategies, of course, must be called into play to deal with sentences of this sort. Sentence (20) would be easier to understand if a relative pronoun were added to indicate the beginning of a new clause:

> (20′) The editor *that* the authors *that* the newspapers hired liked laughed.

Just as an article marks the beginning of a noun phrase, a relative pronoun marks the beginning of a clause. Clark and Clark present this as another specific instance of their general function word strategy (p. 59):

> Whenever you find a relative pronoun (*that, which, who, whom*), begin a new clause.

This strategy has been investigated at length in many psycholinguistic experiments.

In the first experiment in this series, Fodor and Garrett (1967) asked participants to paraphrase (that is, give the meaning of) complex sentences, measuring the amount of time taken to solve the problem and the accuracy of the solution. To take a simple example, compare the following two sentences:

(21) The man the dog bit died.
(22) The man whom the dog bit died.

The sentences are synonymous and both are grammatical. The relative pronoun, *whom*, which appears in (22) can be optionally deleted to produce sentences like (21). The relative pronoun provides a surface clue to underlying relations—namely, that the noun preceding the pronoun, *man*, is the underlying object of a relationship in which the following noun, *dog*, is the underlying subject. Fodor and Garrett hypothesized that the relative pronoun should make sentences like (22) perceptually less complex than sentences like (21), "because the relative pronoun provides a surface structure clue to semantically crucial deep structure relationships." To test this hypothesis, they presented participants with complex sentences with relative pronouns ("full") or with deletion of relative pronouns ("reduced"). The following were some of their sentences, with the deletable pronouns given in parentheses:

(23a) The pen (which) the author (whom) the editor liked used was new.

(23b) The tiger (which) the lion (that) the gorilla chased killed was ferocious.

(23c) The man (whom) the girl (that) my friend married knew died.

Participants performed better on the full sentences than on their reduced versions. That is, they responded more quickly, and more accurately grasped the subject-object relations among the noun phrases of the sentences when the relative pronouns were present. This was true if sentences were read with flat intonation or with appropriate prosody, or if they were presented in writing, or if the full sentences were made longer than the reduced sentences by the addition of two adjectives, or even if the reduced sentences were slowed down by splicing in a bit of blank tape in the position of the deleted relative pronoun. In short, it is much easier for people to figure out the meaning of such a sentence if they have relative pronouns to guide them. These words serve as cues to more clearly identify the constituents of the sentence.

The greater relative difficulty of reduced sentences has also been demonstrated by Hakes and Cairns (1970) using the phoneme monitoring technique. For example, in sentences like (23b), it takes longer to detect the *g* of *gorilla* in the reduced version than if the relative pronoun *that* is present to cue the listener that a new clause has begun. Thus we have two psycholinguistic performance indices pointing to the greater complexity of reduced over full sentences of this type. What might account for these findings?

Fodor and Garrett (1967, p. 290) propose a processing strategy which relies on relative pronouns not only for parsing, but also for interpreting word sequences with noun phrases (NPs) and relative pronouns (rel):

Given the sequence NP_1 rel NP_2 assume the NPs are related to each other as object and subject respectively of the same verb.

For example, consider sentence (22) again:

(22) The man whom the dog bit died.

According to this strategy, as soon as you hear *The man whom the dog . . .*, you expect that a subsequent verb will relate dog to man as subject to object. The relative pronoun plays a central part in this strategy because it is a clue to the underlying relation. But what about the verb? There is more to understanding a sentence than identifying its constituents. Cues like articles and relative pronouns help the listener segment sentences. But he is also attending to meanings. Verbs play an important role in the assignment of meaning.

Determination of Underlying Meanings   Up to this point, the processing strategies we have reviewed pay no attention to meaning. However, Fodor, Garrett, and Bever (1968) have pointed out that the relative pronoun strategy presented above works only with transitive verbs (that is, verbs which can take objects). The strategy would fail for verbs that take complements (e.g., *want*), "middle verbs" (e.g., *cost*), and verbs that take indirect objects (e.g., *give*), as in sentences such as the following:

(24a) The boy that the man wanted Julie to meet was ill.
(24b) The amount that the book cost was excessive.
(24c) The girl that the boy gave the book to was pretty.

Applying the strategies which we have available so far, we would arrive at erroneous interpretations:

(24a′) The man wanted the boy . . .
(24b′) The book cost the amount . . .
(24c′) The boy gave the girl . . .

We will need additional strategies that take account of the types of configurations into which particular verbs can enter. You will recall that verbs are central to grammatical descriptions in terms of case grammar and generative semantics. Numerous psycholinguistic experiments demonstrate as well that the combinatorial possibilities of verbs play a central role in sentence processing strategies. Clark and Clark (1977, p. 64) propose a special strategy on these grounds:

After encountering a verb, look for the number and kind of arguments appropriate to that verb.

For example, encountering *give*, one expects to find an agent, object, and recipient; *put* involves agent, object, and place; and so forth. In processing sentences, then, one is not only doing a surface structure analysis, but one is trying to relate this analysis to underlying semantic configurations. The knowledge of these configurations directs one's anticipation of the speaker's meaning.

Sentence processing strategies are thus constantly involved in the relations between surface and underlying structures of messages. This is because one is trying to make SENSE of speech, at every moment drawing upon knowledge of word meanings and related semantic structures in order to build up possible underlying propositions. Clark and Clark (p. 76) therefore propose another general strategy:

Look for constituents that fit the semantic requirements of the propositional function that underlies each verb, adjective, adverb, preposition, and noun.

For example, just as verbs require certain configurations of noun phrases, adverbs require certain types of verbs (e.g., *intelligently* requires a psychological behavior verb), prepositions require certain types of noun phrases (e.g., *on* requires an object and a surface), and so forth. A semantic configurational strategy aids in detecting underlying prepositions. Consequently, processing strategies rely on linguistic knowledge both of surface syntactic structures and their systematic relations to underlying semantic structures.

Fitting Meanings into Discourse   Determining underlying propositions, however, is only part of the listener's goal. He also wants to know why the speaker might be conveying a particular propositional content. How does a bit of conveyed information fit into the ongoing interaction between speaker and listener? A speaker organizes his discourse to highlight some points and background others: to inform or question or request or threaten or praise, or what have you. The listener must determine the speaker's ATTITUDE towards each proposition and establish its role in their encounter. Much current theoretical work in philosophy (e.g., Cole & Morgan, 1975; Grice, 1975; Searle, 1969, 1975) and linguistics (e.g., Gordon & Lakoff, 1971; Li, 1976; MacWhinney, 1977) deals with the ways in which language expresses conversational and social meanings. Some of these ideas have been brought into the psycholinguistic laboratory.

For example, Haviland and Clark (1974) studied the fact that one looks for IMPLICATIONS in a sentence that can relate it to what has gone before. They measured how long it took people to read and understand pairs of sentences such as:

(25a) Mary got some beer out of the car. The beer was warm.
(25b) Mary got some picnic supplies out of the car. The beer was warm.

The second version takes more time to process, because the reader must draw the implication that the picnic supplies included beer. As Clark and Clark point out (1977, p. 97): "Speakers cannot be bothered to spell out each tiny bit of information they refer to, and so they leave the most obvious pieces for listeners to supply . . ." The listener can supply such pieces only by knowing about the world that the speaker is talking about.

Languages have various syntactic devices to aid the processes of drawing implications, backgrounding some propositions as GIVEN and presenting others as NEW (Chafe, 1974, 1976). For example, consider the sequence of sentences:

(26a) The ballerina captivated a musician during her performance.
(26b) The one who the ballerina captivated was the trombonist.

The indefinite *a musician* of (26a) is replaced by the definite *the trombonist* of (26b). Your knowledge of the world tells you that a trombonist is a musician; the definite article *the* in (26b) signals that this particular musician is the one introduced as new information in (26a). The syntactic structure of (26b) takes all of (26a) and condenses it into a background statement of given information: *The one who the ballerina captivated.* The remaining clause, *was the trombonist,* adds a new bit of information, specifying what sort of musician was captivated. Carpenter and Just (1977) had people read sentences like (26a) and (26b) in a story, with varying amounts of material intervening between the sentences. They measured how long it took to read and understand each sentence. The closer (26b) was to (26a), the more easily it was processed. This indicates that one uses syntactic cues to identify what is new information in a sentence, and that one searches memory to find the link to relevant given information. If (26b) is replaced by a sentence with a different organization of old and new information, such as (26b′), processing is slowed down:

(26b′) The one who captivated the trombonist was the ballerina.

The structure of this sentence presents as given information *someone captivated the trombonist,* but the prior information was not set up this way in (26a). Clark and Haviland (1977) have summarized this discourse-linked aspect of sentence structure as an implicit agreement between speakers and listeners about the use of language for communicative purposes (Clark & Clark, 1977, p. 92):

GIVEN-NEW CONTRACT: The speaker agrees (a) to use given information to refer to information she thinks the listener can uniquely identify from what he already knows and (b) to use new information to refer to information she believes to be true but is not already known to the listener.

By and large, what is given and what is new is not signalled directly, but is signalled by the use of various syntactic forms, such as the examples in Table 2-1. Thus one needs sentence processing strategies not only to identify clauses, but to assess the role of each clause in relation to others.

TABLE 2-1
Given and New Information[1]
Five types of sentences and their given and new information

SENTENCE	GIVEN AND NEW INFORMATION
1. It is the BOY who is petting the cat.	Given: X is petting the cat New: X = the boy
2. It is the CAT which the boy is petting.	Given: the boy is petting X New: X = the cat
3. The one who is petting the cat is the BOY.	Given: X is petting the cat New: X = the boy
4. What the boy is petting is the CAT.	Given: the boy is petting X New: X = the cat
5. The BOY is petting the cat.	Given: X is petting the cat New: X = the boy

[1] Table from Clark and Clark (1977, p. 93).

So far we have conceptualized the listener (or reader) as someone who is trying to determine the underlying meanings of propositions and fit them into a running discourse, figuring out what the speaker (or writer) has left implicit by drawing implications and fitting new information into frameworks of given and background information. The listener must also determine the EFFECT the speaker is intending to produce. Surface form and utterance function do not always match because, as pointed out in Chapter 1, language is often used indirectly. A question can be a command or a request (*Can you be quiet? Could you lend me ten dollars?*). A promise can function as a threat (*I promise never to call you again*). A declaration (*You're a* FINE *student*) can be a compliment or a sarcastic insult or the beginning of a disclaimer, and so forth. These aspects of indirect meaning are structured as well, and must be processed simultaneously with propositional and discourse structures.

We are in no position to lay out all of the processing strategies used by a competent speaker of English—or even by a child, for that matter. But this brief review gives you an idea of the different levels of knowledge which must be called upon during the ongoing processing of speech. The listener attends to grammatical markers to segment utterances into a hierarchy of constituents, assigning meaning to those units on the basis of both verbal and situational factors.

Comprehension and Knowledge

The listener, then, is constantly trying to build an internal representation for the sentences he receives, relying on all available information: grammatical structure, meaning, knowledge of the world, knowledge of the speaker, knowledge of conversational rules, and so forth. No one of these aspects of structured knowledge is sufficient to account for the processes of comprehension. For example, in early psycholinguistic research based on transformational grammar, much effort was devoted in an attempt to demonstrate that syntactic complexity would be mirrored in processing difficulty (as measured in response time, errors, and the like). Various studies showed that passive sentences are more difficult to process than active sentences, reflecting their relatively greater complexity on the formal grounds defined by transformational grammar. In several early experiments (Gough, 1965, 1966; McMahon, 1963; Slobin, 1963, 1966a), subjects were asked to determine whether a given sentence was true or false with respect to a situation. Presented with a picture of a dog chasing a cat, subjects could be asked to verify sentences such as:

(27a) The dog is chasing the cat.
(27b) The cat is being chased by the dog.

The general finding was that passives, like (27b), require more time for response than actives, like (27a).

However, more than syntax is involved in real-life sentence processing. The role of syntax can be quite dramatically altered by manipulating the meaningful purposes to which sentences can be put. For example (Slobin, 1963, 1966a), the distinction between actives and passives, in terms of processing difficulty, can be eliminated by presenting sentences in which only one underlying meaning configuration is possible, as in:

(28a) The boy is raking the leaves.
(28b) The leaves are being raked by the boy.

The two versions of (28) are equally easy to understand, because only one interpretation is possible, whereas the passive version in (27b) can be misinterpreted by over-ready application of the noun-verb-noun strategy. Listeners apparently use every type of available information to guess at the meanings of sentences. This means that a full psycholinguistic model of comprehension must include much more than a grammar, although it certainly must draw upon grammatical rules and categories.

Much current debate in linguistics and psycholinguistics centers on the issue of the role of "world knowledge" (knowledge of possible events, social interactions, human personality, etc.) in building models of linguistic competence and language behavior. The strategies we have reviewed here are sketchy and informal. However, computer scientists have programmed computers with much more detailed rules which make it possible to carry on simple conversations with a computer about a limited topic (e.g., travel plans, moving around a set of blocks of various shapes and colors, patients' medical histories). It turns out that even simple tasks like these are impossible to carry out if the computer is programmed with nothing more than a set of sentence processing strategies. A surprisingly large amount of world knowledge is needed to handle even simple conversations and instructions. The computer must be able to deal concurrently with both syntactic and semantic information, along with an ability to form hypotheses about both the meanings and functions of utterances (e.g., Winograd, 1972, 1973, 1974).

For example, you instruct a computer to act in a simulated robot world of movable blocks and boxes by saying, *Put the block in the box.* The computer must be able to determine that this is a command and that it can only be carried out appropriately if, in the relevant "world," there is one block and one box present (given, of course, that it "knows" about objects, containers, movement, etc.). If there are two blocks, it must be able to reason that the instruction was insufficient and to ask for further information. This simple procedure is not possible unless the computer can parse the sentence syntactically, determine its meaning and function, and relate it to the present situation. At least this much interacting structure must be present in human language users as well. More and more detailed work with computers will fill in the complexities of language processing models, but for our purposes, it is the basic outlines of this endeavor which are important. Terry Winograd, who has done much of the pioneering work in this area, summarizes the minimal components necessary to make a computer model (and, by implication, a human model) of language use (1973, p. 154):[3]

3. For examples of how computers can process sentences, see R. Kaplan's discussions of "augmented transition networks" (1972, 1973). This approach to sentence processing has been applied to psycholinguistics by Eric Wanner and Michael Maratsos (1978). Psychologists and computer scientists at Yale have developed an important general theory of the ways in which knowledge is used in understanding, based on computer programs for the comprehension and production of stories. Much of this work is summarized in a book called *Scripts, plans, goals and understanding* by Roger Schank and Robert Abelson (1977).

The programs can be roughly divided into . . . three domains . . . : There is a syntactic parser which works with a large-scale grammar of English; there is a collection of semantic routines that embody the kind of knowledge needed to interpret the meanings of words and structures; and there is a cognitive deductive system for exploring the consequences of facts, making plans to carry out commands, and finding the answers to questions. There is also a comparatively simple set of programs for generating appropriate English responses.

An important and exciting field of "cognitive science" is growing at the intersection of psychology, linguistics, and artificial intelligence (see Norman and Rumelhart, 1975; and the journal *Cognitive Science*). Eventually it will be possible to be much more precise and detailed about the sorts of structures and processes involved in human intelligence. I hope this brief review leaves you impressed with the complexity of speech processing. It is clear that many levels of knowledge and skill must constantly be called upon in the apparently simple and effortless course of listening and understanding. It should be evident to you that the study of linguistic structures inevitably leads one to questions of the structure of knowledge and of memory. We have seen a bit of how these issues interact in ongoing comprehension of speech. Where do messages go after we have understood them?[4]

REMEMBERING LINGUISTIC MESSAGES

In discussing memory for linguistic form earlier in this chapter, I suggested that once the listener retrieves underlying meanings, surface forms are no longer necessary and can be cast off from memory. Everyday experience shows that while we generally remember quite well what we have just heard, we usually cannot repeat it in the same words in which it was given. Could one even RECOGNIZE exact wording a short time after hearing and understanding a message? Jacqueline Sachs (1967), in a now-classic study, set out to investigate just this question. Following the line of reasoning that listeners quickly unravel meaning and forget syntax, she predicted that: "Form which is not relevant to the meaning is normally not retained."

Sachs' subjects listened to 28 passages of connected discourse. After each passage, the subject was given a test sentence which was either identical to a sentence he had heard in the passage, or had been changed in either form or meaning. There were three delay intervals between the origi-

4. Following traditional work in linguistics and psycholinguistics, our work has focused on comprehension of individual sentences. However, it is obvious that in real-life most sentences are encountered in ongoing discourse of various kinds. Much recent attention has been devoted to the structures of various kinds of discourse (conversation, narratives, stories, fairy tales, etc.) and the ways in which listeners process such connected texts. A review of issues of "text processing" can be found in Kintsch (1977, pp. 356–82). Fredriksen (1975) has studied effects of context on linguistic processing. Psycholinguistic studies of stories can be found in Bower (1977), van Dijk and Kintsch (1977), Kintsch and van Dijk (1975), Just and Carpenter (1977), and Rumelhart (1975, 1977). Ongoing work can be followed in a new journal, *Discourse Processes*.

nal sentence and the test sentence: no delay, 80 syllables (about 27 seconds), and 160 syllables (about 46 seconds). The subject never knew on what sentence he would be tested. The following are examples of the changes used in the experiment:

ORIGINAL SENTENCE: He sent a letter about it to Galileo, the great Italian scientist.
SEMANTIC CHANGE: Galileo, the great Italian scientist, sent him a letter about it.
ACTIVE TO PASSIVE CHANGE: A letter about it was sent to Galileo, the great Italian scientist.
FORMAL CHANGE: He sent Galileo, the great Italian scientist, a letter about it.

When the test sentence was heard with no intervening delay, subjects were able to recognize both semantic and syntactic changes. After only 80 syllables (about 27 seconds) of delay, subjects' recognition of syntactic changes (active-passive and other formal changes) was close to chance, while their recognition of semantic changes remained strong even after 160 syllables (about 46 seconds). In another study (1974), Sachs found that recognition of formal changes dropped to chance level after as short a delay as 40 syllables (7.5 seconds). It is clear that the formal structure of sentences is stored for only a brief period of time. A small change in wording which is related to meaning, however, is easily detected. For example, subjects recognized the following change in meaning with ease after 80 syllables of interpolated material: *There he met an archaeologist, Howard Carter, who urged him to join in the search for the tomb of King Tut*, changed to: *There he met an archaeologist, Howard Carter, and urged him to join in the search for the tomb of King Tut*. However, the following formal change in the original sentence was almost never noted: *There he met an archaeologist, Howard Carter, who urged that he join in the search for the tomb of King Tut*. Sachs concludes that (1967, p. 422):

. . . very slight changes in the words of a sentence had vastly different effects on the experimental task, depending on whether or not the change affected the meaning . . .
The findings . . . are consistent with a theory of comprehension which contends that the meaning of the sentence is derived from the original string of words by an active, interpretive process. That original sentence which is perceived is rapidly forgotten, and the memory then is for the information contained in the sentence.

More recent psycholinguistic research has shown that listeners do not simply remember the underlying meanings of each of the separate sentences they have heard. As I emphasized above, when you listen to speech you try to make sense of it in terms of what you know about the speaker and the situation and the world in which you live. What remains in memory is an abbreviated and schematized version of what you have heard, with some details dropped out and, often, with the addition of details and interpretations which may be plausible (to you), but which were not stated explicitly in the original message. Just as clauses and sentences are way stations between sound and meaning, the meanings which underlie individual clauses and sentences are way stations along the road to long-term memory. Sachs' study demonstrates what may be called "memory as subtraction." Details are left out in short-term recoding. At the same time, one can examine "memory as addition." Listeners interpret speech by filling in plausible elements and schematizing messages according to expectations. Some of these interpretive processes have been demonstrated in the laboratory.

Bransford, Barclay, and Franks (1972) and various co-workers have done numerous experiments to demonstrate that people "do not spontaneously treat sets of individual semantically related sentences as independent objects for storage. Instead information from various sentences is integrated to form holistic semantic structures containing more information than any input sentences expressed" (p. 241). In one study, Bransford, Barclay, and Franks (1972) gave people sentences like (29a) or (29b):

(29a) Three turtles rested beside a floating log and a fish swam beneath them.
(29b) Three turtles rested on a floating log and a fish swam beneath them.

The sentences are similar in surface form and underlying propositions, differing only in one preposition—*beside* or *on*. But (29b) makes it possible to go beyond the information given, based on knowledge of spatial relations: if the turtles were on the log and the fish swam beneath them, then the fish must have swum beneath the log as well. In a subsequent recognition test, people who first received (29b) were likely to think that they had heard (29b'):

(29b') Three turtles rested on a floating log and a fish swam beneath it.

Exposure to (29a), by contrast, rarely led to confusion with (29a') in the recognition test:

(29a') Three turtles rested beside a floating log and a fish swam beneath it.

Many aspects of world knowledge can play a role in building up holistic semantic structures in memory. In another experiment, Johnson, Bransford, and Solomon (1973) presented sequences such as:

(30) John was trying to fix the bird house. He was *pounding/looking for* the nail when his father came out to watch him and to help him do the work.

The version using the verb *pounding* suggests a hammer, while the version with *looking for* does not. Although the word *hammer* does not appear in either version, people often imagined they had read it in the *pounding* version. In a recognition test some people came to the false conclusion that they had read the following sentence:

(30′) John was using the hammer to fix the bird house when his father came out to watch him and to help him do the work.

This false recognition occurred five times as often for those people who had read the *pounding* version than for those who had read the *looking for* version. It is clear that small surface differences can result in large memory differences, since people tend to remember their inferences and interpretations rather than the exact form of the original input.[5] Again, as in the discussion of sentence processing strategies, we are left with the conclusion that knowledge of the world and knowledge of the language interact in the processes of understanding and remembering what we hear and read.

WHAT IS GRAMMAR?

Having considered some psycholinguistic studies of language processing and memory, it is time to return to the question posed at the beginning of Chapter 1: What is grammar? In that chapter we talked of such things as rules, surface structures, underlying meanings, and the like, with the suggestion that such entities play a role in linguistic competence. In this chapter we have talked of such things as sentence processing strategies, computer programs, and memory for meaning. How do these various approaches to grammar fit together? Is there a relation between processing rules and linguistic descriptions?

One relation is obvious: There is a considerable overlap in vocabulary between linguistic and psycholinguistic accounts of language. Strategies are phrased in terms of such units as sentence, clause, verb, relative pronoun, and the like. That is, we take much of linguistic analysis as given. However, not all linguistic units play a role in psycholinguistic models, nor does a grammar specify how linguistic units are to be employed in speech processing. For example, it is a descriptive fact of English grammar that a relative pronoun can introduce a relative clause. It is a PSYCHOlinguistic fact that a listener expects a relative clause upon hearing a relative pronoun, and that deletion of the pronoun, although grammatical, can impose a burden on ongoing processing.

To some extent, the utility of a linguistic unit or linguistic description as an element in a processing model is a test of the psychological status of that linguistic entity. As psychologists, we expect mental structures to have behavioral effects. If we cannot find any way in which a particular linguistic structure can be reflected in language behavior, we are reluctant to consider that structure to be part of our mental apparatus, though it may play an important role in someone's linguistic theory. Thus, although we use linguistic entities in our models, we have different criteria for evaluating such entities.

This point is worth dwelling on, because it reveals differing goals on the part of linguists and psycholinguists. In both fields, models are evalu-

5. These psycholinguistic findings are of considerable importance for such traditional questions as the psychology of testimony (Stern, 1902), the psychology of rumor (Allport & Postman, 1947), and the psychology of memory (Bartlett, 1932). It is clear that memories are CONSTRUCTED—but more of this in Chapter 6.

ated against data. In both fields there are standards for the suitability of models in relation to data. The linguist is concerned with standards of elegance and efficiency. He prefers rules which embrace a number of apparently separate phenomena in one framework. He evaluates his model in terms of its ability to describe a language or a delimited part of a language. His primary data are native speakers' judgments about linguistic forms: their acceptability, their meanings, their relations to one another. Or else he may work with linguistic "texts"—written documents or transcriptions of speech.

The psycholinguist is concerned with rules of language USE. He wants to account for such things as how long it takes people to understand certain forms, what happens to them in memory, and so forth. He is not concerned with an elegant description of the language *per se*, but of the language user.

Let us take a concrete example (following Watt, 1970). Consider these active sentences and their corresponding passives and reduced passives:

(31) The gardener trimmed the hedge.
(32) The hedge was trimmed by the gardener.
(33) The hedge was trimmed.

A linguistic grammar of English should systematically relate these three sentences. An efficient grammar would have a set of rules for generating a common underlying structure at some level for actives and passives, with additional rules for the differences in surface form. All three sentences above would involve an agent acting on an object. A grammar which generated these three sentence types by separate and unrelated sets of rules would be unacceptable. Most grammars would relate the reduced passive of (33) to the full passive of (32) by some sort of rule of agent deletion. As a result, reduced passives should be more complex than full passives, because they involve more linguistic rules.

Psycholinguistically, however, reduced passives do not seem to be more difficult to process than full passives. Each of the three sentences above has its own functions to serve and can be called upon when needed. For example, (33) is the most plausible response to the question: *Why does your garden look different than it used to?* In responding with the agentless form of (33), one focuses on the change of state in the hedge and mention of the agent would be beside the point. An efficient PSYCHOlinguistic model would allow the speaker to express this notion directly, without calling into play the machinery associated with full passives and actives. The speaker may have the abstract knowledge that the three sentence types are related, yet never call upon this knowledge in the course of speaking and understanding.

In making this proposal, however, I suggest that there is a considerable difference between competence from a linguistic point of view and competence from a psycholinguistic point of view. Processing strategies make use of grammatical knowledge, but they involve more than grammatical considerations because they are time- and situation-oriented. Again we have the distinction between temporal behavior and atemporal structures, as discussed in the Introduction. Processing strategies embody knowledge organized for use—the particular use of speaking and understanding. A grammar written by a linguist is organized for a different purpose—namely, to effectively and efficiently describe a language for purposes of analysis and study. It is clear that there will be considerable overlap between these two endeavors to study the nature of language. As I pointed out earlier, psycholinguistics began (Miller, 1962) with the attempt to reduce these two endeavors to one by taking transformational rules to be mental operations. Now the pendulum has swung in the other direction, and some linguists and psycholinguists are asking whether all of linguistic competence can be described in terms of processing strategies. Would a fully elaborated set of processing strategies—at all levels, from phonology to pragmatics—constitute a complete description of a human being's knowledge of language? Or do we also have, tucked away in some corner of our minds, a more systematic description of our language, abstracted from the demands of moment-to-moment use? Does the mind have a "reference grammar" with such information as the fact that there is a systematic relation between active, passive, and reduced passive sentences; that the various auxiliary verbs play similar roles in statements and questions, and that *do* can play the role of a general auxiliary; and so forth? Does the language user need to have such an organized body of linguistic knowledge, or is this just an entity created by linguists for the purpose of abstract and general description and comparison of languages?

The answer to this question is not clear. Perhaps one cannot help but summarize the systematic categories and structures inherent in the collection of processing strategies, and, as a result, we all carry around a grammar which it is the task of linguists to discover. It could be that we are all implicit linguists, and have, unconsciously, constructed grammars in the process of learning language. Indeed, in all areas of life we form implicit general theories which guide behavior. For example, everyone must have a complex personality theory, built up on a lifetime of experience of interacting with people. This theory is realized in the form of "heuristics for encounters" or "processing strategies for human relations." When you meet a new person, you anticipate a certain type of relationship on the basis of cues of behavior and appearance; you implicitly decide on such actions as how close to stand, what topics to discuss, what language style to use, what activities to engage in, and so on. All of these "strategies" come from some general personality theory, but, unlike language, such a "grammar of human interaction" has not been formalized. If, in fact, human heads are full of such general theories, what linguists do is explore that part of their heads where systematic, implicit knowledge of language is stored. (Of course, on the other hand, it may be only linguists, or future linguists, who involve themselves in the construction of such overall summaries of linguistic knowledge!)

Fodor, Bever, and Garrett (1974, pp. 370-72) have an inconclusive discussion of this problem of the relation of a grammar to "the sentence encoding-decoding system." One of the possibilities they consider is that the grammar is a sort of archive of linguistic information which is used in the construction and use of sentence processing heuristics:

> The function of the grammar is to provide a "library" of information about the structures in a language, and the functioning of (some of the) heuristics is to ACCESS the grammar, i.e., to ask what the grammar says about the structure of the particular string of morphemes to which the hearer is attending.

This proposal is provocative, but at present we simply do not know enough about grammars or about language performance systems to resolve the questions of their relations. For now, one can simply state that performance systems embody many grammatical notions, but do not function like the grammars written by linguists. (For a current and lively debate between linguistics and artificial intelligence research on these questions, see issues of the journal *Cognition* for 1976-77: Dresher & Hornstein, 1976; 1977; Schank & Wilensky, 1977; Winograd, 1977.)

The limited success of processing models in psycholinguistics and artificial intelligence has led some linguists to propose serious study of such models in place of traditional linguistic analysis. For example, George Lakoff and Henry Thompson state (1975, p. 295):

> . . . we believe that there is a direct and intimate relation between grammars and mechanisms for production and recognition. In fact, we suggest that GRAMMARS ARE JUST COLLECTIONS OF STRATEGIES FOR UNDERSTANDING AND PRODUCING SENTENCES. From this point of view, abstract grammars do not have any separate mental reality; they are just convenient fictions for representing certain processing strategies.

Earlier I suggested that such an approach may reflect the facts about Russenorsk. It is not clear whether one needs to go beyond a compendium of processing strategies for that case, or for more complex languages. In any event, however, the source and nature of the linguistic categories and structures employed by such strategies remains to be explained.

The issue of the psycholinguistic nature of grammar can be clearly posed in regard to the child's acquisition of language, and we will turn to that problem shortly. The way in which language is acquired casts light on the ways in which it is stored and used by adults. Laboratory research and computer applications have made it clear that much of language use can be thought of in terms of processing strategies. Furthermore, the collection of strategies, in some sense, embodies grammatical knowledge as well as various other sorts of knowledge. Questions of the use and acquisition of language are thus intimately bound up with questions of the structure and development of knowledge in general.

Before examining the development of language, however, there is more to be said about possible relations between grammars and language use. Having looked at grammar from linguistic and psycholinguistic viewpoints, we are in a better position to examine grammar as a psychological entity. Since grammars presumably exist in order to make sentence processing possible, could it be that grammars are—universally—constrained to take certain forms because of the ways in which language must be used? Do constraints of perception, short-term memory, communicativeness, and the like, actually shape grammar? In the next chapter we will consider the extent to which the form of language may itself be determined by psychological factors.

3

Underlying the endless and fascinating idiosyncrasies of the world's languages there are uniformities of universal scope. Amid infinite diversity, all languages are, as it were, cut from the same pattern.

—Joseph H. Greenberg,
Charles E. Osgood,
and James J. Jenkins
(1966, p. xv)

PSYCHOLINGUISTIC CONSTRAINTS ON THE FORM OF GRAMMAR

All languages are cut from the same pattern because they are used by the same species for the same functions of communication and cognition. This short chapter is an exploration of the extent to which the form of human language can be related to its functions.

When one examines a broad sample of the languages of the world, it is evident that, for all their variety, human languages have much in common. In the years since 1961, when Greenberg, Osgood, and Jenkins organized a pioneering interdisciplinary conference on the question of language universals, enough information on the world's languages has been accumulated to reveal striking common patterns (Greenberg, 1978). Of the range of THEO-RETICALLY possible types of rules and rule systems, only a subset actually occurs. A central problem in the study of language is to account for this notable fact. Language universals must be based on psychological and sociocultural universals. An explanation of the species-wide characteristics of language is thus a contribution to a general theory of the nature of human thought and social interaction.

Each language provides conventions for the mapping of communicative intentions onto utterances. These conventions are constrained, for all languages, by: (1) human tendencies to think and image in certain ways; (2) processing demands imposed by a rapidly fading, temporally ordered code (be it auditory speech or visual sign); and (3) the nature and goals of human interaction. I wish to argue that these three types of constraints limit the range of possible human languages. That is to say, language has the form it does because of the uses to which it is put. Let us examine each of these three constraints—ways of thinking, processing constraints, and discourse constraints.

WAYS OF THINKING

The Sensory-Motor Metaphor

As we will see in the next chapter, language begins as an expression of the one-year-old child's sensory-motor understanding of the world. David McNeill (1975), Charles Osgood (Osgood & Bock, 1977), and others, have argued that the organization of sentences in all languages is founded on such very basic ways of thinking. Osgood speaks of a pervasive "naturalness" of the most frequently used word orders across languages: "the order of constraints in sentencing will tend to correspond to the order of components most frequently experienced in pre-linguistic, perception-based cognizing." Consider, for example, the possible orderings of subject, verb, and object. Of the six possible orders, almost all of the languages of the world use only one of three as their basic order (Greenberg, 1963): subject-verb-object (SVO), subject-object-verb (SOV), and verb-subject-object (VSO). What these three orders have in common is the precedence of subject before object. Why should this be so? Action seems to follow from subject to object. Furthermore, subjects tend to be animate, generally human, and therefore of greatest salience or emotional significance to speakers. Actions begin with an intention within an actor, and, in speaking of a situation, we tend to put ourselves into the position of the actor. For peculiarly human reasons such as these, languages are constructed to follow basic thought patterns. (Of course, languages also provide alternative orders, such as passive sentences, to express different orders of attention. Our concern here is with the most neutral, standard sentence type of language.) Similar arguments can be made in regard to other apparently universal basic orders. For example, it is a well-known fact of perception that figures tend to stand out against backgrounds; figure-ground orders are basic in linguistic expression (e.g., *the book is on the table* is a more natural description than *the table is under the book,* or *on the table is the book*). By contrast, some types of expression do not have universal order constraints, and, again, a psychological argument can be offered. For example, qualities of objects cannot be temporally or spatially separated from the objects themselves, so it is just as natural to say *a red book* as *un libro rojo* ('a book red').

Of course, language is used to express abstract notions which go beyond the concrete experience of sensory-motor behavior. However, languages generally seem to express abstract notions by metaphorical extensions of concrete experience. In speaking of such matters as time and abstract ideas, the languages of the world use metaphors based on the human body, located in space, acting on physical objects, looking ahead, and moving forward. Thus, we can speak of LOOKING FORWARD *to tomorrow, meeting* ON *Wednesday, getting* THROUGH *the week,* HAVING, GIVING, TAKING, *and* LOSING *time,* and so on. Such metaphors are widespread, and you can easily add to this list in whatever languages you may know. In the domain of mental experience, we seem to think of the mind as a container filled with ideas and emotions as objects—objects which themselves can have physical characteristics: *filled with grief, full of ideas, grasp an idea, a thorny problem, a hairy theory.* Abstract ideas can also be treated as objects of manipulation: *the plan slipped through my fingers; she held onto that hope.* Or mental contents can themselves become animate subjects: *That idea really grabs me.*

Such physical metaphors have grammatical consequences. For example, prepositions which express spatial relations can also be used temporally (as ON *Wednesday*); nouns which refer to ideas or events can be treated as object nouns or as animate nouns. Furthermore, when new grammatical forms arise, they are generally drawn from such metaphors. Various Indo-European languages have evolved future tense auxiliary verbs based on notions of a human actor striving for as-yet-unrealized events. In English our future tense is drawn from the metaphor of intention (*I* WILL *go*), whereas in Serbo-Croatian the metaphor is that of desire (the future auxiliary comes from the verb 'to want'). Verbs of intention and desire are often drawn on in the formation of future tenses. Passive verb forms are often derived from notions of getting or receiving, as in the passive auxiliary *he* GOT *hit.* (Note the similarity to the active form, *He* RECEIVED *a blow.*) In all of these ways—and many more—the lexical and grammatical structures of language reflect basic metaphors of a concrete human actor. (For further discussion of these issues, see Clark & Clark, 1978.)

The Expression of Complexity

In English we say one *ship* and many *ships;* in Turkish it is *gemi* and *gemiler;* in Egyptian Arabic *márkib* and *maráakib.* Note that, in each case, the plural is longer than the singular. In English a final consonant is added;

in Turkish a whole syllable; in Arabic an infixed syllable. Why should the plural be more complex than the singular? In a sense, these forms can be looked upon as physical metaphors: more things, more sounds. We could imagine languages in which the plural is formed by taking something away from the singular. A computer would have no trouble processing such a language, but languages constructed and used by human beings do not work that way. Again, there is a "naturalness" to grammar based on human thought patterns.

Herbert and Eve Clark (1977, Chapter 14; 1978) propose that there is more at work here than simply a physical metaphor. They advance a general principle: "Complexity of thought tends to be reflected in complexity of expression" (Clark & Clark, 1977, p. 523). Languages are constructed so that what is most simple and expected is expressed with the least complex morphological and grammatical machinery. For example, it is psychologically more basic to assert a fact than to negate or deny it. Negation adds cognitive complexity, and is always reflected in an increase in grammatical or lexical complexity. Consider various ways of negating in English:

AFFIRMATIVE	NEGATIVE
The book is here.	*The book is not here.*
Ellen has some money.	*Ellen doesn't have any money.*
tie	*untie*
confirm	*disconfirm*
ever	*never*
one	*none*

In terms of underlying cognitive complexity, following the discussion of generative semantics in Chapter 1, a state is less complex than a change of state. This is reflected in linguistic complexity:

STATE	CHANGE OF STATE
solid	*solidify*
black	*blacken*
long	*lengthen*
legal	*legalize*

There is an interaction between linguistic complexity and the point of view of the speaker. Generally, what is closest to the present time and location of the speaker is expressed in the relatively simpler form. Clark and Clark suggest that in each of the following contrasting pairs, the second member tends to be more complex linguistically across languages: present-past, present-future, actual-hypothetical, speaker-addressee. Ross (1975; Cooper & Ross, 1975), surveying a number of languages, proposes the "Me First" principle to account for the order of words in "frozen" pairs, such as *this and that* rather than *that and this*. To cite only a few of the many examples of this principle:

SEMANTIC RULE: ORDER THAT ELEMENT FIRST WHICH IS

    CLOSEST TO THE SPEAKER: *this and that, here and there*

    CLOSEST TO THE TIME OF SPEECH: *now and then, sooner or later*

    CLOSEST TO THE GENERATION OF THE SPEAKER: *father and grandfather, mother and daughter*

    AT HOME: *home and away, at home and abroad*

    SOLID: *land, sea and air; solid, liquid and gas*

    ALIVE: *living or dead, life and death*

    HUMAN: *man and beast*

    SINGULAR: *one or more, singular or plural*

Not only are these, and many other pairs, ordered, but the first member of the pair tends to be simpler on a variety of phonological and morphological dimensions. Again, we have evidence that strictly human considerations of importance and complexity are reflected in STRUCTURAL features of language. Language is not an arbitrary mapping of ideas onto utterances; rather, in the very principles of its mapping, as well as in its content, it reflects the concerns and capacities of the species which evolved the system.

In raising the issue of complexity we have touched upon the role of processing constraints. Presumably, things which are closest to the self and which are spoken of most frequently come to be expressed with the least complexity because of matters of efficiency. Leaving matters of the content of speech aside, efficiency considerations in themselves play a profound role in determining the range of linguistic structures which the human mind can process.

PROCESSING CONSTRAINTS

In surveying a large and varied sample of the languages of the world, Greenberg (1963), and others after him, have found curious gaps in the possible combinations of grammatical features which make up a language. As illustration, the basic word order of a language is closely tied to the possible positioning of other sentence elements, besides simple subject, verb, and object. English has SVO order and also uses prepositions to indicate various relations, such as spatial *(Snow fell ON the house)* and temporal *(Rebecca left AFTER the meeting)*. Other languages use POSTpositions—that is, particles which serve the same function as prepositions, but come after the noun which they modify. For example, in Turkish one says *Kar evin ÜSTÜNE yağdi ('Snow house ONTO fell')* and *Rebecca mitingden SONRA gitti ('Rebecca meeting AFTER left')*. Note that the Turkish sentences end with a verb. This is because the basic sentence order in Turkish is SOV. The use of postpositions in an SOV language like Turkish is apparently not fortuitous. Consider the following striking facts about the distribution of pre- and postpositions in 217 languages, classified as to basic word order (after Hawkins, 1976). The numbers represent sums of individual languages of each type:

	DOMINANT WORD ORDER		
	VSO	SVO	SOV
PREPOSITIONS	38	60	5
POSTPOSITIONS	1	23	90

Note that almost all SOV languages (90 out of 95 sampled), like Turkish, use postpositions. Almost all VSO languages use prepositions (97 percent). SVO languages are mixed, but 73 percent of them use prepositions.

Why should there be such striking asymmetry in the distribution of these two features? Certainly one could devise a language of each of the six types; indeed, the cells with small numbers indicate that the unusual types are not completely impossible. But figures like these lead one to look for some sort of psycholinguistic explanation. Consider the two extreme cases, verb-initial and verb-final languages. An "adposition" (that is, a pre- or postposition) functions rather like a verb, in that it relates other elements in a sentence to one another: *on* relates *snow* to *house* in a spatial framework; *after* relates *leaving* to the *meeting* in a temporal sense. In similar fashion, *fell* relates *snow* to its final location *on the house,* and *left* relates *Rebecca* to the time *after the meeting.* If you speak a language in which you are accustomed to placing the verb at the end of the sentence, after mentioning the participants in the relationship described by the verb, it is then consistent to also place the adposition at the end of its phrase, after mentioning the participants in the relationship described by the adposition. Hence a similar processing strategy underlies the use of both postpositions and verb-final position in SOV languages. These two features probably occur together because it is more efficient for the language user to minimize the number of types of sentence processing strategies which he must call upon to produce and comprehend utterances. A similar, but opposite argument would explain the preponderance of prepositions in VSO languages. SVO languages are mixed: the verb "looks back" to the subject, but "looks ahead" to the object. Perhaps this is why speakers of such languages can apparently feel comfortable with either sort of adposition. But note that 73 percent of the SVO languages sampled use prepositions, which indicates a predominant strategy of having both the verb and the adposition precede its objects (compare *Liz read the book* and *Liz wrote IN the book).* (For additional explanations, see Kuno, 1974.)

This is only part of a more complex story. In fact, the position of the verb in relation to the object seems to constrain the placement of a wide range of other features in the sentence (Greenberg, 1963; Vennemann, 1975). Let us collapse the distinction between VSO and SVO types, considering only two basic language types: verb–object (VO) and object–verb (OV). There is a strong statistical tendency[1] for the languages of the world to follow one of the two following patterns in regard to the placement of sentence elements:

1. The discussion in this chapter deals with "pure types." Because of constant historical change, and the existence of competing psycholinguistic pressures on language form, the real world presents only an approximation of the ideal. (See Chapter 7, and Slobin, 1977.)

			relative clause
			possessive
auxiliary	VERB	OBJECT	adjective
			demonstrative
			number

OV LANGUAGES:

relative clause		
possessive		
adjective	OBJECT VERB	auxiliary
demonstrative		
number		

It is indeed striking that these two patterns are the mirror images of one another. Consider an equivalent pair of English and Turkish sentences, in which the Turkish is presented in roughly literal translation:

					POSSESSIVE
The army	had not been able	to capture	the man	who was the leader	of the guerrillas.
SUBJECT	AUXILIARIES	VERB	OBJECT	RELATIVE CLAUSE	

	POSSESSIVE				
The army	the guerrillas'	leader being	man	capture	able not had been.
SUBJECT	RELATIVE CLAUSE		OBJECT	VERB	AUXILIARIES

The Turkish version, no doubt, looks bizarre to you; but take my word that it sounds as natural and easy to process as the familiar English version. The two sentences have a deep and important psycholinguistic commonality: in both cases, the object is directly next to the verb. This is guaranteed by flanking modifying material on either side of this essential verb-object bond. To schematize the above chart:

VO LANGUAGES:

modifiers VERB OBJECT modifiers

OV LANGUAGES:

modifiers OBJECT VERB modifiers

Verb-object is the essential core of the sentence: 'a man was captured'. The subject, if it is relevant, is stated at the outset. In discourse, however, the subject is most often already known and can be referred to by pronoun, or it can simply be omitted if the verb bears information about the subject (person, number, gender, etc.). The linguistic universal of modifier placement seems to exist in order to facilitate sentence processing: interposing too much material between verb and object would place a burden on short-term memory. For example, consider an SVO language with the modifier placements characteristic of OV languages: *The army to capture had not been able the guerrillas' leader being man.* Not only are verb and object far apart, but intervening nouns, such as *guerrillas* and *leader* stand in danger of being interpreted as object, given the sort of sentence processing strategies discussed in the previous chapter.

These two sentences illustrate another psycholinguistic constraint on grammatical form. In both language types, the modifiers flank the verb-object bond; but note that the VERBAL modifiers are always adjacent to the VERB and the NOMINAL modifiers adjacent to the object NOUN. This seems obvious, but, of course, it is not logically necessary. An artificial VO language could function perfectly well with a rule to the effect that preverbal modifiers relate to the object and postobject modifiers relate to the verb. However, for such a language to function, the computer would have to do a considerable amount of checking back and forth, storing preverbal object modifiers while processing the verb, retrieving them upon encountering the object, and so on. Computers are good at this sort of short-term storage, search, and retrieval, but the demands of ongoing communication would make this a very inefficient sort of language to be used by speaking and listening people with human brains. Rather, languages are constructed to conform rather closely to a very simple and human principle ("Behagel's First Law," Behagel, 1923): "What belongs together mentally is placed close together syntactically." Again, we have a psycholinguistic constraint on the possible forms of grammar.

DISCOURSE CONSTRAINTS

In reading through the literature of linguistics and psycholinguistics, one can easily get the impression that a sentence is an entity which functions to prove a linguistic point or to measure an experimental subject's response. However, almost all of the sentences which have ever occurred in the world have been spoken in the context of other sentences in an ongoing interaction between people who alternate as speakers and hearers. This most basic function of human language cannot help but determine the form of the linguistic code. A computer could function most conveniently with a single and simple means of encoding each proposition type. However, as we have seen in Chapter 1, language presents a vast array of means for saying roughly the same thing. This is because one does not simply attempt to convey propositions, but to focus, direct, and tantalize the listener's attention, by weaving sentences into a coherent and pleasing flow of speech, or by grappling for the expression of ideas, or by attempting to hold the floor in a conversation, and so on.

The basic assumption of the listener is that he will be guided from what he already knows to what he does not know. Accordingly, sentences tend to begin with stating a definite topic which is given or known, and move on to present new information as comment. Givón (1975, p. 76) presents this as a universal word order principle "that the leftmost constituent is the MORE TOPICAL ONE, i.e., the one more likely to NOT constitute new information, while the rightmost constituent is the FOCUS for new information." The sentence type best corresponding to this universal is the simple, active, affirmative, declarative sentence. Much of syntactic complexity exists to signal the listener that this communicative assumption is not being followed. For example, in English we have special grammatical means to bring focused information to the front of the sentence, using such means as stress (*THAT professor I wouldn't trust*), topicalization (*As for Jones, I wouldn't trust him*), and various complex forms (*It's Jones that I wouldn't trust, Jones is not to be trusted*). Beginnings and ends of temporal units seem to have special attention value to human perceivers, and languages are constructed to exploit this tendency by favoring these positions to signal special features of messages. We have just noted the use of first position, plus grammatical signals, to convey special emphasis or attention. Interrogatives are another set of sentence forms which deviate from the listener's neutral expectation of simple declaratives. Questions are always expressed by more complex syntactic means than declaratives and generally have a special marker at the beginning (such as a question word) or end (such as rising intonation) or both. There are many complex issues of the ways in which grammar serves to express communicative functions. These issues are receiving increasingly detailed attention from linguists and social scientists (e.g., papers in Givón, 1979; and in Li, 1976). Let us briefly consider the role of syntax in lending coherence to a stretch of discourse.

Syntax is used to guide the listener's attention to the thread of an argument. For example, consider the following brief statement:

Last night I was going to the concert at that place where Judy used to perform, but it had been cancelled.

A relative clause and a passive construction knit this series of propositions together with a minimum of repetition. Lacking this complex syntactic apparatus, one would have to say something like:

1. *Last night I was going to a concert.*
2. *Judy used to perform at a place.*
3. *The concert was at that place.*
4. *I went to that place.*
5. *They had cancelled the concert.*

Not only is the "simpler" version longer, but it lacks smoothness and directed attention. The attention is switched from *concert* at the end of the first sentence to *Judy* at the beginning of the sentence, although Judy is not the topic of the discourse at all. Again, there is no smooth flow from *place* at the end of the second sentence to *the concert* at the beginning of the third. The awkwardness of the second, third, and fourth sentences can be resolved by the use of the complex syntax of relative clauses, as in the original version. And lack of a passive construction requires the introduction of an anonymous *they* as subject (but hardly discourse topic) of the last sentence. Complex syntax thus makes speech compact and coherent. One needs means to refer back to what was said before, to qualify what is being introduced, and to coordinate the point of view of speaker and hearer. Such discourse pressures—both temporal and social—are constantly at work in shaping the form of language.

We can see the results of some of these factors in the study of historical language change (Li, 1977; Slobin, 1977). Others can be observed in the present time, as pidgin languages become adapted to carry out more complex and varied discourse functions in developing societies. (More of this in Chapter 7.) Try to imagine a flowing and engaging conversation in Russenorsk! The following example of pidgin English, from Margaret Mead's (1930) classic study of New Guinea, may give you some additional feeling of the discourse functions of syntax. In this selection the owner of a pig is presenting his claim for compensation to a district officer's court. Mead notes: "The endless circumlocutions of pidgin English combined with the exceedingly complex nature of native economic affairs often leads . . . to unfortunate misunderstandings in court." A native defendant explains to the officer (p. 178):

"Now me sell 'em along one fellow man, he man belong one fellow sister belong me fellow. All right. This fellow man he sell him along one fellow man, he belong Patusi, he like marry him one fellow pickaninny mary belong 'em. He no pickaninny true belong 'em that's all he help 'em papa belong this fellow mary. All right . . ."

Lacking the complex grammar needed for embedding, possession, pronominal reference, and the like, it is hard to discern that what was intended was something like (p. 179):

'Now I gave the pig to a man, who is my sister's husband. This man gave the pig to a man in Patusi who was planning to marry a daughter of his. She was not his own daughter, but he had inherited his father's position . . .'

It is fascinating to discover that since Margaret Mead studied in New Guinea some 50 years ago, Melanesian Pidgin English has been evolving into a full-fledged language with native speakers (Sankoff & Brown, 1976). In the process, the language has developed a more complex and regular syntax, including a means for producing relative clauses. It has been a combination of processing constraints and discourse needs which has contributed to the rapid change of this language. Presumably, similar factors were at work in the evolution of human language generally, resulting in the particular structural features of the communication system used by our species.

In sum, as we come to understand more of the functional pressures on language, we will be better able to account for the particular form that human language has taken.

4

... for I was no longer a speechless infant, but a speaking boy. This
I remember; and have since observed how I learned to speak. It was
not that my elders taught me words ... in any set method; but I,
longing by cries and broken accents and various motions of my
limbs to express my thoughts, that so I might have my will, and yet
unable to express all that I willed, or to whom I willed, did myself,
by the understanding which Thou, my God, gavest me, practise the
sounds in my memory. ... And thus by constantly hearing words, as
they occurred in various sentences, I collected gradually for what
they stood; and having broken in my mouth to these signs, I
thereby gave utterance to my will. Thus I exchanged with those
about me these current signs of our wills, and so launched deeper
into the stormy intercourse of human life ...

—Saint Augustine,
The Confessions [c. 397 A.D.]
(1949, p. 11)

LANGUAGE DEVELOPMENT IN THE CHILD

The mystery of how a child learns to speak has intrigued and puzzled adults since antiquity—undoubtedly for millennia before St. Augustine's speculations. Questions of the origins of human knowledge and abilities have always been central to philosophical theories. The mental abilities of a little child seem to be rather limited in many ways, yet he[1] masters the exceedingly complex structure of his native language in the course of a short three or four years. What is more, each child, exposed to a different sample of the language, and generally with little or no conscious teaching on the part of his parents, arrives at essentially the same grammar and rules of language use in this brief span. That is to say, each child rapidly becomes a full-fledged member of his language community, able to produce and comprehend an endless variety of novel yet meaningful utterances in the language he has mastered.

Earlier in this book there are hints that one's theory of the nature of language is closely related to one's theory of the acquisition and use of language. Modern linguistic theories, phrased in terms of productive rules, have posed a serious challenge to psychological learning theories. The problem was posed in Chapter 1, in the discussion of transformational grammar: If all of the linguistic structure is not evident in the surface forms of utterances, how do children acquire such structures? More and more, we have come to believe that children come to the task of language acquisition equipped with cognitive strategies which enable them to decipher and form the rules of the code. Until recently, behavioristic psychology looked upon language, and the task of initial language learning, as just another form of human behavior which could be reduced to the laws of conditioning. The picture we are now beginning to form, however, is that of a child who is creatively constructing his language on his own, in accordance with innate and intrinsic capacities—a child who is developing new theories of the structure of the language, modifying and discarding old theories as he goes. This picture differs radically from the traditional picture of a child whose learning is governed by variables such as frequency, recency, contiguity, similarity, and reinforcement. The study of child language has thus become central to a long-standing debate between nativism and empiricism—that is, between the doctrine of inborn knowledge and the doctrine of knowledge acquired through sensory experience. Of course, all theories of mental growth require that the child have experience of the outside world. The issue is one of the degree to which the mind is structured at birth, and the degree to which experience can shape inborn structures. After reviewing

1. After much consideration, I have decided to avoid the valuable but cumbersome innovation of bisexual pronouns such as *s/he* and *his or her*. What is gained in sexual equality must be offset by the resulting loss of ease in reading (e.g., "he or she masters the exceedingly complex structure of his or her native language . . . "). All of the statements made in this chapter hold for boys and girls alike. There are no important sex differences in the process of language acquisition. In fact, a recent review of "the myth of female superiority in language" concludes: "In the present state of language assessment the only tenable position is that there is NO significant difference between the sexes in linguistic ability" (Macaulay, 1978, p. 361). Similar conclusions apply to adult ability. Throughout the book, therefore, remember to read *he* in its generic sense, calling to mind general statements about HUMAN language capacities. The conventions of English (and all languages that mark gender grammatically) require that it is the male form which is used in the generic sense. I have followed this convention for the sake of ease of style, using plurals or terms like *human being* and *people* whenever possible. On the grounds of readability, rather than ideology, I offer my apologies to readers who would prefer the bisexual linked or hybrid pronoun.

some of what has been learned about language acquisition in the past twenty years or so, we will be in a better position to examine this debate. Chapter 5 poses the problem again, in a biological and cross-species framework.

What is there about child language which makes it so interesting and relevant to issues associated with such names as Descartes and Kant and Locke, Pavlov and Skinner and Piaget? To set the stage for a more detailed discussion, consider an apparently simple interchange between a mother and her three-year-old son:

MOTHER: Where did you go with Grandpa?
CHILD: We goed in a park.

The mother has asked a QUESTION about DIRECTED MOTION, TO A GOAL, INVOLVING THE LISTENER AND A PARTICIPANT, IN THE PAST. The child's answer indicates that he has understood all of these elements of the mother's utterance. What does the child have to know about English in order to carry out this feat? To identify this utterance as a question, he must recognize the role of the initial question word, *where,* and the question intonation. The meaning of this word, along with the meaning of *go,* indicate that the question is about directed motion and that it is the goal which is being questioned. The pronoun *you* and the preposition *with* indicate that it is the listener and another person, *Grandpa,* who were involved in this activity. The form of the auxiliary, *did,* places the action in the past. The child cannot reply appropriately without this general knowledge of English grammar and semantics; yet these facts of form and meaning are not immediately evident in the utterance. What the child hears is a stream of sounds, which is not even obviously separable into words. If you look at the English sentence, with no word boundaries, you get some idea of the problem:

wheredidyougowithgrandpa

It is hard to abandon your knowledge of English in looking at this string of letters, or in listening to the succession of sounds. To make the point more clearly, consider the Turkish equivalent of the same question:

dedenlenereyegittinsen

Unless you know Turkish, you will be at a loss to segment this string into words, even knowing its meaning. How many words do you think there are, and where are their boundaries? Even provided with a segmentation into meaningful elements, the meaning of the whole is not immediately obvious:

dede-	n-	le	/	ne-	re-	ye	/	git-	t-	in	/	sen
grandpa	your	with		question	place	to		go	past	second-person		you

The seven-word English utterance is equivalent to a four-word Turkish utterance, with the sequence of meaningful elements: 'grandpa your with question place to go past second-person you'.

Now perhaps the achievement of the three-year-old in understanding an apparently simple question will appear more dramatic to you. Not only must he segment the stream into meaningful units, but he must know how to combine them to arrive at the intended underlying propositions. This knowledge is not directly provided by parents, nor is it immediately obvious in the nature of the signal. Without knowledge of Turkish, or of English, the child could never answer the question. Children must have special and powerful mental abilities which enable them to arrive at such knowledge.

The child's answer indicates not only that he has the knowledge to decipher the utterance, but that he has developed rules to produce appropriate utterances of his own. For example, the use of *we* responds to the mother's use of *you . . . with grandpa; goed* responds to *did . . . go;* and so on. What appear to be errors, from the adult point of view, reveal the productive knowledge of the language that the child has achieved. Although he has not heard *goed,* his production of this form indicates a grasp of the rules for past tense formation in English. By saying *in a park,* he shows that he has partially mastered the English rules for talking about the goals of directed motion. In speaking of enclosures we say, for example, *he is in the house* and *he went in the house;* but, for some reason, we treat parks as enclosures when speaking of location *(he is in the park),* but treat them as non-enclosed entities when moving towards them *(he went to the park).* The child's "error" is simply an incomplete analysis of this portion of English.

Learning to speak thus involves the mastery of abstract and general patterns of a language. These patterns correspond, in their broadest outlines, to the linguistic universals discussed in the last chapter. Perhaps linguistic universals exist, in part, because children have to learn language. That is to say, language has the form which it does because no other sort of linguistic structure could be learned by children. If this is the case, then there is a close fit between the universal nature of language and the nature of the child's language acquisition strategies. The philosophical import of this position should now be obvious: if the child is able to acquire the abstract and general patterns of language, it is because he is, in some sense, "pretuned" to do so. This position, in its most extreme form, is consonant with philosophical theories of innate ideas and with nativistic theories of animal behavior. Opposing theories seek to explain language acquisition in terms of general learning principles which, guided by linguistic stimuli, result in the necessary generalizations.

There are two broad issues in question here: (1) Do you believe, with the empiricists, that learning is primarily a matter of applying general principles of association by contiguity and similarity to structured stimulus input; or do you believe, with rationalist nativists, that the organism begins with fairly complex inner structures which are elaborated in directed interaction with the outside world? (2) If you favor the latter position, that learning is heavily guided by innate structural principles, do you believe that there are special principles evolved for the task of language acquisition, or is it sufficient to have general principles of cognitive learning?

My position is that language acquisition is guided by innate structural principles, some of which are unique to this particular task, and some of which are more general. The position advocated here can thus be characterized by such terms as "nativist," "constructionist," "interactionist," "cognitive," "structuralist." You, of course, will sample the evidence (hopefully going beyond what is presented here), and come to your own conclusions. The evidence presently available certainly does not determine any clear conclusion. Regardless of your philosophical bent, the facts of child language are engaging in their own right and have obvious practical implications to questions of education, child rearing, and speech therapy. Let us review some of the facts, and then return to the theoretical issues.

LANGUAGE BEFORE GRAMMAR

The infant's early attempts at vocal communication are quite different from human language in important ways. There is a repertoire of inborn noises expressing a spectrum of need states. However, it will take a long time before vocalizations are used to designate objects or events, to ask and answer questions, and so on. Normally, by the end of the first year the child can produce a number of clearly differentiated sounds, and parents begin to hear what they identify as "first words" coming out of the infant's babblings. These first words often have the force of entire sentences and have been referred to as "one-word sentences." All babies seem to go through a one-word stage sometime before they reach age two. The meaning of such minimal utterances varies with the situation, and so *mama* can mean 'Mama come here', or 'That's mama', or 'I'm hungry', or any number of things. We cannot speak of the child's ACTIVE grammar because he has not yet combined any of his words into longer utterances. However, it is clear that the infant's knowledge of language goes beyond the collection of separate words that he knows.

On the perceptual level, even very young infants can discriminate some of the acoustic cues necessary for speech comprehension. For example, Eimas et al. (1971) have found that infants as young as one month in age can discriminate the subtle acoustic cue that distinguishes voiced consonants, like *b,* from unvoiced consonants like *p.* By eight months, infants can respond differentially to falling and rising intonation contours (E. L. Kaplan, 1969). The basic perceptual apparatus for deciphering the linguistic code is present long before the child begins to speak. It has long been known that very young children can understand many adult words and commands, responding by participation in pointing games and other verbally guided interactions with adults. Only recently, however, has some light been shed on the extent to which infants can interpret aspects of structural, combinatorial meaning in adult utterances.

"Passive Grammar"

In the first edition of this book, after introducing the notion of "one-word sentences," I wrote: "We cannot speak of the child's ACTIVE grammar because he has not yet combined any of his words into longer utterances. It is possible that he already has a 'passive' grammatical system; that is, he may be able to understand some grammatical patterns in adult speech, but this delicate and complex research question has not yet been submitted to investigation." From a linguistic point of view, grammatical knowledge is needed for both comprehension and production. You know from foreign language study that it is easier to understand what you hear than to marshall the entire speech apparatus to produce foreign utterances. Perhaps the infant is in a similar condition. If we could determine the sorts of STRUCTURED utterances an infant can respond to appropriately, we would be in a position to examine the early roots of linguistic competence. Thanks to some careful research, we can now begin to talk about the issue which was only a possibility a few years ago.

Janellen Huttenlocher (1974) regularly visited four infants in their homes, beginning when the children were 10–13 months old. She tested the children's active vocabulary as well as their ability to understand adult speech. The children were able to find named objects, even if they did not yet use the names in their own speech. But beyond this early comprehension of names, Huttenlocher found remarkable early comprehension of word combinations. For example, one child, Craig, at one-and-a-half, produced only two words: *di,* when seeing the family dog or other animals, and *uh-uh,* when refusing an adult request. A new baby sister entered the scene, and after two weeks Craig was able to distinguish between *your bottle* and *baby's bottle, your diaper* and *baby's diaper,* going to get the appropriate objects from another room. He also distinguished between *show* and *give,* holding up an object in response to the first command, and taking it to someone in response to the second. The most dramatic evidence of combinatorial understanding came a few weeks later. In Huttenlocher's words (1974, pp. 348–49):

> *1 year, 5 months, 30 days.* On my next visit I try out commands that have three contrasting terms of the form Give (show) Mommy (me) the baby's (your) bottle. I have the two bottles standing on the high chair in the kitchen. Each time, before a request is made, Craig is put in the living room where he can see neither the bottles nor the two people to whom he was to show or deliver them. Each of the eight possible commands is given twice over a short period of time and is always correctly carried out.

As Huttenlocher points out, a number of cognitive skills are necessary for such performance. In long-term memory the infant must store both the sound patterns for particular words and concepts about objects and events, along with the relations between the words and the referents. Furthermore, he must store some knowledge of how combinations of words are to be interpreted. In short-term, active memory, he must access this stored information and relate it to the current situation.

It seems clear that children as young as Craig can hold several words in memory and determine the resultant meaning of the combination. Sachs and Truswell (1976) have provided further evidence that children at the one-word stage of speech development can productively make inferences based on more than one word from an utterance. These investigators provided infants with novel instructions, presenting words they already understood in unfamiliar combinations, such as *tickle book, smell truck,* and *kiss ball.* Children whose own utterances were never more than one word long were able to perform correctly to such strange instructions. Thus it is clear that before the child begins to produce connected speech of his own, he already knows something about the meanings of words and word combinations in his language.

Meanings of One-Word Utterances

One-word utterances are clearly used with communicative intent. Parents interpret such utterances and respond to them, and dialog is possible. Language is used meaningfully, but there has been much recent debate in the psycholinguistic literature about the extent to which meanings can be attributed to such brief and unstructured utterances. The speech of very young children can only be understood in context. Verbal signals are but one part of a complex interactive situation, including gestures oriented towards present people and objects, direction of gaze, and intonation pattern of speech. The use of tape recordings along with detailed contextual notes, and, more recently, videotape, has made it possible to examine speech contexts in detail, and many investigators have satisfied themselves that it is possible to impute fuller communicative intent to the child than would be indicated by the meaning of the single word alone. The issue is one of characterizing the COMMUNICATIVE FUNCTIONS of utterances. If a child says *daddy* when pointing to a picture of his father, the function of his utterance is one of naming; while if he says *daddy* while finding daddy's slipper, he is communicating some relationship (possession, or habitual association) between his father and the object, without naming the object.

Greenfield and Smith (1976) have made one of the most thorough attempts to demonstrate the functional meanings of one-word utterances, arguing that many of the relational notions expressed more fully in later stages of language development are already present before the onset of combinatorial speech. Like many investigators, they have been stimulated by Fillmore's case grammar (see Chapter 1) to classify children's utterances in terms of such underlying notions as agent, object, goal, location, etc. For example, any utterance relating to a situation in which daddy is throwing a ball requires the child to cognize that an agent is acting on an object. Greenfield and Smith argue that if a child says *ball* in such a situation, the one-word utterance is not just the name of a thing, but indicates the object of action in a total situation. Similarly, in saying *daddy,* the child would not only be naming the father, but naming the agent of ball-throwing.

Studying two boys from the ages of 7 to 22 months, Greenfield and Smith found a common order of emergence of the expression of various semantic functions—an order which has been supported, in broad outline, in other studies of early development as well. The earliest utterances do not name objects or events, but are the vocal parts of ritual actions, such as saying *byebye* while waving. Other early utterances serve to express the child's desires in relation to adult action: *down* when wanting to be taken down from a high chair, *no* when refusing food, and so forth. When the child begins to use words beyond these simple rituals and demand situations, there seems to be a fairly stable order of development of the notions expressed, as shown in Table 4-1. Broadly, the earliest relational utterances refer to a relation between an entity (an agent or an object) and an action; then relations between two entities are expressed; and towards the end of the one-word stage the child begins to speak of modifications of events. Thus, early in development, the child may say *daddy* when hearing daddy come up the steps (agent) or when giving something to daddy (recipient), and only later will say *daddy* when finding daddy's slipper (animate being associated with object).

TABLE 4-1
Onset of Semantic Functions in a Child's One-Word Utterances[1]

Semantic function	Age	Instance
Performative	7(22)	hi, as accompaniment to waving
Performative Object	8(12)	dada, looking at father
Volition	11(24)	nana, turning away from stairs in response to mother's no[2]
Dative	11(28)	dada, offering bottle to father
Object	13(0)	ba(ll), having just thrown ball
Agent	13(3)	daddy, hearing father come in door and start up steps
Action or State of Agent	13(16)	up, reaching up, in answer to question Do you want to get up?[2]
Action or State of Object	14(6)	down, having just thrown something down
Object Associated with Another Object or Location	14(29)	caca (cracker, cookie), pointing to door to next room, where cookies are kept
Location	15(20)	bo(x), putting crayon in box
Animate Being Associated with Object or Location	15(29)	fishy, pointing to empty fish tank
Modification of Event	ca. 18(1)	again, when he wants someone to do something for him again

[1] Table from Greenfield and Smith (1976, p.70). The examples are from the development of one child, Matthew. Ages are given in months and days, and they represent the first occurrence of each type of utterance. The terms for semantic functions are those of Greenfield and Smith.

[2] These imitative examples are used because of clear behavioral evidence of comprehension; none of the other examples in this table are imitative.

Two important points emerge from this sort of analysis: (1) one-word utterances express underlying relational notions; (2) the order of emergence of notions expressed reflects the child's maturing cognitions about entities and events. Both points closely tie language to cognition. The first point suggests that, when grammar begins to develop in child language, it serves to express relational notions which the child already conceived of at an earlier stage. The second point indicates that the range of notions expressed in speech reflects the child's understanding of the world. To place this point in fuller perspective, we must consider the emergence of symbolic communication within the broader framework of cognitive development.

Language and Cognitive Development

A number of cognitive prerequisites lie behind the emergence of communicative speech. The child must be able to perceive, analyze, and store verbal messages; he must conceive of a stable world, with objects and events and human participants; and he must be able to engage in social interaction for the achievement of various personal and interpersonal goals. The ultimate basis of these prerequisites lies in the evolution of our species and is genetically prepared before the child is born. This genetic potential unfolds in the course of interaction with people and objects and sights and sounds long before the onset of speech. The terms of case grammar, or generative semantics, or other frameworks for describing the semantic content of child language, all assume that the child conceives of a world of animate beings and objects, in which beings act upon objects to move them or change their states, in which beings have experiences, and so forth. Piaget (1951, 1955), in detailed studies of infants, has traced the development of this world understanding which underlies all language and thought. The beginnings of intentional communication arise in later stages of sensory-motor development, preceded by at least a year of active exploration of the world, in which the infant comes to know that objects and people exist outside of himself, and that he and other people can have an effect on the world.

The immediate cognitive precursors to language are the capacities for SYMBOLIC REPRESENTATION and TOOL USE. The child's memory and inner structures must mature to the point that he can represent events to himself—that is, hold them in mind and deal with them in their absence. And he must realize that he can use people—through communication—as means for the realization of desired ends. All of these capacities emerge somewhere around the beginning of the second year of life.

Symbolic representation can be seen in the development of imitation and play. Piaget (1951, p. 63) reported an example of delayed imitation in his daughter at age 1;4 (one year, four months). She had been visited by a little boy who threw a temper tantrum, trying to get out of his playpen by screaming, pushing the playpen backwards, and stamping his feet. The little girl imitated this scene when in her own playpen, 12 hours later, and again two weeks later, after a visit from the same boy. Piaget noted that the time delay between the original event and its imitation is evidence that the child had some representation of the event, some means of holding it in memory. At the same age, she began to use words that she had only heard earlier in given situations, such as saying *in step* while walking, though she had not used these words before, and they had not been uttered by an adult in the immediate situation. Symbolic play also emerged at this time, again indicating an ability to represent absent objects and events. For example, the child rubbed her hands together and pretended to wash them, saying *soap,* though no soap or water were present.

These symbolic capacities follow on the heels of related capacities of tool use. By this stage the child has already learned that he can approach goals indirectly, using other means than immediate grasp. For example, if a doll is placed on a blanket, the younger child will crawl toward the doll, while the older child is able to pull in the blanket in order to get the doll. The child is now able to conceive of chains of causal sequences, in which something other than his own body can be a source of causality. An important instrument in the outside world is, of course, an adult. Only at this stage does the child turn to an adult, establishing eye contact and signalling with gestural and vocal means in an attempt to enlist aid in achieving a goal (Bates, Camaioni & Volterra, 1975; Bates, 1976). Bates (1976, p. 56) points out that such gestures as pointing become communicatively significant in the context of using adults as "tools":

Those actions that were originally means for reaching a goal himself— i.e., orienting, reaching, grasping—are gradually separated from the concrete attempt to reach objects and become instead signals. They are produced in a ritualized fashion, more appropriate for communicating desire to an adult than for filling those desires himself.

In order to use a communicative gesture or sound, the child must shift his orientation from the desired goal to the adult, holding the goal in mind, just as a goal must be held in mind while a child searches for and uses a tool. In both cases, there is an increase in "distancing" between the child's immediate need state and his activity. Bates (p. 61) discusses the emergence of communicative pointing in a one-year-old girl. Pointing began at nine months as a private activity, keeping the child's attention on what she was looking at, rather than establishing contact with an adult. At a later stage, when she began to give objects to adults, she also began to use the pointing gesture in communication. There was an interesting transitional period, however, which shows clearly how the child was trying to put together pointing for herself and pointing as communication.

She would first orient toward the interesting object or event, extending her arm and forefinger in the characteristic pointing gesture while uttering a breathy sound of surprise, *Ha!*, that often accompanies these sequences; then she swung around, pointed at the adult with the same gesture, and returned to look at the object and point toward it once again. This series of steps—point at object, point at adult, point at object—puts together in a chained form the components that eventually form the smooth deictic [i.e., indicating] act of simultaneously pointing at an object while turning to the other for confirmation.

There are obviously close psychological links among these abilities which arise between nine and twelve months of age. Symbolic play and imitation and tool use all involve internal representation and a decrease in impulsive, stimulus-bound behavior. With increased understanding of causal sequences, both tools and adults can be conceived of as intermediaries between desires and goals. Communication arises as the child realizes that, by attracting and directing the adult's attention through speech and gesture, the adult can be used as a means towards those goals. Here we have the precursor of the IMPERATIVE use of language. The child can also seek adult attention as an end in itself, first presenting actions and objects to the adult, and later making utterances about actions and objects. Here we have the precursor of the DECLARATIVE use of language. The sequence of communicative intentions summarized by Greenfield and Smith reflects a development of what it is in the realm of actions and objects that a child can attend to, beginning with actions upon objects, and later conceiving of relations between objects and the qualities of objects. All of this cognitive apparatus is developed before the acquisition of grammar, which we will consider shortly.

It is significant that the constellation of language-related mental capacities emerges during a single period in development. Bates et al. (1977), in a detailed study of twenty-five infants, found that the emergence of the capacity for vocal and gestural naming was strongly correlated with imitation, tool use in problem-solving, and complex object-to-object manipulations in play. There is also evidence from language-impaired children that these skills are especially important for language. Snyder (1975), for example, found that speech-delayed children were normal on a number of cognitive measures, but were delayed in tool-use capacities—just those capacities which seem to be linked to language development. Bates (1977) has recently suggested that there is a very general change in the maturation of memory and attention which serves as a cognitive prerequisite for these symbolic, instrumental, and communicative developments. They all require "an ability to (1) interrupt a goal-system, (2) maintain that goal-system in memory, while (3) simultaneously carrying out a search for alternate means. In short, this may be a very general ability to interrupt and recover complex activities" (p. 5).

Language is thus embedded in a complex network of cognitive abilities. When children first begin to put two words together, somewhere around the end of the second year of life, much of the preparatory work for language use has been carried out. What happens next?

THE DEVELOPMENT OF GRAMMAR

The Emergence of Two-Word Utterances

By the end of the one-word stage the child has a considerable vocabulary, augmented by intonational means for distinguishing requests, statements, questions, complaints, and so forth. Many investigators have noted a period, shortly before the emergence of longer utterances, of successive single words spoken in the same situation, but somehow linked in meaning. Lois Bloom (1973, p. 41) has discussed this period in detail in a book appropriately called *One Word at a Time*. Each of the single words sounds like a full utterance:

> The prosodic pattern that distinguished such words as these said in succession, as single-word utterances, was unmistakable. Each word occurred with terminal falling pitch contour, and relatively equal stress, and there was a variable but distinct pause between them, so that utterance boundaries were clearly marked.

For example, consider the following transcript from Bloom's recordings of her daughter Allison at age 1;6. Context is given on the left, and child speech on the right, with slashes separating single-word utterances with falling pitch.

(Daddy had 'cut' a piece of peach that was in the bowl of a spoon, with a knife. Allison ate both pieces, then picked up another piece of peach and held it out to Daddy)	peach/Daddy/
(Allison picking up the spoon)	spoon/
(Allison giving peach and spoon to Daddy)	Daddy/peach/ cut/

It sounds as if Allison has already conceptualized the whole situation, but is not yet ready to speak of it in one connected utterance. There is no particular order to the individual words, but they are elements of what must be an underlying proposition on a cognitive level—namely, that Daddy is to cut a peach (with a knife) on a spoon. It is only the knife which is not mentioned in this succession of single words. (And it is interesting to note that later, in the period of two-word utterances, mention of the instrument is also rare. Apparently instruments are less salient to child cognition than actors, actions, objects, and places.) From here on, the task of learning a language is to figure out which parts of a situation are to be encoded, and how those parts combine into structured utterances. At 1;6 Allison apparently has a limited utterance programming "window" through which only one word can pass at a time. As this window expands with maturation, more words can be uttered within one span, and the problem of productive grammar emerges.

Even at the one-word stage, the child must choose which particular word to utter in a situation. In the example above, Allison begins by holding out a new piece of peach and saying *peach*. This is obviously the new element in the situation. There is some evidence that children choose to encode the most salient aspect of a situation first. Greenfield and Smith (1976) propose that the child, limited to one word, chooses the most "informative" element to speak about—that is, the element which is least certain or least presupposed by the situation. For example, Matthew, at 18 months, points to his toy car and says *car*. Then, as he pushes his car, he says *byebye*. First the car is in the focus of his attention, then the action performed with the car. At the two-word stage, he would be able to say *car byebye* in a single utterance. Later, when the car falls, he says *down*. Given that the car has been obviously present up until that point, the single word *down* encodes what is new—namely, the change in the situation. Again, at the two-word stage, *car down* would be possible. At that stage, then, the child can fill in some of the background, or given information, rather than leave it to be contextually presupposed.

The advent of the two-word stage does not represent an advance in what the child is capable of speaking about, but rather an advance in how much of a communicative intention can be coded in a single utterance. This point finds further support if we examine the content of early two-word utterances. Various semantic schemes have been proposed to categorize the meanings of early utterances (e.g., Bloom, Lightbown, & Hood, 1975; Braine, 1976; Brown, 1973; Schlesinger, 1971; Slobin, 1970; Wells, 1974; and many others). Regardless of the scheme, the categories reflect cognitions which have been available to the child for some time before the emergence of two-word utterances. Furthermore, the categories seem to be the same regardless of the particular language being acquired. For example, consider the child utterances from a half-dozen languages presented in Table 4-2, which could be expanded to include many more languages, and which could be classified in various ways. The important thing about tables such as this one is to show that early utterances arise from the framework of the child's thought, action, and social interaction. Speech arises from a cognitive and interpersonal matrix before it bears the stamp of any particular language. By and large, the child begins by mapping communicative intentions onto utterances according to his own plan and must later adapt that expressive mapping to the conventions of his speech community.

At this point in our developmental story, there are two major paths to explore. As the child grows, there are more things he is able to think about, and hence more things he wants to talk about. Increase in communicative intent is one source of language development. At the same time, the child learns more about the structure of his particular language, and can map his intentions onto more complex utterances. The child is always working on two planes at once: the plane of content and the plane of form. The plane of content is determined by universal aspects of mental growth (see Edwards, 1973). The plane of form is language specific, but the forms of a particular language can only be discovered if the child has general strategies for the acquisition of linguistic knowledge, since he cannot know in advance which language he is meant to learn. Let us look a bit more at the first problem—the development of communicative intentions—and then turn to the problem of the acquisition of grammar itself—that is, the problem of mapping intentions onto the particular structured forms of a given language.

The Growth of Propositional Complexity

Let us assume that, from the one-word stage onward, the child is attempting to encode PROPOSITIONS in terms of the generative semantics model presented in Chapter 1. That is, the child has in mind a semantic configuration involving a predicate and its associated argument or arguments. This is, of course, only one of many analytic schemes one could use in describing child speech;[2] but it is one which has been fully developed and applied to linguistic development (Antinucci & Parisi, 1973; Parisi & Antinucci, 1974). How can we validate this assumption, and what can we learn about development using this approach?

Antinucci and Parisi followed two Italian-speaking children in detail between the ages of 1;4 and 2;4, recording two hours of spontaneous speech every two weeks and carefully noting the contexts in which utterances occurred. (This is the standard method for gathering data of this sort, developed in the early 1960s by Roger Brown, Susan Ervin-Tripp and Wick Miller, and Martin Braine.) One cannot read a child's mind, but Antinucci and Parisi satisfied themselves that they were able to ascertain communicative intentions using several criteria: close examination of the circumstances in which utterances occurred, mothers' interpretations of child speech, and the child's comprehension and response to adult utterances. These criteria are familiar to you from our discussion of the meanings of one-word utterances. For example, it is only through a knowledge of the context of the child encountering his father's slipper that one can attribute a possessive meaning to the utterance *daddy*.

Let us consider a number of utterances spoken in contexts in which the child either gives something to another person, or receives something. The underlying semantic configuration for utterances describing object

---

2. Leonard (1976) summarizes over a dozen analytic schemes used by various investigators to systematize the facts of semantic development.

TABLE 4-2
Functions of Two-Word Sentences in Child Speech,
with Examples from Several Languages[1]

				LANGUAGE			
Function of Utterance	English	German	Russian	Finnish	Luo	Samoan
LOCATE, NAME	there book that car see doggie	buch da [book there] gukuk wauwau [see doggie]	Tosya tam [Tosya there]	tuossa Rina [there Rina] vettä siinä [water there]	en saa [it clock] ma wendo [this visitor]	Keith lea [Keith there]
DEMAND, DESIRE	more milk give candy want gum	mehr milch [more milk] bitte apfel [please apple]	yeshchë moloko [more milk] day chasy [give watch]	anna Rina [give Rina]	miya tamtam [give-me candy] adway cham [I-want food]	mai pepe [give doll] fia moe [want sleep]
NEGATE[2]	no wet no wash not hungry allgone milk	nicht blasen [not blow] kaffee nein [coffee no]	vody net [water no] gus' tyu-tyu [goose gone]	ei susi [not wolf] enää pipi [anymore sore]	beda onge [my-slasher absent]	le 'ai [not eat] uma mea [allgone thing]
DESCRIBE EVENT OR SITUATION[3]	Bambi go mail come hit ball block fall baby high-chair	puppe kommt [doll comes] tiktak hängt [clock hangs] sofa sitzen [sofa sit] messer schneiden [cut knife]	mama prua [mama walk] papa bay-bay [papa sleep] korka upala [crust fell] nashla yaichko [found egg] baba kreslo [grandma armchair]	Seppo putoo [Seppo fall] talli 'bm-bm' [garage 'car']	chungu biro [European comes] odhi skul [he-went school] omoyo oduma [she-dries maize]	pa'u pepe [fall doll] tapale 'oe [hit you] tu'u lalo [put down]

INDICATE POSSESSION	my shoe mama dress	mein ball [my ball] mamas hut [mama's hat]	mami chashka [mama's cup] pup moya [navel my]	täti auto [aunt car]	kom baba [chair father]	lole a'u [candy my] polo 'oe [ball your] paluni mama [balloon mama]
MODIFY, QUALIFY	pretty dress big boat	milch heiss [milk hot] armer wauwau [poor dog]	mama khoroshaya [mama good] papa bol'shoy [papa big]	rikki auto [broken car] torni iso [tower big]	piypiy kech [pepper hot] gwen madichol [chicken black]	fa'ali'i pepe [headstrong baby]
QUESTION[4]	where ball	wo ball [where ball]	gde papa [where papa]	missä pallo [where ball]		fea Punafu [where Punafu]

[1] The examples come from a variety of studies, published and unpublished. Data from the three non-Indo-European languages are drawn from the doctoral dissertations of Melissa Bowerman (Harvard, 1973: Finnish), Ben Blount (Berkeley, 1969: Luo), and Keith Kernan (Berkeley, 1969: Samoan). (Luo is spoken in Kenya.) The examples given here are representative of many more utterances of the same type in each language. The order of the two words in the utterance is generally fixed in all of the languages except Finnish, where both orders can be used freely for some utterance types by some children.

[2] Bloom (1970) has noted three different sorts of negation: (1) nonexistence (e.g., *no wet*, meaning 'dry'), (2) rejection (e.g., *no wash*, meaning 'don't wash me'), and (3) denial (e.g., *no girl*, denying a preceding assertion that a boy was a girl).

[3] Descriptions are of several types: (1) agent+action (e.g., *Bambi go*), (2) action+object (e.g., *hit ball*), (3) agent+object (e.g., *mama bread*, meaning 'mama is cutting bread'), (4) locative (e.g., *baby high chair*, meaning 'baby is in the high chair'), (5) instrumental (e.g., *cut knife*), (6) dative (e.g., *throw daddy*, meaning 'throw it to daddy'). (The use of terminology of grammatical case is suggestive here; cf. Fillmore's (1968) discussion of deep cases as underlying linguistic universals.)

[4] In addition to wh-questions, yes-no questions can be made by pronouncing any two-word sentence with rising intonation, with the exception of Finnish. (Melissa Bowerman reports that the emergence of yes-no questions is, accordingly, exceptionally late in Finnish child language.)

transfer is a predication ('give') with three arguments: an ACTOR who causes an OBJECT to move to a RECIPIENT. Examining a number of one- and two-word utterances of a one-and-a-half year old girl, Claudia, Antinucci and Parisi found that all of these elements of the underlying configuration could be expressed, though no single utterance, of course, could contain all of them. For example, Claudia said the following (as translated into English):

ACTION
    Give   (Giving something to her mother)

OBJECT
    Water   (Asking her mother for some water)

RECIPIENT
    To me   (Asking Francesco for something)

RECIPIENT + OBJECT
    To me candies   (Asking for candies)

ACTION + OBJECT
    Give ball   (Asking for a ball)

ACTION + ACTOR
    Give mommy   (Asking for something from her mother)

RECIPIENT + ACTION
    Mommy give   (Giving something to her mother)

Antinucci and Parisi conclude that all of these utterances reflect the same underlying structure, with a limitation in "lexicalization span"—that is, the number of elements of the structure which can be expressed as words under the time pressure of producing a single utterance. Note that Claudia, at this stage, could lexicalize one or two of the semantic elements at a time, and across the whole collection of utterances, all of the possible elements occurred. Basing themselves on Claudia's actions and apparent intentions in producing such utterances, the investigators (1973, p. 611) propose:

> When she says *da* [give], it is difficult to suppose that she does not know who must give, what must be given, and who must receive, as in that case we should be supposing that she does not execute the mental operations—which we call semantic components—corresponding to all these elements.

Further evidence comes from the advent of three-word sentences at a later stage. Such sentences, with *give,* reflect an expansion in the lexicalization, or sentence programming span, but no increase in underlying propositional complexity:

ACTION + ACTOR + RECIPIENT
    Give grandma cookie   (Grandma gives cookie to Claudia)

Now Claudia is able to lexicalize two arguments along with the predication.

Looking at all of the utterances from an early stage of development, regardless of length, Antinucci and Parisi found that the two children they studied were limited to the expression of a simple proposition involving a single predicate and its arguments. At this early stage, only the NECESSARY semantic components of a sentence could be attributed to the children. All of the arguments were single nouns or pronouns. There was no elaboration—of modification of nouns, of mention of time or place of action; nor were propositions linked to one another. Apparently we can look upon the entire first period of language development as a gradually increasing ability to encode more and more components of basic propositions which are cognitively available almost from the onset of speech.

A major advance in semantic complexity comes when the child is able to produce utterances which include two underlying semantic predicates. This important structural change is not an advance in utterance length, but in underlying complexity. Two things are added at the same time: adverbials and noun modifiers (Parisi & Antinucci, 1974). Consider adverbials first. A two-word utterance like *doll sleeps* expresses a proposition with a single predicate: *doll* is the single argument semantically required by the predicate *sleep*. But an utterance like *sleep bed* is semantically more complex. The predicate does not require mention of a location. What we have here is a proposition with two predicates: (1) something happens in a bed, namely, (2) someone sleeps. Parisi and Antinucci diagram this proposition in two parts, involving a nucleus and an adverbial:

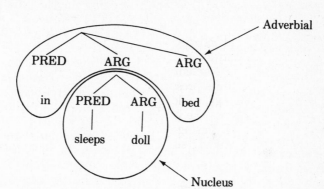

Utterances like *sleep bed,* although apparently simple on the surface, do not occur during the first period. That period, as pointed out above, is limited to expressions of the nucleus. During the second period, a variety of locative and temporal adverbials occur. They do not, at first, add surface complexity. In fact, the child may already be using four-word utterances for nuclear expressions, yet be limited to one- or two-word utterances involving adverbials (e.g., *later, play now, wait here*). This suggests that the addition of an adverbial takes additional effort, leaving the child less "processing space" for the lexicalization of other parts of the semantic configuration.

Parisi and Antinucci list a number of types of adverbials which emerge during this period: (1) locative *(wait here),* (2) temporal *(come tomorrow),* (3) addition *(draw again, Francesco too),* (4) manner *(draw like this),* (5) instrumental *(works with pliers),* (6) comitative *(play with Paola).*

At the same time, the nouns and pronouns that are arguments of the nucleus begin to be modified. An utterance like *Broken Tata's car,* meaning 'Tata's car is broken', also encodes a complex proposition: NUCLEUS: 'car is broken' and MODIFIER: 'car belongs to Tata'. Possessives and adjectives enter at the beginning of this period, followed later by more extended modifiers expressed as relative clauses (I draw the elephant with the tail). Both adverbials and noun modifiers map two configurations onto one surface utterance—an obligatory nucleus and an optional addition. The important advance is not a matter of the number of words that a child can pack into an utterance, but the number of separate predicates that he can conceive of and attempt to express simultaneously.

The remaining advance in propositional complexity is the embedding of one sentence in another. This comes toward the end of the period studied by Antinucci and Parisi. For example, the child can use a causative verb to express the relation between his action and a result (I made Lellina cross; I'm making it spin). Modal verbs, like can and have to, relate one semantic structure to another (I have to go home). Complement verbs, like know, can embed one sentence in another (Do you know we're going skiing?). At this point, causal and temporal adverbials can also be expressed as full sentences (I want some wine because I'm thirsty; When I've finished a cookie I take another one).

By this time, after about two years of life, the child has demonstrated knowledge of the basic underlying semantic configurations of language: he expresses complex propositions containing a nucleus and non-nuclear structures, both of which can be realized as full sentences. A similar pattern has been confirmed for a number of English-speaking children by Johnston (1976). And so, with the characteristic optimism of developmental psycholinguistics, I will suggest that this pattern of development is universal. It SHOULD be universal because it seems to reflect a growth in general abilities (1) to conceive of relations of time, space, causality, purpose, obligation, and the like, and (2) to lexicalize more and more of communicative intent in a single coherent utterance.

Given a development in the structured content that a child wishes to express, and an increase in the ability to produce sentences under time constraints, we can now turn to the problem of how the child figures out the means of expressing his intentions in the language of the particular speech community he has been born into.

The Mapping Problem

We are now in a position to consider in greater detail the problem of mapping communicative intentions onto utterances. Imagine a child who is able to conceive of a nuclear proposition about object transfer. He has segmented his language into words; he knows word meanings; his processing span has reached the point where he can encode all of the elements of the underlying semantic configuration. What remains to be learned? Let us suppose that the child wishes to report that he received a ball from his father. He knows that he has to say something about an actor, an object, a recipient, and an action that relates these three participants. In English he could say: Daddy gave me the ball—one word for each of the basic elements, and an extra word, the. The task seems straightforward. It appears that the child simply has to learn the proper order for these terms—which in English is ACTOR-ACTION-RECIPIENT-OBJECT. And in English he must indicate, in addition, whether the object was definite *(the)* or indefinite *(a)*.

But if we look across languages, it becomes evident that there is more to the task than meets the eye. Why indicate that the object, and only the object, was definite? And why indicate definiteness by a little word that precedes the object name? And why NOT indicate other facts, which are also obvious—like the sex of the actor and/or recipient, or that the action took place recently, or that balls are round? It is evident that there are many things that COULD be said about this situation, but that English requires only that the basic elements be named, with an indication that the action was in the past and the object was definite. The child must discover which of the myriad of known aspects of this situation are obligatorily encoded in his language. Compare English and a closely related language, German:

Daddy	*gave*	*me*	*the*	*ball.*
ACTOR	ACTION	RECIPIENT	(DEFINITE)	OBJECT
	(PAST)			

Der	*Vater*	*gab*	*mir*	*den*	*Ball.*
(DEFINITE)	ACTOR	ACTION	RECIPIENT	(DEFINITE)	OBJECT
(SINGULAR)		(PAST)		(SINGULAR)	
(MASCULINE)		(3rd PERSON)		(MASCULINE)	
(SUBJECT)		(SINGULAR)		(OBJECT)	

The child must learn the same word order rule in both languages. In German, as in English, the child is required to mark the object as definite. But German articles, unlike English *the,* also encode gender, number, and case. The German equivalent of *the ball—den Ball—*says, in the single word *den,* that the ball is a definite object which is also singular and considered as masculine. Unlike English, German requires that the actor must also be marked by an article, indicating that it is definite, singular, masculine, and the subject of the sentence. And the German verb indicates not only tense but number. So the mapping problems differ. The semantic elements given in parentheses above are language specific, elaborating in seemingly arbitrary ways the nuclear proposition.

Consider several other examples. In Hebrew the verb tells more about the actor than German, indicating also the sex of the actor; but this information is not expressed in the word for the actor, as it is in German. And whereas the German article, *den,* encodes both object and definiteness in one word, Hebrew uses a separate particle, *et,* to indicate that the following noun phrase is an object:

Aba	*natan*	*li*	*et*	*ha*	*kadur.*
ACTOR	ACTION	RECIPIENT	(OBJECT PARTICLE)	(DEFINITE)	OBJECT
	(PAST)				
	(3rd PERSON)				
	(SINGULAR)				
	(MASCULINE)				

Again, the order of elements is the same. English, German, and Hebrew differ in how much must be said about number, gender, and definiteness of the participants, and where and how this information is to be encoded.

The order of elements, of course, is not universal. In Turkish, for example, the order is 'father to-me ball gave', where each of the four words compresses information encoded by separate words in other languages:

Babam	*bana*	*topu*	*verdi.*
ACTOR	RECIPIENT	OBJECT	ACTION
(POSSESSED BY		(DEFINITE)	(PAST)
SPEAKER)			(3rd PERSON)
			(SINGULAR)
			(WITNESSED BY SPEAKER)

The word for 'ball'—*top*—has an ending which indicates that it is definite and an object. The Turkish child is required to indicate that it is 'MY father' who acted, and that he knows of this action by direct experience. A different verb ending would be required if the child knew of the action by inference or hearsay. Again, the mapping problem is not at all straightforward beyond the basic four elements.

This list of additional facts required by various languages could go on and on—but not indefinitely. In Chinese one does not indicate whether the action took place in the past, but whether or not it was completed. In Navaho an obligatory verb particle would indicate that the object given was round in shape. Looking across all of the languages of the world, we would find a finite list of those aspects of situations which the grammar requires one to encode—aspects of the temporal nature of the act, physical characteristics of the objects, and various psychological, physical, and social aspects of the human interactants. Many other things which the child knows and feels about the situation are never encoded in obligatory grammatical structures. Probably no language REQUIRES one to mark, somewhere in the sentence, whether the ball was pretty, or whether the action was performed on a warm day, or indoors, and so forth. The general point is this: the child must somehow know what aspects of his vast knowledge of the world are likely to find obligatory grammatical mapping in human language; he must discover which particular aspects are in fact encoded by the grammar of his language; and he must discover the particular means (word order, affixes, particles, etc.) employed by his language. Thus there is a long way between a COMMUNICATIVE INTENTION, which may be present in basic form even at the one-word stage, and the SEMANTIC STRUCTURE containing that particular array of notions which must be mapped onto a grammatical utterance in a specific language. The preschool years are spent in discovering these mapping principles. (For more detail, see E. Clark, 1973, 1975, 1977.) By examining children's initial attempts to produce structured utterances, we can reveal some of the strategies involved in the construction of grammar—for each child must construct for himself anew the grammar of his native language.

The Child Creates Order

Early in the two-word stage one can observe regularity and originality in children's utterances. Consider, for example, a child who says *allgone milk* upon draining a glass of milk. His utterance does not seem to be a simple imitation, since it is unlikely that parents say things like *allgone milk*.

From adult utterances like *The milk is allgone,* the child has determined a general meaning for *allgone,* and he produces his own constructions, such as those of a child studied by Martin Braine (1963), who said *allgone sticky* after washing his hands, and *allgone outside* after the door was shut, apparently noting that *the outside is allgone.* These utterances, and dozens like them, follow a simple positional formula (Braine, 1976), with *allgone* in first position. This is a simple sort of order, but at first the formulas may be limited to specific words or meanings—the child may always mention the actor first in actor-action constructions, he may always indicate location in second position *(shoe here, book there),* and so forth.

At some point, he must arrive at more general principles. For example, nouns are always pluralized in the same way in English, regardless of whether they are functioning as actors or objects or recipients or instruments. Along the way to these generalizations, the child may make some premature guesses as to the notions which are grammatically marked in his language. For example, in Russian the direct object of a verb is marked by an accusative inflection. Yet, one Russian child studied by Gvozdev (1949) at first put the accusative inflection only on nouns which were objects of direct action or manipulation. In utterances like the equivalent of *throw ball* or *tear paper,* he added the appropriate suffix to the noun, but failed to do so for utterances like *read book* or *see clock.* Apparently he made only a partial generalization—that the inflection encodes direct physical action upon an object. This error shows that the child has indeed made a grammatical generalization, but one that does not entirely correspond to the input he has received. Again, he has not simply imitated adult Russian, but has come to an initial conclusion about the function of a grammatical inflection—in this case a conclusion which is quite in accord with a two-year-old's action-based view of objects.

Child speech deviates from adult speech—but it deviates in systematic fashion, leading one to believe that the deviations are creatively constructed by the child on the basis of a partial analysis of the language. Close examination of deviations reveals the child's propensity to form regular systems, ignoring or avoiding the irregularities of adult speech. The child's creative and regularizing contribution is clearly revealed in the overregularization of grammatical inflections, where consistently deviant utterances appear in all languages. Parents and school teachers know, for example, that English-speaking children say things like *comed, breaked, goed, doed,* and so on. That is, the irregular (or "strong") verbs are inflected for past tense as if they were regular (or "weak") verbs. You have probably also heard regularizations of other sorts—say, of the plural, as in *foots, mouses,* and the like. This tendency to regularize continues well into elementary school for some children.

Now, from a traditional point of view of psychological learning theory, we would expect to find that children begin by using some regular forms correctly—like *walked* and *helped* and so on—and that they extend (or OVERextend) this rule to the irregular verbs. The real story, however, is much more interesting. The irregular verbs are the most frequent in English, and children begin by learning a number of these forms, like *came* and *broke* and *went,* as unanalyzed vocabulary items. So the first past tenses used by the child are grammatically correct, but not based on a productive rule, since there are no clear rules for forming these past tenses. The child must memorize that *broke* means 'break in the past' while *made* means 'make in the past', though the two verbs sound the same in the present. Then, shortly after learning only one or two regular past tense forms—like *smoked* and *played*—the child replaces the correct but irregular past tense forms with their incorrect overgeneralizations from the regular forms. Thus children actually say *it came off, it broke,* and *he did it,* before they say *it comed off, it breaked,* and *he doed it.* Even though the correct forms may have been practiced for several months, they are driven out of the child's speech by the overregularization, and may not return for years.

This phenomenon is rather puzzling from the point of view of some approaches to the psychology of learning. The correct irregular forms were already learned, practiced, presumably reinforced. Then suddenly the child begins saying things like *goed*—which could not be imitations, since he has never heard such forms from his parents, and which are certainly not reinforced by his parents. (These facts are true of first-born children of educated families.) Yet these overgeneralizations persist, sometimes for years. The crucial point is that the strong verbs, though they are frequent, do not follow a regular pattern, and evidently children are especially sensitive to patterned regularities. As soon as a pattern is noticed, the child will try to apply it as broadly as possible, thus producing words which are regular, even if they have never been heard before. One cannot help but be impressed with the child's great propensity to generalize, to analogize, to look for regularities—in short, to seek and create order in his language.

It is important to the theory of language acquisition to discover what sorts of order children are sensitive to. Comparison between the acquisition of different types of languages can cast light on this question (Bowerman, in press; Slobin, 1973; 1978). Let us compare the ways in which two different types of languages mark the noun as direct object, or accusative. In many languages (called "inflectional" languages) some marker is attached to the noun which functions as direct object. In Turkish the inflection is totally regular, applying to all nouns in the language in similar fashion. One simply adds a final vowel to the noun, matching the vowel of the suffixed inflection to the preceding vowel in the word ("vowel harmony"). In the example given earlier, *top* means 'ball' and *topu* means 'ball functioning as definite direct object' (the ball which is thrown, given, seen, etc.). The final vowel, *u,* is a rounded vowel produced in the back of the mouth, like the *o* vowel of the word it is attached to. Vowel harmony is quickly and easily acquired by children—it is almost an automatic result of holding one's mouth in roughly the same position for a succession of vowels in a word. Turkish children also quickly learn that word endings indicate grammatical relations, and well before the age of two they productively and correctly use a range of suffixes indicating such notions as direct object, location, source, goal, and possession (e.g., *topta* means 'on the ball', *toptan* 'from the ball', *topum* 'my ball').

The idea of mapping such notions onto word endings comes easily to small children, and even if the inflectional system is not as regular as Turkish, inflections always appear at an early age. Slavic languages, for example, also use suffixed inflections, but—characteristic, alas, of Indo-European languages—the system is quite irregular. Whereas Turkish has a uniform rule of adding a final harmonized vowel, in these languages the accusative inflection has many forms, depending on whether the noun is considered masculine, feminine, or neuter; whether it is singular or plural; whether it refers (if masculine) to an animate being; and what kind of sound it ends in. Let us consider one corner of the complex inflectional paradigm (which includes six cases and three genders)—the singular accusative, which has been studied developmentally in Russian (El'konin, 1973; Gvozdev, 1949; Slobin, 1966; Zakharova, 1973) and Serbo-Croatian (Radulovic, 1975). Compare the nominative form with the accusative. (The nominative is the base form of the noun, used when the noun is subject of the sentence, or simply being named, e.g., *This is a ball* or *The ball is red.*) The Russian suffixes are given below, but the paradigm is almost the same in Serbo-Croatian, and the developmental findings are the same for both languages. The symbol Ø ("zero") means no ending is added.

	MASCULINE		NEUTER	FEMININE
	ANIMATE	INANIMATE		
NOMINATIVE	Ø	Ø	*-o*	*-a*
ACCUSATIVE	*-a*	Ø	*-o*	*-u*

Several facts are striking in this paradigm—facts which one would expect to delay acquisition. For one thing, note that the accusative is often not marked at all: for masculine inanimate and neuter nouns, the nominative and accusative forms are identical. Where the accusative is marked, there is no common principle. If a noun refers to a masculine animate being, an ending in *-a* indicates the accusative; but the same ending indicates the nominative for feminine nouns. (For example, *drug* means 'friend', and 'the friend that I love' becomes *druga;* but *podruga* means 'girl friend', and 'the girl friend that I love' becomes *podrugu!*)

The child, of course, does not see this paradigm laid out on a page, as you have it here. Rather, he hears many different nouns in many different sentences and must determine the relational meanings marked by the suffixes. (The entire system is far more complicated, since most of the suffixes, like *-a,* have several meanings.) Yet the Slavic-speaking child does not simply throw up his hands in despair. At about the same age as the Turkish child—that is, somewhere before his second birthday—he begins to use suffixed inflections productively, appropriately encoding such meanings as direct object, indirect object, location, and others. The notion of inflectional marking of grammatical relations can be easily discovered even in a system as complex and irregular as this one—suggesting, as we will see later, that the child may have language acquisition strategies which are well adapted to the discovery of certain kinds of grammatical structures.

However, like the English-speaking child learning the past tense forms, the Russian or Serbo-Croatian child constructs a more regular system than he has heard. Examine the paradigm presented above and ask yourself what you would do if you wanted to find a clear accusative inflection. The feminine *-u* ending is the only unique and clearly marked indicator of the accusative in the system—and this is the ending chosen by children for all accusatives. That is, the form of overregularization in this situation consists in marking all nouns, regardless of gender, with a final *-u* when they function as direct object in a sentence. In effect, these Slavic children have made their language much like Turkish, with a single, unique suffix indicating direct object for all nouns. They spend the next four or five years sorting out all of the separate cases and irregularities. The abundance of inflections allows for many more overgeneralizations than in English. Again and again a form which has been highly practiced will suddenly be driven out by another, more regular form, and only much later will a proper balance be achieved. However, the imposition of order, and the early sensitivity to suffixes as grammatical markers, are revealed—in all of these examples and more—as basic "operating principles" which guide the child in the discovery and construction of grammar. (See Slobin, 1978, for a summary of cross-linguistic findings on language acquisition.)

Grammatical Rules and the Growth of Processing Capacity

We have encountered the notion of processing capacity, or sentence programming span, several times already. In early stages of development, the child is limited in the number of words he can produce in one connected utterance and the number of semantic configurations he can encode. At later stages, grammatical complexity imposes burdens on processing capacity, and children may be forced to delete or simplify grammatical elements in order to produce a complete utterance within the available "time window." The ways in which grammar is altered under such time pressures reveals something of the child's underlying syntactic rules.

For example, Ursula Bellugi (Bellugi-Klima, 1968) studied the development of questions with "wh-words" *(what, who, why,* etc.) in English-speaking children. As mentioned in Chapter 1, children frequently utter questions such as *What the boy hit?* Other typical forms are: *What he can ride in?; What he wants?; Where I should put it?;* and *Why he's doing it?* In all these examples, the child has correctly performed one grammatical operation—preposing the question word; but he has failed to perform another—inversion of subject and auxiliary. Bellugi found that at the same stage at which a child produced wh-questions like *What he can ride in?* he also produced inverted yes-no questions like *Can he ride in a truck?* Thus the child was also able to perform the grammatical operation of inversion, or transposing. It seems, therefore, that both preposing and transposing are "psychologically real" operations for the child, for we have evidence that each can be performed singly. Apparently there is some performance limitation, some restriction on "sentence programming span," which blocks the application of both operations together at this stage of development.

Sentences such as *Where I can put them?* are clearly PRODUCED by the child. They could not have been imitated from adult speech. Furthermore, when asked to imitate such a sentence a child will often filter it through his own rule system:

ADULT: Adam, say what I say: "Where can I put them?"
ADAM: Where I can put them?

It is as if the child even imposes his own structure on what he hears. Again, as in Chapter 2, we see the phenomenon of an ACTIVE perceiver, processing heard speech according to his own inner structures.

Bellugi suggests that small children operate under a performance restriction on the number of operations they can perform in producing a sentence. At the stage just discussed, the child is apparently limited to one of the two operations of transposing and preposing, and will fail to transpose in sentences where the adult system requires both operations. At a later stage the sentence programming span apparently increases, and the child is able to perform both operations on one sentence, producing appropriate sentences such as *Why can he go out?* At this stage, however, he cannot produce appropriate adult sentences when three operations are called for. This is clear when the operation of negation is introduced. The negative element must be attached to the auxiliary, and the child demonstrates his control of this operation by producing such sentences as *He can't go out.* But note what happens when negation is called for along with preposing and transposing: the child says *Why he can't go out?* failing to transpose, although he transposes correctly in the corresponding affirmative, *Why can he go out?*

Bellugi demonstrated this phenomenon very clearly with the little boy who is referred to in the literature as Adam. She played a game in which Adam had to ask questions of a puppet shaped like an Old Lady:

ADULT: Adam, ask the Old Lady where she can find some toys.
ADAM: Old Lady, where can you find some toys?
ADULT: Adam, ask the Old Lady why she can't run.
ADAM: Old Lady, why you can't run?

Bellugi (1968, p. 40) gave numerous problems of this sort to Adam. She concludes: "In his responses, all affirmatives were inverted, all negatives were not. The interpretation again fits with the notion of a limit on the permitted complexity at one stage."

Slobin and Welsh (1973) have used the technique of elicited imitation to probe in detail a two-year-old girl's understanding of complex grammatical constructions. For example, consider the following simplification in imitation:

ADULT: Say: "The man who I saw yesterday got wet."
CHILD (age 2;4): I saw the man and he got wet.

Although this child does not yet produce embedded relative clauses of the sort offered by the adult model, it is clear that she is able to process them, since her imitation preserves the meaning of the complex sentence, breaking it down into two simple sentences within her sentence programming capacities. Again, the child's knowledge of grammar is revealed by deviations from the adult model, as well as by acquisition of that model. But what does it mean to say that a child "knows grammar"?

What is a "Rule"?

The discussion so far in this book has made reference repeatedly to the speaker's knowledge of the rules of his language and to the emergence of various sorts of rules in the child. It is time to examine this notion more carefully, before going on to consider how one may account for language acquisition. You will remember the proposal in discussing grammar that the great productivity of human language—the ability to produce and understand endless novel sentences—requires that one speak in terms of the formation of grammatical rules, rather than the learning of large numbers of specific word combinations. But the notion of "rule" can be easily misunderstood in the psychological realm as can related notions such as "processing strategies," "knowledge of underlying structure," and the like. Psycholinguistic writing may lead you to think that we believe people can state explicit rules of grammar, and that children learn such rules; or that one consciously applies various strategies in acquiring or using language. This, of course, is not what we have in mind. None of us, for example, can state all the rules of English. Perhaps this important notion of rule can be clarified by asking about the sorts of behavioral evidence that would enable one to say that a person "possesses" or "acts as if he knows" a rule, or that he is "operating according to a particular strategy," or the like. (The approach outlined below can be applied to other realms of social behavior and its related cognitive structures, although the discussion here deals with rules in terms of grammatical development in childhood.)

There are various levels of evidence for rules, ranging from weak to stringent. The simplest sort of evidence comes from analysis of natural behavior—in our case the spontaneous speech of the child. For example, at the elementary level of two-word utterances, regularities can already be detected, since not all possible word combinations actually occur, and certain word orders seem to be preferred. This is the earliest sort of evidence for rules ontogenetically—REGULARITIES OF BEHAVIOR.

A more stringent criterion for the existence of rules is the search for the extension of regularities to new instances. As we have seen, the spontaneous speech of the child can furnish such evidence, as when one encounters utterances such as *it breaked* or *two mouses,* or the overextension of the Russian and Serbo-Croatian feminine accusative suffix. Jean Berko (1958) developed an explicit test of children's ability to extend morphological rules to new cases, and her method has been widely used in the developmental study of various rule systems in a number of languages (Ferguson & Slobin, 1973). She presented children with new words, inviting them to apply their linguistic knowledge to the use of these words. For example, a child is presented with a picture of a little creature called a *wug,* and then is asked to name a picture showing two such creatures. If he says *two wugs,* one has clear evidence that he knows how to produce this particular English plural ending, since he has clearly never heard the word *wug* before. (This technique, for obvious reasons, has become widely known as "The Wug Test.")

But there are even more stringent tests, or definitions, of a rule. Later on in his development, the child will demonstrate a NORMATIVE sense of rules—that is, he will be able to judge if an utterance is correct with respect to some linguistic standard. This is what linguists refer to as a "sense of grammaticality." Several levels of evidence of a sense of grammaticality emerge with age, demonstrating increasing linguistic self-awareness on the part of the child (Sinclair, Jarvella, & Levelt, 1978).

Once again, the earliest evidence comes from spontaneous speech. When a child stops and corrects himself, one can infer that he is monitoring his speech against some notion of correctness. By age three, self-corrections are frequent. For example, the following was recorded in the free speech of a three-year-old girl: *She had a silly putty like me had . . . like I . . . like I did.* It is evident that this girl was checking her speech against her linguistic rules as she went along. What is equally evident from other utterances is that she was using her OWN rules as the standard for her sense of grammaticality, and not those of adults. For example, later on in the same sample she "corrected" herself as follows: *Why . . . why . . . why ducks have not . . . why ducks have no hands?*

Perhaps a more stringent test of the sense of grammaticality is met when the child detects deviations from the norm in the speech of others. Three-year-olds are also heard to correct the speech of other children (and even of their parents), though the developmental relation between self-correction and correction of others has not been clearly established.

The most stringent criterion of grammatical judgment (or other normative judgments, such as appropriateness or meaningfulness) is response to a direct question. One can ask the child, for example, if it is "better" or "more correct" to say *two foots* or *two feet*. This is a major type of data for the linguist working with adult informants. The ability to make such overt grammatical judgments is late to develop in childhood, and, unfortunately, of little use in dealing with very young children. The frustrations resulting from such attempts are aptly captured by what has come to be known as the "pop-go-weasel effect," described by Roger Brown and Ursula Bellugi (1964):

INTERVIEWER: Now Adam, listen to what I say. Tell me which is better . . . some water or a water.
ADAM (two years old): Pop go weasel.

So far, then, we have the following evidence for rules. We can be fairly sure that a child has some rule system if his production is regular, if he extends these regularities to new instances, and if he can detect deviations from regularity in his own speech and the speech of others. This is generally what psycholinguists mean when they speak of the child's learning, or forming, or possession of linguistic rules. Note that I have left out the most stringent test for the existence of rules, namely: Can the individual state the explicit rule? As I pointed out before, using this as evidence, of course, we would all fail the test. Since no complete and adequate grammar of English (or any language) has yet been written, in fact none of us KNOWS the rules of English according to this criterion. We can follow them and use them implicitly (in some as yet unknown psychological sense), but we can state them only rarely, imperfectly, and with uncertainty. Explicit statement of rules is irrelevant to our concerns here, and is an entirely different sort of ability than we are now considering. From the point of view of the scientific observer, it is possible to describe the speaker's behavior in terms of "rules" (or "strategies," or "heuristics," or what have you). Such a description, however, should not be taken to imply that the particular descriptive terms devised by the scientist are actual entities existing inside the individual in a definite psychological or physiological sense. In very rough and brief form, the sorts of behavior I have just listed constitute evidence for behaving, in Susan Ervin-Tripp's terms, "as though one knew the rules" (in Slobin, 1967, p. x).

Developmental psycholinguists have collected much evidence of this sort, indicating that children speaking a variety of languages and growing up in a variety of cultural and social settings, develop, discard, and refine linguistic rule systems. Although there are individual differences in the child's approach to the task of language acquisition (Nelson, 1973), the evidence suggests that individual children go through strikingly similar stages of development in acquiring the grammar of the same language (Bloom, Lightbown, & Hood, 1975; Brown, 1973; de Villiers & de Villiers, 1973). The remaining issue in this chapter is to try to account for children's accomplishments as unconscious linguists.

THEORIES OF LANGUAGE ACQUISITION

Nativism vs. Empiricism

The direction of theory and research in developmental psycholinguistics over the past fifteen years or so has been to emphasize universality and the existence of innate, biological determinants of such universality. We will examine biological aspects of the human language capacity in the next chapter. Here let us examine the philosophical and psychological issues. The nativist hypothesis has been proposed most strongly by Chomsky (1965, 1968, 1975), and has given rise to heated debate. You have encountered this position several times already. Put in its barest form, the problem is this: All that the child is exposed to is the occurrence of speech in situations. How does he end up with an abstract and productive knowledge of the language? Chomsky has argued that the "primary linguistic data"— the speech that a child hears—cannot be the source of linguistic competence. Language acquisition is only possible if the child comes to the task prepared, in some way, to process data of that sort and to form the kinds of structures which are characteristic of human language. The impact of transformational grammar in the 1960s—along with work in ethology, perceptual and cognitive development, and other areas—revived the interest of psychologists in nativistic aspects of the growth of intelligence. To many psychologists the postulation of complex, genetically programmed perceptual and cognitive mechanisms has become quite plausible—if not obligatory. The problem of language acquisition has long been central in this debate. In recent years the debate has shifted, to some extent, from an argument between nativism and empiricism to an argument about what kind of nativism is appropriate to issues of language acquisition. Does the child have strategies which were specifically evolved for the task of language acquisition, or can one account for this process on the basis of more general human cognitive capacities (which also have their own innate bases)? This issue is far from being resolved, though I suspect that both general cognitive principles and principles specific to language are at play in the child's construction of his native language. In the final section of this chapter, I sketch out part of a general approach to this problem. But first let us look again at the question of why language acquisition is difficult to account for in terms of traditional empiricist theories of knowledge.

An empiricist theory of learning, such as American S-R (stimulus-response) behaviorism, imputes a minimum of innate structure to the organism, relying mainly on a built-in capacity to form associations between stimuli and between stimuli and responses on the basis of similarity and contiguity. Structure exists in the outside world, and the individual comes to reflect that structure. However, as we have seen repeatedly, what the child acquires in the course of language development is not a collection of S-R connections, but a complex internal rule system of some sort. He is never exposed to the rule system itself, but only to individual sentences in individual situations. How, then, does he acquire the underlying linguistic system on the basis of such evidence?

Chomsky (1965, pp. 58–59) has posed the problem in the following terms, emphasizing the limitations of the speech sample available to the child (what he calls "the degenerate quality" of the data), and the fact that almost all children, even if retarded or speech delayed, generally master a grammar, however rudimentary, of considerable formal complexity. In his words:

> . . . knowledge of grammatical structure cannot arise by application of step-by-step inductive operations (segmentation, classification, substitution procedures, filling of slots in frames, association, etc.) of any sort that have yet been developed within linguistics, psychology, or philosophy . . . It seems plain that language acquisition is based on the child's discovery of what from a formal point of view is a deep and abstract theory—a generative grammar of his language—many of the concepts and principles of which are only remotely related to experience by long and intricate chains of unconscious quasi-inferential steps. A consideration of the character of the grammar that is acquired, the degenerate quality and narrowly limited extent of the available data, the striking uniformity of the resulting grammars, and their independence of intelligence, motivation, and emotional state, over wide ranges of variation, leave little hope that much of the structure of the language can be learned by an organism initially uninformed as to its general character . . . On the basis of the best information now available, it seems reasonable to suppose that a child cannot help constructing a particular kind of . . . grammar to account for the data presented to him, any more than he can control his perception of solid objects or his attention to line and angle. Thus it may well be that the general features of language structure reflect, not so much the course of one's experience, but rather the general character of one's capacity to acquire knowledge—in the traditional sense, one's innate ideas and innate principles.

Reinforcement

Let us examine some of the major theoretical concepts of psychological learning theory in the light of Chomsky's arguments.[3] A classical approach to acquisition problems such as the one we have been examining is to say that the child is "reinforced" for his performance (both positively and

---

3. Chomsky's (1959) review of Skinner's *Verbal Behavior* presents a forceful and extended exposition of the position against psychological learning theory taken here.

negatively), and that, on the basis of reinforcement, he "generalizes" his future behavior pattern to be closer to that required by the reinforcing agent. Now let us imagine a highly improbable, but theoretically perfect reinforcement situation: every time the child utters a grammatical sentence he receives positive reinforcement, and every ungrammatical sentence receives negative reinforcement. Could this schedule of reinforcement result in grammatical speech? Conceivably it could, but it would tell us nothing of the process whereby the child arrived at the underlying notions of grammar which would make correct performance possible. To find out that a given utterance was in error does not tell the child exactly what he did wrong in producing that utterance, and it certainly does not tell him how to correct it the next time (if he ever chooses to utter that particular sentence again). Nor does positive reinforcement give any discriminative information about what was correct about the grammatical construction just uttered. We are still left with the problem of how the child comes to realize the proper relationship between sounds and meanings; how he arrives at the principles of ordering words and parts of words so that they make sense.

For example, suppose a child says *I called up her* and then receives negative reinforcement for an ungrammatical utterance. How does he know what to do next? He has formed this utterance, probably, on analogy with sentences like *I called up Kathy.* Now he has to learn that when the object of a verb-particle construction is a pronoun (like *her*) it must always go between the verb and the particle (*I called her up*), but when the object is a noun, it can go either between the verb and the particle or after the particle. The mere fact that *I called up her* is wrong gives the child no clue as to what is right. Maybe he should have said *I called up she*, or *I call-upped her*, or any number of other things. And even if he is given the correct form, how does he know what generalization to make? There are indefinitely many possibilities: maybe the rule only holds for feminine pronouns, or animates; maybe it holds for some kinds of verbs and not others; maybe it only holds in the past tense; and so on. The point is that reinforcement could only tell the child that a sentence is globally correct or incorrect. His own cognitive facilities and language acquisition skills are needed in order for him to make use of reinforcement. And it is just these skills and facilities which are the core interest of psycholinguistics.

There are several other important things to say about reinforcement. For one thing, you have seen above (in the discussion of overregularization) that reinforcement could not be a very effective means of shaping language. Certainly, if children receive reinforcement for grammar at all, they receive negative reinforcement for overregularizations of the English past tense, or the Slavic accusative inflection. Yet these errors are very persistent.

Moreover, parents seem to pay little attention overall to the grammatical correctness or incorrectness of their children's speech (Slobin, 1975). What they are most interested in is what the child has to say—whether it is true or appropriate or clever—and not the sentence structures he uses. Roger Brown and his co-workers at Harvard have carried out a detailed longitudinal study of three children between the ages of about one and a half and four (Brown, 1973). Spontaneous interaction between mother and child was recorded weekly over the course of several years.

Brown and his co-workers (Brown, Cazden, & Bellugi, 1969) examined their data to see if mothers are sensitive to the grammaticality of their children's utterances. If they are not, it would be difficult to maintain that child language develops as a result of conscious tuition, or reinforcement, on the part of mothers. Following this argument, the investigators looked at cases in which a child's utterance was followed by an expression of approval or disapproval on the part of the adult. There was no evidence that parental responses could play a role in shaping the child's sense of grammaticality. In the cogent summary of Brown et al. (1969, pp. 70–71):

> What circumstances did govern approval and disapproval directed at child utterances by parents? Gross errors of word choice were sometimes corrected, as when Eve said *What the guy idea*. Once in a while an error of pronunciation was noticed and corrected. Most commonly, however, the grounds on which an utterance was approved or disapproved . . . were not strictly linguistic at all. When Eve expressed the opinion that her mother was a girl by saying *He a girl* mother answered *That's right*. The child's utterance was ungrammatical but mother did not respond to the fact; instead she responded to the truth value of the proposition the child intended to express. In general the parents fit propositions to the child's utterances, however incomplete or distorted the utterances, and then approved or not, according to the correspondence between proposition and reality. Thus *Her curl my hair* was approved because mother was, in fact, curling Eve's hair. However, Sarah's grammatically impeccable *There's the animal farmhouse* was disapproved because the building was a lighthouse and Adam's *Walt Disney comes on, on Tuesday* was disapproved because Walt Disney comes on, on some other day. It seems then, to be truth value rather than syntactic well-formedness that chiefly governs explicit verbal reinforcement by parents. Which renders mildly paradoxical the fact that the usual product of such a training schedule is an adult whose speech is highly grammatical but not notably truthful.

Imitation

The notion of "reinforcement" is thus not a very convincing candidate for the explanation of language development. What other notions are available? If you ask the proverbial "man-in-the-street" how children learn to talk, he will hardly think this is a serious question. The typical reply is something like, "They just imitate what they hear." The traditional assumption has been simply that the child acquires new linguistic forms from the speech of his parents through mimicking what they say: he hears something new, repeats it, and so practices the new form. It is only through such practice—it has been thought—that the child's speech can change. For a time the new form is dependent on parental models; later it breaks free.

You have already read a number of arguments against this simple answer. Even in discussing two-word sentences we found that we couldn't account for all of the child's utterances on the basis of reduced imitations of adult speech, because strange combinations occur. Furthermore, Bellugi's examples, along with those of Slobin and Welsh, and others, suggest that the child cannot imitate structures which he is not yet capable of producing on his own. David McNeill (1966, p. 69) quotes a passage from Roger Brown's transcripts which shows dramatically that even if a parent is trying to actively teach a linguistic form to a child, the child persists in imitating according to his own rules of grammar:

> CHILD: Nobody don't like me.
> MOTHER: No, say "nobody likes me."
> CHILD: Nobody don't like me.
> [Eight repetitions of this dialog follow.]
> MOTHER: No, now listen carefully; say *"nobody likes me."*
> CHILD: Oh! Nobody don't likes me.

Beyond this, of course, as I have just argued above, even if a child could successfully imitate all of the utterances he hears, we would not understand how he goes on to produce new utterances which he has not heard before.

Even stronger arguments against the necessity of imitation for language acquisition come from examples of linguistic knowledge in children who have not engaged in imitation of speech. We discussed an early example in Huttenlocher's study, where children at the beginning of the one-word stage—long before imitation of any multiword utterances—already understood such utterances. Yet more striking evidence comes from cases of children who cannot speak at all, due to some disturbance in articulatory ability, but who can hear normally. Eric Lenneberg (1962) reported the case of a boy who was unable to articulate speech, yet who learned to understand the complexities of English utterances. Obviously, at some deep level, the same linguistic knowledge must underlie both the production and interpretation of speech. Surely it is clear that a speechless child could never have imitated speech nor have been reinforced for speaking—yet these handicaps do not interfere with his acquisition of linguistic competence.

Why, then, DO children imitate speech? Imitation seems to be a way of practicing what you are in the process of learning. Various studies of imitation (Bloom, Hood, & Lightbown, 1974; Ervin-Tripp, 1964; Slobin, 1968) suggest that the child does not spontaneously imitate forms which he has long since mastered; nor does he imitate forms far beyond his scope. Rather, he imitates those forms which he is in the process of acquiring. In Piagetian terms, imitation is the external indication of the child's attempt to accommodate his linguistic schemata to new material. Thus imitation does play a role in language acquisition, but its role is not to insert new structures into the child's rule system.

The Role of Input

Even if the child does not learn language through imitation and reinforcement, there is a persistent belief among psycholinguists that the nature of parental speech—the "input" to the child—must play a significant role in guiding the process of language acquisition. Chomsky has been taken to task by a number of writers for referring to "the degenerate quality and narrowly limited extent of the available data" (1965, p. 58). These investigators have pointed out that most of parental speech to small children is made up of short, simple, grammatical sentences (see papers in Snow and Ferguson, 1977). If you have followed the theoretical arguments presented above, however, it should be evident to you that the basic problem remains. Even if the input to the child is perfectly regular in form and adapted to his processing span and cognitive capacities, he is still faced with the problem of discovering implicit structure and the principles of mapping communicative intentions onto utterances in the particular language to which he is exposed. The child must make use of parental input to discover the UNDERLYING, UNSPOKEN regularities of his language. (This point has been persuasively argued by Newport, Gleitman, and Gleitman, 1977, who have shown that the way the child attends to parental speech is shaped by what he already knows about the language.) A perfectly tailored input, like a perfectly tailored reinforcement schedule, does not account for the child's ability to fashion a grammar based on that input.

Furthermore, a close examination of parental speech reveals that the problem facing the child is even more complex than we have characterized it thus far. The child does not grow up in a linguistic world in which particular situations are uniquely mapped onto particular utterances types (as you will recall from the discussion of the various ways to ask someone to 'heat the coffee' as discussed in Chapter 1). The mapping problem is not just one of determining the way in which a particular language expresses such notions as 'daddy gave me a ball'—because communicative intentions are mapped onto a variety of utterance forms. For example, in one tape-recorded session of interaction with a two-year-old, a mother is trying to get her daughter to sit still and have her hair curled.[4] The first attempt is made when the mother says: *C'mon and let me set your hair.* If this sentence were simply repeated again and again, we would be faced with the mapping problem as described above. That is, the child must discover what aspects of the situation receive obligatory grammatical expression in English. However, in the course of a half-hour the mother tries to express the same general intention again and again, in different words. All of the following utterances occur, scattered throughout the session, interspersed with other conversation:

C'mon and let me set your hair.
Don't you want to have curls for this afternoon?
Why don't you lemme put your hair up?
You won't have any curls when you go down to see Betty and Alice.
Alice has lots of little curls in her hair.
Why don't you lemme fix your hair?
You won't have any curls.
Why don't you fix his hair [a doll's] and I'll fix your hair?
You fix his hair and I'll fix your hair.
Sit up here on the chair so I can fix your hair.
You'll look like Mag Snatch with a pretty dress on and no curls.

4. These data are drawn from unpublished transcriptions of Roger Brown (described in Brown, 1973). My thanks to him for permission to use these examples here.

You'll look awful.
You don't want to go out and look awful.
How would you like to have your face combed?
Lemme get the snarls out of your hair.
Can I comb your hair?
Let me comb your bangs.
Lemme fix your hair.
Why don't you lemme fix your hair?
You gotta go lemme fix your hair first.

This girl must discover the semantic equivalence of *set your hair, put your hair up, fix your hair, have your face combed, get the snarls out of your hair, comb your hair,* and *comb your bangs.* She has to know that imperatives can be expressed directly or by means of indirect questions or by means of description of the negative consequences of failure to comply. It should be evident that the mapping problem, as we considered it cross-linguistically, revealed only half of the problem. This two-year-old girl must figure out that an entire diverse range of utterances expresses essentially the same communicative intent. To be sure, what she discovers about rules of English grammar and discourse must be based on what she has heard. But parental input does not solve the problem of theory construction for the child. It only presents the data for the task. How the child uses the data is based on her linguistic and cognitive capacities at a particular level of development.

Acquisition Strategies

We are left, then, with the problem of the source of internal structure. While linguists and psycholinguists have been adept at pointing out the inadequacies of psychological learning theories, we have only the broad outlines of a problem-solving, hypothesis-testing, cognitive theory of language acquisition. A frequent approach has been to propose various "strategies" used by children in deciphering and acquiring various aspects of linguistic structure, such as word order (Bever, 1970), spatial terms (E. Clark, 1973, 1975, 1977), temporal verb forms (Bronckart and Sinclair, 1973), morphological structures (MacWhinney, 1978), and so forth. What we have here is a partial response to Chomsky's claim, quoted above, that "knowledge of grammatical structure cannot arise by application of step-by-step inductive operations . . . of any sort that have yet been developed within linguistics, psychology, or philosophy" (1965, p. 58). The aim is to devise new sorts of operations, tuned to specific sorts of cognitive and linguistic tasks. A set of strategies for language acquisition is not a "step-by-step inductive" system, because it is not solely guided by speech input. Rather, the strategies limit in advance the range of possible outcomes. We are not even in sight of a general language acquisition theory of this sort. As an example of where this kind of approach might lead, I conclude this chapter with discussion of a few general "operating principles" which may play a role in guiding grammatical development, based on available data on the acquisition of some 40 different languages from 14 major language families. (For more detail see Slobin, 1973; for discussions of problems of the "strategy" approach, see Cromer, 1976, and Maratsos, in press.)

OPERATING PRINCIPLES FOR
THE CONSTRUCTION OF GRAMMAR

It has been implicit throughout this chapter that certain linguistic forms are more "accessible" or more "salient" to the child than others. For example, rules based on consistent meaning—like the regular past tense in English, or the Turkish direct object inflection—are more easily acquired than rules which do not exhibit a one-to-one mapping of meaning onto surface form. The Slavic inflectional system is difficult to master because one must take account of various factors which have no direct bearing on underlying semantic relations (such as gender, animacy, etc.). Small children appear to have little difficulty in segmenting the speech flow into word units, and in discovering meaningful parts of words, like suffixes. Inversions of word order pose problems to the child. If we could rank formal linguistic devices in terms of ease of acquisition, we would have a clue as to the kind of strategies which the child first applies in the task of language acquisition. If segmentation into words and morphemes appears early in development, and if combinations of meaningful elements are assigned meanings which go beyond the meanings of each of the elements taken separately, we can state that the child operates, early on, with principles of analysis and combination. Such operating principles are, in a sense, initial expectations about how language works. If we were programming a computer for deciphering a linguistic system, we would equip it with heuristics to break utterances into pieces and keep track of the meanings of various combinations of these pieces. The claim is that children are equipped with such heuristics, which I have referred to as "operating principles." (What follows is a condensed discussion of Slobin, 1973.)

The child must carry out several kinds of tasks concurrently. He must listen for meaningful elements in adult speech, and he must understand how such elements are mapped onto his understanding of the world. When speaking, he must find means for going from thought to utterance. The problem becomes especially clear—as always—when we compare different types of languages. When the child becomes ready to express certain notions—say, notions of spatial relations—he must figure out how to express these particular notions in his native language. The notions develop on nonlinguistic grounds, before the child has mastered the relevant mapping system. Children are able to conceive of notions of containment ('in') and support ('on') long before they can speak. In all languages, children express locative notions at the two-word stage, with no formal marking (such as prepositions, postpositions, inflections) of the locative relation. For example, a child may say *pot stove* (or its equivalent in various languages) to encode this locative relationship, perhaps relying only on a word order regularity to indicate which is the referent object and which the supporting object. If we assume that such spatial notions arise at the same stage of cognitive development in all children, we can then look across languages to see how long a time delay there is between the first appearances of utterances like *pot stove* and the acquisition of the full adult form, like *the pot is on the stove*. It turns out that there are striking cross-linguistic differences.

Consider two types of languages—those that use prepositions (the Indo-European languages, including English) and those that use suffixes or postpositions (Altaic languages like Turkish, Korean, and Japanese; Uralic languages like Finnish and Hungarian). For example, in Hungarian there are noun suffixes which regularly indicate relative position and movement between objects: *hajó* means 'boat', *hajóban* 'located in the boat', *hajóból* 'moving out from inside of the boat', *hajótól* 'moving away from next to the boat', and so on. In Turkish one says the equivalent of *pot stove on,* in which the word for 'on' is a POSTposition, rather than *pot on stove,* with a PREposition. It turns out that locative markers placed AFTER the noun (suffixes and postpositions) are easier for children to acquire than locative markers placed BEFORE the noun. We can conclude, for various reasons of attention and memory, that children find ends of words and utterances more salient than beginnings and middles. There is much cross-linguistic evidence for this generalization. Phrased in terms of operating principles, one can propose:

OPERATING PRINCIPLE A: PAY ATTENTION TO THE ENDS OF WORDS.

This principle assumes that the child is looking for grammatical elements to indicate meaning relations between words, and that a salient place for the detection of such units is in postposed material. Thus we must propose another operating principle as well:

OPERATING PRINCIPLE B: THERE ARE LINGUISTIC ELEMENTS WHICH ENCODE RELATIONS BETWEEN WORDS.

This is an operating principle which guides the child in constructing mapping relations between underlying meanings and surface utterances.

Taking these two operating principles together (along with several others, which would account for such things as the discovery that words make reference to objects, the discovery that phonological forms of words can be systematically modified, and so forth), we can now predict a language acquisition universal:

Universal 1: For any given semantic notion, grammatical realizations as postposed forms will be acquired earlier than realizations as preposed forms.

This universal finds support in a number of other linguistic domains. Remember, for example, the difference between direct object marking in German, where there are various forms of the article preceding the noun, in contrast to Russian, Serbo-Croatian, and Turkish, where suffixes are used. The German case inflectional system is acquired later than these suffixed systems, presumably because of the same operating principles. Prenominal articles are simply a less salient place to attend to in an utterance and to expect to find the encoding of relational notions.

Other sorts of operating principles have to do with the kinds of rule systems children are most likely to form as a first guess at the nature of language. Remember that children seem to prefer consistent and regular systems, often going beyond the degree of regularity of the adult language. This can be phrased as a general operating principle for the formation of grammatical rules:

OPERATING PRINCIPLE C: AVOID EXCEPTIONS.

This principle accounts, in part, for such overgeneralizations as the English past tense and the Slavic accusative. Again, we can go beyond to predict an acquisitional universal, which can be checked cross-linguistically:

Universal 2: The following stages of linguistic marking of a semantic notion are typically observed: (1) no marking, (2) appropriate marking in limited cases, (3) overgeneralization of marking, (4) full adult system.

Not only does the child want his rules to be exceptionless, but he wants them to relate clearly and directly to underlying semantic notions. Several operating principles can be proposed in this regard:

OPERATING PRINCIPLE D: UNDERLYING SEMANTIC RELATIONS SHOULD BE MARKED OVERTLY AND CLEARLY.

A grammatical system is easier to learn if each element of meaning corresponds to a separate surface element. For example, in the Turkish inflectional system, separate particles encode number and case, in that order:

el 'hand'	*eller* 'hands'
eli 'hand + accusative'	*elleri* 'hands + accusative'
elin 'of the hand'	*ellerin* 'of the hands'

This contrasts with Indo-European systems, like the German and Slavic inflections discussed above, where a single article or suffix has a FUSED meaning of, say, 'singular + accusative + masculine + animate'. Analytic inflectional systems, like Turkish, are acquired more easily by children than synthetic systems, like the Indo-European languages. From these facts we can predict:

Universal 3: The closer a grammatical system adheres to one-to-one mapping between semantic elements and surface elements, the earlier it will be acquired.

A related Operating Principle comes into play when a language presents children with grammatical markers which are not directly related to the core semantic notion expressed. For example, in English it makes no semantic sense that the plural of a small collection of nouns should be formed by vowel change rather than suffix (e.g., *mice, feet, geese).* Or, to take another widespread example, it is semantically irrelevant to the notion of plurality that a particular noun is conceived of as masculine or feminine, yet many languages have different plural endings for nouns of different genders. Children have difficulty in acquiring such semantically unmotivated grammatical rules, suggesting that another kind of operating principle is at work in the initial construction of grammar:

OPERATING PRINCIPLE E: THE USE OF GRAMMATICAL MARKERS SHOULD MAKE SEMANTIC SENSE.

On the basis of this principle, we can predict the sorts of errors which will occur in early speech. For example:

Universal 4: When selection of an appropriate inflection among a group of inflections performing the same semantic function is determined by arbitrary formal criteria (e.g., phonological shape of word stem, number of syllables in stem, arbitrary gender), the child initially tends to use a single form in all environments.

Thus the Russian or Yugoslav child consistently uses the feminine *-u* suffix to mark the accusative of nouns of all genders, adhering to Operating Principle D that this notion should be marked overtly and clearly, and also following Operating Principle E, that the inflection should make semantic sense.

If we followed principles of this sort through in detail, we would be in a position to predict both those types of errors which occur, and those which do not occur. For example, Roger Brown (1973) has found that the

English progressive is the only inflection which is never overextended by children. One does not find errors like *She's knowing how to read* or *I'm liking cookies.* This is because there is a clear semantic distinction between those verbs which can take the progressive inflection and those which cannot. The progressive cannot indicate an involuntary state, but only a process (e.g., *running, melting,* etc.). The child has to memorize by rote which verbs take irregular past tenses, or which nouns have irregular plurals, but the class of verbs which do not take the progressive inflection can be semantically defined, and therefore errors of overgeneralization of the inflection do not occur. One can predict, accordingly:

Universal 5: Semantically consistent grammatical rules are acquired early and without significant error.

These operating principles and their resulting universals are, of course, only a sketch of what might be a theory of language acquisition. The important thing to remember is that the structure of language is intimately related to the structure of the mind and the mental processes involved in thinking and speaking. Therefore the acquisition of language must be guided by a rich collection of procedures for the perception and analysis of speech, along with procedures for developing knowledge of structure and using that structure in the process of speaking and understanding. Ultimately, general operating principles must develop into specific language processing strategies of the sort discussed in Chapter 2. As you can see, however, the task accomplished by the child in a few years will take us many more years to explain. A great Russian children's writer, Kornei Chukovsky, has aptly described the accomplishment that we are trying to account for (1963, p. 10):

It is frightening to think what an enormous number of grammatical forms are poured over the poor head of the young child. And he, as if it were nothing at all, adjusts to all this chaos, constantly sorting out into rubrics the disorderly elements of the words he hears, without noticing as he does this, his gigantic effort. If an adult had to master so many grammatical rules within so short a time, his head would surely burst—a mass of rules mastered so lightly and so freely by the two-year-old "linguist." The labor he thus performs at this age is astonishing enough, but even more amazing and unparalleled is the ease with which he does it.

In truth, the young child is the hardest mental toiler on our planet. Fortunately, he does not even suspect this.

READING

The following is a small selection of readings on child language development. Detailed bibliographies can be found in Slobin (1972) and Abrahamsen (1977). Topical bibliographies can be found in the readings listed below. Current research is reported in the *Journal of Child Language,* and in various journals reporting developmental psychology (e.g., *Child Development, Developmental Psychology, Journal of Experimental Child Psychology),* psycholinguistics (e.g., *Journal of Verbal Learning and Verbal Behavior, Journal of Psycholinguistic Research),* and cognition (e.g.,

Cognition, Cognitive Psychology). Useful introductory textbooks are Bloom and Lahey (1978), Dale (1976), and de Villiers and de Villiers (1978). Books of readings on language development have been edited by Bar-Adon and Leopold (1971), Bloom and Lahey (1978), Ferguson and Slobin (1973), Lahey (1978), Lenneberg and Lenneberg (1975), Morehead and Morehead (1976), and Schiefelbusch and Lloyd (1974). Collections of theoretical papers can be found in Hayes (1970), Macnamara (1977), Moore (1973), and Slobin (1971). The following are useful reviews of special topics. GRAMMATICAL DEVELOPMENT: Brown (1973). SEMANTIC DEVELOPMENT: Bowerman (1976), Leonard (1976). SEMANTICS AND SYNTAX: Bowerman (1978). EARLY COMMUNICATION: Bruner (1975), Carter (1975), Halliday (1975). DEVELOPMENT OF DISCOURSE: Ervin-Tripp and Mitchell-Kernan (1977), Ochs and Schieffelin (1979). PARENTAL SPEECH INPUT: Snow and Ferguson (1977). LANGUAGE AND COGNITIVE DEVELOPMENT: Cromer (1974, 1976). LANGUAGE INTERVENTION: Schiefelbusch (1978). CHILDHOOD LANGUAGE DISORDERS: Lahey (1978). CROSS-LINGUISTIC STUDIES: Bowerman (in press), Slobin (1973, 1978).

5

*For it is a very remarkable thing that there are no men, not even
the insane, so dull and stupid that they cannot put words together
in a manner to convey their thoughts. On the contrary, there is no
other animal, however perfect and fortunately situated it may be,
that can do the same. And this is not because they lack the organs,
for we see that magpies and parrots can pronounce words as well as
we can, and nevertheless cannot speak as we do, that is, in showing
that they think what they are saying. On the other hand, even
those men born deaf and dumb, lacking the organs which others
make use of in speaking, and at least as badly off as the animals in
this respect, usually invent for themselves some signs by which they
make themselves understood by those who are with them enough to
learn their language . . . . Furthermore, we notice variations among
animals of the same species, just as among men, and that some are
easier to train than others. It is therefore unbelievable that a
monkey or a parrot which was one of the best of its species should
not be the equal in this matter of one of the most stupid children,
or at least of a child of infirm mind, if their soul were not of a
wholly different nature from ours.*

—René Descartes,
Discourse on Method [1637]
(1956, p. 37)

BIOLOGICAL FOUNDATIONS
OF LANGUAGE

It is attractive to set ourselves off from the other animals, just as it is also attractive to see our similarities. We sense continuities and discontinuities across species. The most striking discontinuities are those of language and culture. Modern science is not comfortable in drawing a definitive line between the behavior and physiological structures of animals and humans. At least since Darwin it has not been possible to claim that animal psychology is "of a wholly different nature from ours." But the basic outline of Descartes' argument is still compelling. As we will see in this chapter, language can develop in humans even in the presence of severe cognitive or physical defect. Indeed, deaf children deprived of sign language will invent their own. Chimpanzees, with detailed training, however, CAN acquire some portion of a humanly-constructed language system, but the debate as to where to draw the line between chimp and human still continues—displaced to somewhere WITHIN the domain of linguistic capacity. And now—beyond Descartes' seventeenth century speculations—we know a good deal about the anatomical equipment involved in the use of language. Special features of our brain and our articulatory apparatus make it clear that the language capacity has a distinct biological foundation in our species. Species-specific behavior, accompanied by distinct neural and anatomical structures, is good evidence for the special evolution of those capacities, preserved in the genetic code which makes us mature into speaking creatures. The uniquely human biological foundations of language thus support the theoretical and empirical arguments for inborn language capacities in human beings, developed in the previous chapter.

This chapter is not a detailed exposition on the neuroanatomy of language (see Lenneberg, 1967; Luria, 1970; Segalowitz & Gruber, 1977; Whitaker & Whitaker, 1976, 1977) or on the evolution of language (see Harnad, Steklis, & Lancaster, 1976; Lieberman, 1975; Stross, 1976). Rather, I want to present a general picture of language as developing and functioning within a uniquely human biological matrix. First we will examine the specialization of the human speech apparatus and brain and then try to place this system in a maturational scheme. Finally we will wonder how far other primates—lacking this special equipment—can go towards "becoming people."

SPECIALIZATION OF
THE HUMAN SPEECH APPARATUS

Think of the limbs of various species: the digging paws of the mole, the wings of birds, the webbed feet of waterfowl, various sorts of hoofs and claws and fingers. We attribute the diversity in these homologous structures to the different evolutionary histories of these species and the functions they succeeded in performing in various environments. A similar story can be told for the articulatory apparatus. Although we share with other animals structures of mouth, tongue, lips, hinged jaw filled with teeth, and the ability to use breath to make sounds that resonate in the oral and nasal cavities, there are vast differences in the sound-producing mechanisms of animals, just as there are in their limbs. In the case of Homo sapiens, it can be shown that our oral and respiratory systems did not just evolve to serve functions of eating and noisemaking, but to serve the particular functions of producing articulate speech. Chimpanzees may be able to learn some elements of manual sign language, as we will see below, but they cannot learn to speak because they are not built to do so. This suggests that, a very long time ago, there were selection pressures for hominids who could voluntarily produce strings of distinctly different sounds in rapid sequence. (At the same time, there must have evolved specific perceptual mechanisms to process such complexly patterned and rapidly fading auditory information.) All of the terms of the above description are important for characterizing the vocal capacities of our species: VOLUNTARY, DISTINCT SOUNDS, IN COMPLEX TEMPORAL PATTERNS.

Chimpanzees, and other mammals, can certainly produce and perceive sounds. The question is how they do it and what the sounds are used for. Primates emit distinct calls in social interaction—roars, pants, barks, growls, screeches, screams, and squeaks—expressing threat, playfulness, desire, fear, and so forth. Many of these sounds—and their accompanying facial expresssions, gestures, and postures—appear to be unlearned and are emitted involuntarily under appropriate conditions of emotional arousal. We humans partake of the heritage of ancient sounds and body expressions shared with our primate relatives. I have heard children who have been deaf and blind since birth spontaneously burst out with completely normal-sounding laughs and whines, together with matching facial expressions, in appropriate situations. Such sounds are apparently of a reflexive nature and do not require auditory feedback. But it is extremely difficult to condition a chimpanzee to produce a voluntary vocalization in response to an arbitrary stimulus (say, the flash of a light). These emotive calls, which we share with the other primates, do not make reference to events outside the communicator but serve to express his present condition. They do not work through the higher cortical, cognitive system involved in symbolic communication.

An important part of the human means of producing SPEECH sounds, then, is its voluntary aspect. Indeed, the same can even be said of the human production of emotive sounds. Except under extreme stress, we can choose to communicate feelings or to refrain from doing so. Emotive expression loses much of its reflexive nature and comes under cognitive control in human beings. Much of our social learning, in fact, involves learning when NOT to cry, or scream out in pain, or laugh out loud, and so on. So even our emotive expression, which is undoubtedly closely related to that of our primate relatives, may be controlled differently and can be brought into the service of culturally mediated functions.

Furthermore, the human system for producing sounds is distinct, and this distinctness cannot be simply traced to factors of diet and posture. We have especially strong and well-developed muscles around the lips, and our cheeks are almost all muscle. In addition, we have a smaller mouth than other primates—that is, we cannot bare all of our teeth. Inside, at the back of our mouth, the tongue can be pressed against the pharyngeal wall. This makes it possible to close off the oral cavity at either end, building up air pressure and maintaining or releasing it to produce a large range of sounds. Our tongue is higher than that of other primates, and it can easily be brought into contact with the front teeth, allowing for a range of rapidly moving articulations, breaking up the flow of air. In the back of the oral cavity, because of the relation of the tongue to the pharynx, we can produce a variety of vowel sounds not accessible to other primates. (For acoustic and anatomical details of these comparisons, see Lieberman, 1975.) Subhuman primates breathe through the nose, even when the mouth is open, because the oral cavity can be closed in back by bringing the epiglottis and palate together. (See Figures 5-1 and 5-2.) This means that the nasal cavity is the major resonator, and, since it has no moving parts like the mouth, the range of sound variation is quite limited. In Homo sapiens, where the epiglottis has descended, air can flow out freely through the mouth. In short, only in our species is it possible to use the tongue, cheeks, and lips, together with the teeth, to make articulated sounds, differentially using both the oral and nasal cavities as resonators.

So far we have considered the periphery of the speech system—that is, the parts far from the brain. However, the muscles that make this system work are centrally controlled—and Lenneberg (1967, p. 91) estimates that there are at least 100 of them. Considering the normal rate of speaking to be something like 14 phonemes per second, he notes: "Since the passage from any one speech sound to another depends ultimately on differences in muscular adjustments, fourteen times per second an 'order must be issued to every muscle,' whether to contract, relax, or maintain its tonus." These commands, of course, must be issued by the brain in the proper rate and order to insure the production of speech sounds. Because the various parts of the articulatory system are not at all at the same distance from the brain, the order in which the commands are issued is different than the order in which the motor events occur. For example, it can take 30 msec

FIGURE 5-1
The Adult Human Vocal Tract[1]

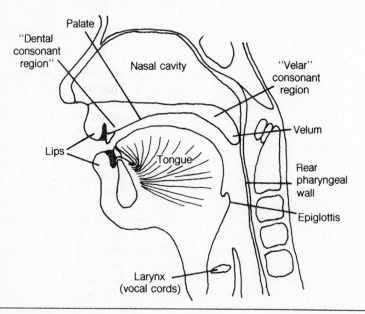

[1]Figure from Lieberman (1975, p. 60).

FIGURE 5-2
Head and Neck of a Young Adult Male Chimpanzee
Sectioned in the Midsaggital Plane[1]

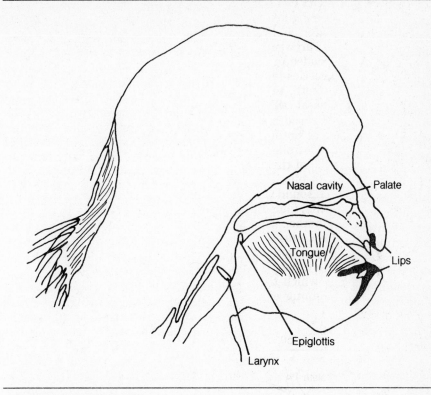

[1]Figure from Lieberman (1975, p. 106).

longer for a nerve impulse from the speech center to reach the laryngeal muscles than the muscles of the oral cavity. This means that the neural message to the larynx to produce a given speech sound must be sent out earlier than the messages to the mouth if the two parts of the system are to function at the same time in producing that sound. So, in addition to the special adaptations of the peripheral musculature and associated articulators and resonating cavities, the area of the brain involved in sending signals to the speech mechanism must have evolved complex means of timing and sequencing motor commands to make the rapid articulation of successive speech sounds possible. And, in order for such signals to be interpreted, other parts of the brain must be able to rapidly decode such information.

Much more could be said about the articulatory system and language capacity. It is enough here to simply make the point that this system appears to be a specific adaptation in our species to the demands of speaking. Most of the interesting questions about the organization of language, however, relate to the central nervous system. Does the human brain exhibit specialization for language? Is there a neurological basis for any of the constructs of linguistics and psycholinguistics?

BRAIN SPECIALIZATION AND LANGUAGE

Brain Size, Language, and Intelligence

Human beings have relatively large brains; they are intelligent; they can speak. The human brain weighs about 1,350 grams; the chimp brain about 450 grams; the rhesus monkey brain about 90 grams. The human brain has a higher cell count than the brain of any other animal of the same body weight. Undoubtedly, our special place in the animal kingdom has something to do with the size of our brains. But is it in terms of size alone that our special mental abilities can be explained? Apparently not, because there are humans with brains of 400 grams who learn to talk. Lenneberg (1967, pp. 69–70) has described cases of so-called *nanocephalic,* or "bird-headed" dwarfs—human beings who grow to about three feet in height, but have normal body proportions. Their head size and brain weight are barely larger than normal newborn infants, and they have a smaller number of brain cells than normal adults. (The individual cells are not abnormal.) Such dwarfs are mentally retarded, reaching a mental age of about six. Brain size, then, appears to play a role in general intelligence. However, in Lenneberg's words: "All of them acquire the rudiments of language including speaking and understanding, and the majority master the verbal skills at least as well as a normal five-year-old child." From what you have learned in the previous chapter, such language ability is considerable (and, anticipating later discussion, seems to exceed the current language attainments of specially trained chimpanzees). Thus, although a small brain reduces general intellectual ability, the capacity for basic language acquisition is intact.

The combination of language development and mental retardation demonstrated by bird-headed dwarfs is consonant with Descartes' observation "that there are no men, not even the insane, so dull and stupid that they cannot put words together in a manner to convey their thoughts." Similar pictures emerge from other studies of mental retardation, with normal brain size. In the case of mongolism (Lenneberg, 1967, pp. 309–320), for example, we see a normal but very much slowed down course of language development in children with IQ scores as low as 50. Lenneberg notes (1967, p. 124):

> An IQ of 50 is deficient enough to keep a child from learning the most elementary concepts (counting, social distance, rules of kindergarten parlor games), yet it is high enough to use correctly plurals, tenses, question transformations, etc. THE GENERAL PROBLEM THAT EMERGES FROM THESE CONSIDERATIONS, AND WHICH IS CENTRAL TO PSYCHOLOGICAL THEORIES AT LARGE, IS: WHY ARE CERTAIN TASKS EASIER THAN OTHERS FOR A GIVEN SPECIES . . . ? [Emphasis added.]

The answer must be that these tasks are based on a specific neurological capacity—in this case, the capacity for language. This capacity must be based on a fairly specific, genetically determined propensity to acquire language in human beings. It must be the ORGANIZATION of the brain, rather than its mass, which underlies this propensity. Let us examine this organization, first in regard to control of the muscles involved in speaking, and then in terms of the cortical representation of various language functions.

The Motor Cortex

Different parts of an animal's brain control different aspects of its body, behavior, and mental processes. A map of the brain, indicating the size and distribution of areas related to various functions, reveals a good deal about the life-style that the organism was evolved to carry out. Consider, for example, maps of the motor cortex of human and monkey, as shown in Figures 5-3 and 5-4. These figures represent the part of the brain devoted to controlling muscles, showing the relative proportion of motor cortex devoted to the control of various organs. The larger the organ depicted in the schematic drawing, the greater proportion of cortex devoted to controlling that organ. Looking at the monkey drawing, it is clear that this is an animal that has great use—and equally great use—of hands and feet, involving separate control of all digits. The tail is also well represented, and we can infer that the animal uses its hands, feet, and tail for prehension and locomotion. The hands and feet are much more fully represented than the mouth and its organs, suggesting that the use of the mouth is less complex in this animal than are the various uses of the hands and feet. The human drawing, by contrast, looks almost like an intentional caricature of our species: a lot of talk and a lot of manipulation, on a fairly spindly and

FIGURE 5-3
Diagrammatic Representation of the Proportions
of the Human Motor Cortex[1]

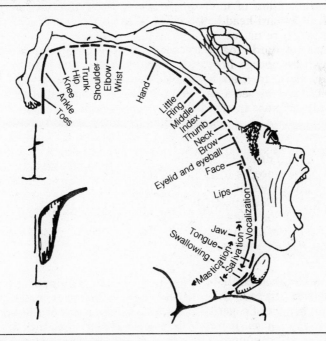

[1]Figure from Penfield and Rasmussen (1968, p. 57).

FIGURE 5-4
Diagrammatic Representation of the Proportions
of the Monkey Motor Cortex[1]

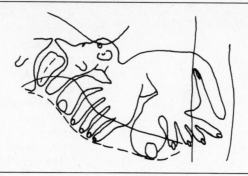

[1]Figure from Ruch (1951, p. 155), after Woolsey and Settlage (1950, p. 140).

poorly developed body! The hand vastly outmeasures the foot in cortical representation, with considerable cortex devoted to each finger and the famous opposable thumb. There is a disproportionately huge representation for the lips, and, overall, the representation of the face and oral system seems to be as great as that of the hand and fingers. It is evident that the peripheral speech apparatus discussed above is abundantly mapped onto cortical control areas.

What do these comparisons tell us? Clearly, that the human brain evolved to control a number of complex hand and mouth movements. We can speculate on the significance of this cortical organization. In a book fittingly called *The Evolution of Man's Capacity for Culture* (Spuhler, 1959), the anthropologist Sherwood L. Washburn (pp. 28-29) notes that

> the areas of the cortex concerned with speech are very large . . . The frontal lobes of man are greatly expanded also, and these areas are, at least in part, concerned with elaboration of thought and planning. Foresight and planning are essential to any complicated social life, and in the future it may be possible to demonstrate that the expansion of much of the cortex is directly related to new selection pressures associated with the evolution of complex social systems. OUR BRAINS, THEN, ARE NOT JUST ENLARGED, BUT THE INCREASE IN SIZE IS DIRECTLY RELATED TO TOOL USE, SPEECH, AND TO INCREASED MEMORY AND PLANNING. The general pattern of the human brain is very similar to that of ape or monkey. Its uniqueness lies in its large size AND IN THE PARTICULAR AREAS WHICH ARE ENLARGED. [Emphasis added.]

The Two Hemispheres

The right and left halves of the nervous system in animals are generally symmetrical. In humans, however, there are distinct asymmetries—in both structure and function—between the two hemispheres of the brain. Schematized (and often exaggerated or oversimplified) accounts of "left and right hemisphere thinking" have recently become part of common lore.

Here I want to dwell primarily on the implications of this asymmetry for the discussion of language capacity. As we will see in more detail below, the left hemisphere of the brain is specialized for certain language functions in right-handed people, and in a large proportion of left-handed people. (For other left-handers, the corresponding language functions are carried out by the right hemisphere, or, rarely, in little-understood sharing of functions between the hemispheres.) There is also preliminary evidence that portions of the left hemisphere related to language function are significantly larger than the mirror-image portions of the right hemisphere (Geschwind & Levitsky, 1968), and such asymmetry has been found in newborn infants (Witelson & Pallie, 1973) and even in fetuses (Wada, Clarke, & Hamm, 1975). There is also evidence that some of the areas involved in language function mature later than other parts of the brain, suggesting that they are of relatively recent evolutionary origin. The difference between the two halves of the brain is thus deeply rooted in our biology. We are a long way from understanding the reasons for this asymmetry. Indeed, the basic facts are just beginning to come to light (see, for example, Harnad et al., 1976; Segalowitz & Gruber, 1977). One can argue, however, that the demands of language processing have contributed to a "division of labor" between the hemispheres, requiring that a significant portion of the brain be devoted to language and language-related functions.

Up until recently, the major source of evidence about human hemispheric functioning came from the study of people with abnormal or damaged brains—particularly people with *aphasia* (brain-based language disturbance) caused by tumors, strokes, and bullet wounds. (It is a sad fact that our most significant body of knowledge about the neural bases of language has been gathered in military and veterans' hospitals.) More recently, techniques have been devised for monitoring or assessing differential hemispheric functions in normal, healthy people as well (who are, by grim contrast, referred to as "intact subjects" or "intact preparations" in the literature). All of this evidence clearly demonstrates lateralization of language, and predominantly left lateralization. (For convenience of discussion, I will discuss only these cases, which constitute the overwhelming majority. What is important is the FACT of lateralization, and not the particular side.) Brain damage to the left hemisphere is far more likely to implicate language than is damage to the right. In surgical cases where it is necessary to cut the connections between the two hemispheres, allowing them to function separately, it is the left hemisphere that retains most control of language (Gazzaniga, 1967, 1970; Nebes, 1974). And in monitoring brain function in normal individuals, it is the left hemisphere which predominates in tasks of language processing. Let us look at this specialization more closely.

Analytic Capacity in the Left Hemisphere   As you probably know, each hemisphere of the brain receives information primarily from the opposite side of the body, and there are connections between the two hemispheres allowing each half to "know" what is happening in the other. If language is "located" in the left hemisphere, the right ear, accordingly, should be more adept at language processing than the left. One can test this proposal by presenting information simultaneously to both ears, asking listeners to report what they have heard. Doreen Kimura (1973) has developed such a "dichotic listening task," and she has found that listeners report verbal material presented to the right ear more accurately than material simultaneously presented to the left ear. (There is no differential ear advantage for the detection of pure tones, so the matter is not one of general perceptual advantage in the right ear.) What is it about verbal material that the right ear (i.e., left hemisphere) is especially sensitive to? For one thing, it is apparently the SOUND of language which is important, because the right ear is also superior for nonsense syllables and even for speech played backwards or speech in an unknown foreign language. However, the left hemisphere is not set to perceive speech sounds in general, but only speech sounds in a language-like context. The right ear advantage disappears for separate vowels but is present for consonant-vowel combinations, suggesting that the syllable is a basic unit in speech perception. If, however, listeners are told to pay attention to the emotional tone of a message, there is a left ear advantage (Haggard & Parkinson, 1971), suggesting that the right hemisphere can process nonlinguistic aspects of speech. Thus, the left hemisphere is apparently finely tuned to attend to language-like sounds, for the purposes of strictly linguistic or acoustic processing. The right hemisphere is superior at detecting nonlanguage environmental sounds and musical melodies.

Can we say, then, that the specialization of the left hemisphere lies in the processing of speech sounds, and the right hemisphere in processing other kinds of sounds (environmental sounds, emotional tone, music)? The matter is not so simple. It seems that the differences between the hemispheres is one of HOW input is to be processed, rather than the source of the input. For example, Papçun, Krashen, Terbeek, Remington, and Harshman (1974) have found that Morse code operators have a right ear advantage for Morse code signals, while naive college students do not. The sounds are the same for operators and nonoperators, but the knowledge involved in serially processing and interpreting these sounds is located in the left hemisphere, like language. It is apparently a facility for such tasks—tasks of analysis and serial processing of discrete units of information—which is the domain of the left hemisphere. Bever and Chiarello (1974) have demonstrated that even music perception need not be a right hemisphere function. They had people perform various tasks of melodic analysis and recognition, using one ear at a time. One group of subjects was musically experienced (having had at least four years of music lessons and currently playing or singing music); the other group was inexperienced in these terms. They found that melodic recognition was better in the right ear for experienced listeners, and better in the left for inexperienced. Apparently part of musical training involves learning to take an analytic approach to melodies, whereas naive listeners tend to hear melodies as holistic patterns (as has been demonstrated classically by Gestalt psychology). In contrast to the ANALYTIC capacities of the left hemisphere, a large body of research suggests that the right hemisphere is specialized for tasks of synthetic and holistic perception (facial recognition, pattern perception, visualization, etc.). Language is thus embedded in a general cognitive matrix which involves abilities to analyze wholes into units, to combine those units in various ways, and to process them serially. The special abilities of the left hemisphere are thus in accord with the picture of language processing developed in psycholinguistics.

Limited Language Capacity in the Right Hemisphere Is there any language capacity in the right hemisphere? Even though the left hemisphere is dominant for language, there seem to be some aspects of language which can be dealt with by the hemisphere which is not specialized for rapid analytic processing and propositional thinking. The contrast between "right and left hemisphere language" serves to heighten the unique characteristics of fully developed human language. Since the two hemispheres are connected, it is difficult, normally, to assess the abilities of either hemisphere separately, except by techniques such as those mentioned above. In some cases, however, it has been necessary to separate the hemispheres surgically in order to control severe epilepsy. Such "split-brain" individuals can function fairly normally, but psychological testing providing stimuli to only one isolated hemisphere can reveal special hemispheric functions. We cannot review all of the intriguing findings from these unusual cases here (see Gazzaniga, 1967, 1970; Nebes, 1974), but will limit ourselves to the question of right hemisphere language.

The right hemisphere, in split-brain individuals, cannot express itself through speech, since the left hemisphere controls the speech apparatus. But it can read written messages sent to the right visual area of the brain alone, demonstrating comprehension by appropriate activity with the left hand; and, similarly, it can respond to auditory messages. For example, the left hand can pick out a pencil from an array of objects when the word *pencil* is given to the right hemisphere in writing or in speech. By comprehension testing, the right hemisphere appears to have a small vocabulary and very limited grammatical ability. For example (Gazzaniga & Hillyard, 1971), this hemisphere is shown a picture (via the left visual field) along with two statements, read by the experimenter. The subject is to nod when he hears the appropriate description of the picture. The right hemisphere in split-brain subjects is not able to distinguish active from passive sentences, present from future, or singular from plural; but positive and negative statements are distinguished. The experimenters suggest that the right hemisphere cannot recognize the relationship between subject, verb, and object. (The left hemisphere performs normally on these tasks.)

On other sorts of tasks, the right hemisphere has the advantage. In tasks of copying drawings or block constructions, the left hand performs far better than the right. The same advantage holds for tasks involving matching part to whole, as in matching an arc to a complete circle. Interestingly, the left hemisphere has difficulty in associating names to faces (Levy, 1972), while the right hemisphere does not. Presumably the right hemisphere can conceive of faces as patterns, while the left hemisphere can only make specific partial associations (as, for example, trying to remember that the face called *Leah* has glasses and short, dark hair). In a review of this research, Nebes (1974, p. 10) concludes: "This suggests that in man it is the right cerebral cortex which is responsible for forming, from the incomplete information provided by our senses, the spatial and cognitive map of our surroundings in which the planning and organization of behavior take place."

In an "intact" human being, of course, these two sets of hemispheric functions constantly interact. Of special interest to us is the fact that the right hemisphere—presumably less equipped for language acquisition from birth—has only a rudimentary grasp of language. This rudimentary grasp includes words and meanings, but very little grammar. And it is grammar which seems to reflect, par excellence, the special capacities of the left hemisphere.

Maturation and Hemispheric Specialization

Left Hemisphere Function in Infancy   Why should there be any language capacity in the right hemisphere at all? Presumably, early in development, a sort of "insurance policy" is taken out against possible damage to the left hemisphere, setting down a core of language which may be able to develop into mature language capacity if necessary. If the left hemisphere is damaged or removed early in life, language does develop in the surviving right hemisphere. But even infantile hemiplegia of the left hemisphere sustained in the first year of life has effects both on the course of language development and adult capacity. The acquisition of single words is not delayed, but the development of word combinations is retarded—in consonance with the findings discussed above. And even in adulthood, syntactic capacity—although adequate—does not fully reach normal levels (Dennis & Whitaker, 1977). Normal right hemisphere functions may also be affected, suggesting that the division of functions between the two hemispheres may be required because of the exceptionally high demands of human cognitive functioning—of both the right and left hemisphere variety.

Recent research has demonstrated that the left hemisphere is sensitive to some aspects of language from birth. Infants as young as one day show relatively greater left hemisphere electrical activity to speech sounds, and relatively greater right hemisphere activity to nonspeech sounds (Molfese, 1977). In a dichotic listening task with infants as young as 22 days, Entus (1977) found the normal right ear advantage for spoken syllables and left ear advantage for musical notes (played on piano, viola, bassoon, and cello). Furthermore, in complex acoustic experiments with infants, it appears that infants are sensitive to just those acoustic distinctions which are used to signal phonetic distinctions in human language, showing the same kinds of speech perception patterns as adults. (Eimas, Siqueland, Jusczyk, & Vigorito, 1971; Eimas, 1974). The left hemisphere thus appears to be "preset" to speech sounds, already prepared to analyze those sounds in language-like ways.

Critical Age for Language Acquisition   There may well be a "critical age" for the left hemisphere to develop language functions, as well as a critical age for the right hemisphere to take over such functions in the event of damage to the left. Recovery of language following left hemisphere damage is significantly poorer if the damage occurs after puberty, suggesting a maturationally based decrease in the ability of the right hemisphere to master language. In addition, language experience itself may be necessary for the full development of lateralization and the functioning of the left hemisphere. The most striking evidence in this regard comes from the tragic but highly informative recent case of "Genie," a girl who was locked away and deprived of all language and social interaction until she was discovered at age thirteen and a half (Curtiss, 1977). Genie could not speak at all, but eventually mastered a degree of language. By age eighteen, after very slow development, she was able to speak short sentences, with a minimum of grammar. She followed English word order and learned meaningful words, including prepositions (which make reference to spatial locations) and some means of negation. But virtually everything of syntax was lacking: there were no auxiliaries, no reorderings (as for questions), no question words, no pronouns or other forms which replace concrete words in English. (Curtiss calls these "proforms," including relative pronouns, indefinite pronouns, demonstratives, and wh- question words.) Yet in regard to right hemisphere functions—such as pattern perception, facial recognition, and part-whole judgments—her performance was normal or even superior to normal. In dichotic listening tasks it appeared that ALL listening functions were carried out by the right hemisphere, although she could hear normally in both ears and was right-handed. Curtiss concludes that Genie uses the right hemisphere for both language and nonlanguage functions, suggesting that "a kind of functional atrophy" had occurred in the left hemisphere, brought about by disuse due to inadequate language stimulation in childhood. Genie began to learn language after puberty, using the right hemisphere, and her level of language mastery probably represents the scope of language capacity available to the nonlanguage hemisphere of the brain.

The language hemisphere is thus apparently predisposed to acquire language AT AN APPROPRIATE MATURATIONAL STAGE. That is to say, learning to speak is conditioned by the complex timetable of physical growth. (The critical age remains to be clearly defined: some aspects of language development seem to have a cutoff at age five; others at puberty [see Witelson, 1977].) Genie's case demonstrates the sort of language that can be acquired by the nonlanguage cortex, outside of the critical period. Curtiss suggests (1977, pp. 210–11) that this sort of language—essentially lacking in syntax—is seen in three other groups: (1) adults who have had the left hemisphere removed and must reacquire language in the right, (2) normal children in the earliest stage of language development, and (3) chimpanzees attempting to learn a language-like system (as we will see later in this chapter). She notes that in all three groups, the attempt to learn language is carried out either by cortex which is not "predisposed or 'programmed' to process language in the normal brain" or "outside of the appropriate maturational stage" (i.e., too young for normal children, too old for left-hemispherectomized adults). By characterizing the degree of language mastery accessible to these cases, we can, by contrast, delineate the specifically human, left-hemisphere language capacity. Curtiss characterizes the capacity of "nonlanguage" cortex in the following terms (p. 211):

> It is as if there are specific limitations to how much and what aspects of language "nonlanguage" area cortex, or the immature cortex can acquire. "Nonlanguage" cortex in humans may be the right hemisphere in general, and possibly the left hemisphere outside of the appropriate maturational state in development. In chimpanzees it is possibly the cortex in general. Such cortex can acquire vocabulary, simple two-, three-, and four-word utterances, negatives, and, in general, greater semantic than syntactic abilities. None of the groups above has been reported to have acquired proforms, movement rules, or AUX

[auxiliary] elements. Genie's acquisition of language, therefore, resembles that of (1) humans attempting to reacquire language utilizing their right hemispheres, (2) humans attempting to acquire language in the "noncritical" period, or (3) other species acquiring language.

What is left then to distinguish us (full-fledged human beings) from these other groups seems to lie, in great measure, in the domain of syntax. Beyond basic abilities to symbolize, we can use COMBINATIONS of symbols which have predictable meanings, given a general system of grammatical knowledge. In order for such syntactic abilities to function, (1) it is necessary to use words to stand for other words, or to represent general underlying notions (such as case, time, person, number, and the like); and (2) one must be able to systematically rearrange the orders of meaningful elements in a sentence (words and grammatical particles) in order to express various combinations and alterations of meaning. In both cases, what seems to be involved is an ability to operate on linguistic entities themselves: to permute, delete, rearrange, and substitute one word or structure for another.

These findings and speculations, however, must be taken very tentatively. We are just beginning to gather detailed data on all of the sorts of issues discussed above. The important conclusion to remember is (1) that the human language capacity has a specific neurological base, (2) with a degree of inborn potential, (3) tied to a maturational timetable. It remains for us now to explore the nature of language representation in the left hemisphere. Here we rely upon studies of aphasia to reveal the interrelations and separability of various language functions.

Language Functions in the Left Hemisphere

When the brain is damaged (by illness or by bullets), language disturbance often results. In about 97 percent of the cases of permanent language disorder, it is the left hemisphere which is damaged (Geschwind, 1972). Speech disorder caused by brain damage is called *aphasia,* and the victims are called *aphasics.* Often one aspect of language is interfered with more than another. Such selective disturbance provides evidence for separability of various language functions. Postmortem examination of the brains of aphasics has made it possible to localize the areas of the brain involved in specific language functions. Broadly, there is neurological evidence that phonology, syntax, vocabulary, and word meanings are distinct entities. The literature on aphasia is complex and often contradictory. What I present here is a schematic summary for psycholinguistic purposes. (For more detail on aphasia, see Geschwind, 1972; Goodglass & Geschwind, 1976; Goodglass & Kaplan, 1972; Jakobson, 1971; Whitaker, 1971; and the journal *Brain and Language.*)

In Figure 5-5 you see a schematic flowchart of the left hemisphere of the brain. This is an idealization of what has been learned from more than a hundred years of aphasia studies. Let us take a brief "tour" of this chart, trying to determine functional areas and their connections.

The first modern contribution to our understanding of the relations

FIGURE 5-5
Schematic Diagram of the Lateral Aspect
of the Left Cerebral Hemisphere[1]

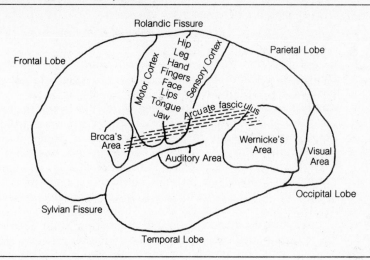

[1]Figure adapted from Palermo (1978, p. 67).

between brain and language was made in the 1860s by the Frenchman, Paul Broca; and, accordingly, one of the language areas of the brain is named after him. Broca's area is in the motor cortex, right in front of the portion which controls the muscles involved in speech production. Broca discovered that damage to this area is related to difficulty in speaking, but not in comprehending. The disturbance is specifically linguistic, since the same muscles—muscles of the lower face, jaw, tongue, palate, and vocal cords—can still function for nonspeech purposes, apparently through right hemisphere control. In addition, the linguistic disturbance is clearly lateralized, since damage to the corresponding area in the right hemisphere does not interfere with speech. Not only is speech slow, effortful, and distorted in pronunciation in "Broca's aphasia," but the nature of the remaining speech shows an interesting selective disturbance. It is primarily the grammatical elements which are missing: grammatical particles and noun and verb endings. For example, a Broca's aphasic is shown a picture which the investigators (Marin, Saffran, & Schwartz, 1976, p. 874) describe as follows:

> In this picture, a man has just run out of his house to remonstrate with a girl passerby, thinking that she must be responsible for his broken window. We also see a boy in baseball garb hiding behind a fence and can reasonably assume that he, not the girl, is the culprit.

The patient is limited to the following, halting description, consisting almost entirely of separate nouns (p. 876):

> Like the door . . . crash . . . like, pants . . . shirt . . . shoes . . . the boy . . . the dress . . . I dunno.

In reading, this patient has difficulty with the same kinds of grammatical words which are lacking in his speech:

SENTENCE	PATIENT'S VERSION
Dinner is on the table.	*Dinner . . . dinner is . . . the table.*

The problem is not just one of organizing speech into sentences. Such patients apparently cannot access grammatical words, even if they can pronounce identical, homophonous words (i.e., words with the same sound). For example, the patient is asked to read words like *would* (a grammatical function word) and its homophone *wood* (a content word) (Marin et al., 1976). He is more successful in reading *wood* than *would.* (Other pairs, with similar results, were: *which-witch, be-bee, us-bus, and-end.*) In speech and in reading these patients have difficulty with personal pronouns, relative pronouns, prepositions, articles, conjunctions, and particles. The interesting conclusion for psycholinguistic purposes is that here we seem to have a situation in which the lexicon is maintained, but syntax is lost, suggesting that syntax is, indeed, a distinct linguistic system. Furthermore, word order is maintained—as it is in Genie's speech and early child language—suggesting that this portion of the grammar is of a different level than the use of grammatical markers.

The opposite disturbance—syntax with an impaired lexicon—also occurs, but with damage to a different brain location. Shortly after Broca's discovery, Carl Wernicke discovered patients who speak rapidly, using normal syntax, but with little content. These patients have damage in a posterior region of the brain, close to the place where auditory input is processed. Although these patients can have normal hearing of nonverbal sounds and music, their comprehension of speech is seriously impaired. For example, such a patient described the broken window picture as follows (Marin et al., 1976, p. 874):

> This guy did something, right there . . . He ran . . . and she's there like she didn't even know. (Tester: "Who broke it?") She would never do it—she looks like a really nice kid. He's really getting mad (pointing to the man) . . . HE did it (pointing to the boy); he broke it. (Tester: "How?") I can't tell you but I know what it is. . . .

The speech of such aphasics has a small number of content words, generally nonspecific, and a preponderance of pronouns. In such patients the syntactic system appears to be retained, but it functions with an extremely limited lexicon, with few content words available. Again, we have evidence for the distinct storage of grammar as a separate system. In Wernicke's aphasics, Broca's area is intact and can program grammatical utterances, but it does not receive sufficient information to produce fully meaningful utterances.

If Broca's area programs rapid serial coordination of the speech musculature, and Wernicke's area is involved with comprehension, we can predict the results of a lesion in the fibers which connect these two areas (the arcuate fasciculus). A patient suffering such a disconnection of these two language areas should speak fluently, but with little content, because Broca's area is still functioning. And comprehension should not be disturbed, because Wernicke's area has not been damaged. However, he should not be able to repeat the speech he hears, because the auditory information reaching Wernicke's area cannot be transmitted to Broca's area. Such patients ("conduction aphasics") do indeed exist, lending further evidence to the picture presented above.

It is also possible to block access to the lexicon, leaving comprehension, syntax, and articulation intact, resulting in what is known as "anomic" or "amnesic" aphasia. (The location of lesions producing this sort of aphasia is not as predictable as in the aphasias discussed above. The means of storage of the lexicon is still an open question.) Such patients can often produce paraphrases while searching for a given word. For example, presented with a pair of scissors, the patient might say *for cutting.* However, he accepts *scissors* when suggested by the investigator, rejecting other names (e.g., *knife, pliers,* etc.). Here we seem to have a disconnection between words and meanings.

Surgical studies also show that words—as utterable entities—are stored separately from the concepts which underlie them (Penfield & Roberts, 1959). In the course of brain surgery, the patient is conscious (with only local anesthesia) and it is necessary for the surgeon to probe the brain with electrodes, monitoring the patient's physical and verbal responses in order to locate specific areas in the brain. Often the consequences of stimulation are either speech or the suppression of speech. For example, the patient is shown a picture of a butterfly while an electrode is applied to a given location in his brain. He says, "I know what it is," and falls silent. After the electrode is withdrawn, he says: "Now I can talk—butterfly. I couldn't get that word *butterfly,* and then I tried to get the word *moth.*" Another patient is shown a picture of a foot and says: "Oh, I know what it is. That is what you put in your shoes." After the removal of the electrode he is able to say *foot.* These examples suggest that the patients were, temporarily, in a state which is chronic in some sorts of aphasics (and familiar to all of us from everyday groping for words!). Their comprehension was intact, and word meanings were accessible to them, but they could not produce specific words. In everyday life, we say "it's on the tip of my tongue." These neurological studies show that the acoustic-articulatory form of a word (the form that can be executed by the tip of the tongue) is distinct from its meaning. Presumably, when a word is "on the tip of the tongue," the speaker is keeping the tongue waiting while holding the meaning in mind. In the words of Dr. Wilder Penfield, who pioneered in brain stimulation research, "an individual normally presents a concept to the speech mechanism and expects an answer" (Penfield & Roberts, 1959, p. 228). Cases of direct brain stimulation, aphasia, and normal momentary struggles with expression all demonstrate that these two functions—access of concepts and access of words—are separate.

A Philosophical Footnote

I will not continue with these impressionistic summaries of research in "neurolinguistics." This rapidly growing field promises to contribute much to our understanding of the organization of language functions. Hopefully there will be further convergence between the analytic categories created by linguists and psycholinguists and the functional structures revealed by neurological research. In concluding this section, though, I want to leave you with a puzzle about language and thought—a problem which will engage our attention more fully in the next chapter.

Cases of selective impairment of abilities raise intriguing questions about the nature of human consciousness and cognition. What are we to make of patients who can deal with concepts but not name them, who can speak but not understand, and so on? The noted aphasiologist Norman Geschwind (1965) has speculated on such issues in describing a patient who had a disconnection of the motor cortex of the right hemisphere from the speech area in the left hemisphere (rather like the split-brain patients discussed above, but occurring naturally). The man could carry out verbal commands with his right hand, but not with his left; he could write and type with the right, but not the left. If an object—say, a hammer—were placed in his left hand, he could not respond to the command, "Show me how to use a hammer"; yet, he could use a hammer correctly with the left hand.

Geschwind discusses this case in terms of philosophical considerations of "the whole man" and "the unity of consciousness," suggesting that consciousness is more a system of connected parts than a unified entity. Speaking of his work with this patient, he writes (1965, pp. 637–38):

> We were constantly dealing with questions such as "If he can speak normally and he knows what he's holding in his left hand why can't he tell you?" We had to point out that we couldn't say that "the patient knew what was in his left hand" and that "the patient could speak normally," since that part of the patient which could speak normally was not the same part of the patient which "knew" (non-verbally) what was in his left hand. . . .
>
> . . . It would no doubt be startling to suggest that the patient . . . had separate consciousness in each hemisphere; it would on the other hand be a little difficult to understand just what would be meant by saying that his consciousness was unitary. If the ability to give a verbal account is a prerequisite of consciousness then only the left hemisphere was conscious; if the ability to respond in a highly organized manner and to use the results of past experience constitutes consciousness then he had multiple consciousness.

In introducing Wundt's formulation of psycholinguistics at the beginning of the book, and throughout the discussion of grammar, we repeatedly encountered the problem of the existence of organized knowledge which is prior to, and outside of, the production of speech. In the discussion of early child language, again, it was necessary to introduce the notion of knowledge structures antedating and guiding the emergence of linguistic expression. In the next chapter I will argue for distinctions between language and thought. And now, on neurological grounds as well, we have evidence that language and speech do not constitute the whole of consciousness or cognition.

THE HUMAN CAPACITY OF LANGUAGE INVENTION

I think it should be clear to you by now that the language capacity has a distinct neurological and anatomical basis in human beings, organized at birth according to the various separate systems and their interconnections which make up a full human language. Normally, this capacity is set into operation by direct linguistic stimulation from the environment. In the remaining two sections of this chapter we will consider two significant deviations from this normal situation. First, we will ask whether human children, deprived of linguistic input, can invent some linguistic system of their own, relying on their inborn capacities. And then we will consider attempts to teach language to closely related, intelligent species (the higher apes), whose brains lack the specialization for language reviewed above. In this way, examining Descartes' claims in the light of modern evidence, we will be in a position to more fully evaluate the ways in which our language capacity is a species-specific endowment.

You will remember that Descartes said that "even those men born deaf and dumb . . . usually invent for themselves some signs by which they make themselves understood by those who are with them enough to learn their language." Unfortunately, we do not know what evidence was available to Descartes on the invention of sign language by the deaf. But recently a group of researchers at the University of Pennsylvania have documented six different cases of the invention of sign languages by deaf children of hearing parents (Goldin-Meadow, in press; Goldin-Meadow and Feldman, 1977). These cases provide striking evidence of the ways in which the language capacity functions "on its own." These children were being raised by parents who did not believe in the use of the sign language of the deaf (which is a structured language system acquired in normal fashion by deaf children of deaf, signing parents). Whatever language these children used, therefore, was not based on linguistic input from parents and was not part of the normal auditory-vocal system. Yet each of these children did invent a sort of gestural sign language, going through what appears to be a normal sequence of development—both in terms of content and structure. The language was apparently taught TO the parents by the children—as Descartes suggested—since those mothers who eventually communicated gesturally used the system in more limited fashion than their children, having a smaller sign vocabulary and always being at a less complex stage of development than the child. It was the children who invented the signs. Let us examine the extent to which these invented languages can be said to be structured and developmentally sequenced.

The children went through developmental stages of speaking in one-sign utterances, two-sign utterances, and then longer utterances, similar to speaking children, and to children learning American Sign Language. The developmental constraints on length of utterance thus seem to be based on maturation of some general processing capacity. Since these children did not speak or hear speech, it cannot be that the stages of utterance length are systematic features of parental communication. The children began producing combinatorial, two-sign utterances before their mothers did. Thus the notion of combination of meaningful units is not derived from input but is provided by the child.

The meanings of sign combinations are the same as those produced by speaking children at the two-word stage and are produced at about the same age. For example, a child pointed at a shoe and then to a table, requesting that the shoe be put on the table. Or a child extended an open palm, signifying 'give', and then pointed to his chest, indicating that he wanted a particular object to be given to him. Signs were invented for various actions, such as producing a twisting motion in the air to indicate opening of a jar, sliding the hand along in a palm-down position to indicate 'go', and so forth. Like the normal, hearing children discussed in Chapter 4, these children used two-sign utterances to communicate nuclear propositions of one-place predicates (e.g., *bridge fall, father sleeps),* two-place predicates (e.g., *chew cookie,* meaning 'I am chewing the cookie'), and three-place predicates (e.g., *toy give,* meaning 'you give me the toy'). Like normal children, they communicated earlier about actions and locations, later about attributes, and still later about instruments and beneficiaries of actions. The stage of simple statements was followed by a stage of conjoined and modified utterances. It was possible to describe the children's signed utterances using the terms of case grammar—ACTOR, PATIENT, RECIPIENT, and so on. These unusual children clearly show that the sequence of development of communicative intentions arises naturally, independent of linguistic input. This sequence must be based on the maturation of a symbolic capacity which underlies normal language development as well. These cases also reveal the basic capacity for the expression of propositions, encodable in combinable meaningful entities.

Furthermore, these combinations are structured, in that clear word order tendencies were present. At the two-word stage, the children produced PATIENT-RECIPIENT utterances (e.g., *book mother,* requesting that a book be given to mother), but no RECIPIENT-PATIENT utterances. There was a tendency to adhere to the order of PATIENT-ACT (e.g., *drum beat)* and ACT-RECIPIENT (e.g., *give mother,* meaning something was to be given to mother). We thus have a general order rule, which Goldin-Meadow and Feldman (1977, p. 402) summarize as follows:

CHOOSE ANY TWO MAINTAINING ORDER:
Phrase → (PATIENT) (ACT) (RECIPIENT)

As we will see in the discussion of chimpanzee acquisition of sign language, the notion of sign order is a difficult one for chimps to master, even though it is present in the language in which they are being trained. Yet these deaf children, with no exposure to a system of ordered signs at all, have invented regular orders on their own. You will recall that Genie's speech adhered to word order rules, and that word order is not disturbed in Broca's aphasia, when the rest of the grammatical system crumbles. Pidgin languages, lacking in most grammatical devices, are characterized by regular word order. All of this evidence suggests that the notion of using order as a symbolic device is deeply rooted in the human language capacity.

These exciting data on spontaneous language invention suggest that there may be a biological basis for the sorts of "operating principles" for language acquisition proposed at the end of Chapter 4. As Goldin-Meadow has put it (in press, pp. 55-56): "It may not be unreasonable to suppose that the child, hearing or deaf, brings to the language learning situation certain predispositions which narrow down the field of potential languages to be acquired." These predispositions may include the organization of semantics into the sorts of predicate structures considered in this book, the symbolization of elements of these structures by discrete units (sounds or gestures), and the use of order and combinatorial rules to encode propositions and combinations of propositions. Goldin-Meadow concludes (in press, p. 56):

> Whatever the explanations of the substantive structures constituting human language, the fact of structured early communication without structured conventional linguistic input is clearly demonstrated here. Even under adverse circumstances, the human child has the natural inclination and the capacity to develop a structured communication system. It is this capacity to "make do" under less than perfect conditions which allows us to conclude that humans are prepared for language learning, even when their linguistic environments are not prepared for them.

Finally, let us ask whether chimpanzees are prepared for language learning, even when their evolution and normal habitat have not required them to demonstrate a language capacity. If humans provide a linguistic environment for chimpanzees, are they prepared for language learning? To the extent that they are prepared, we must place our story about the biological foundation of human language in a broad evolutionary perspective, speaking of common primate neurological structures and functions. And the limits of chimpanzee language capacity (when they are eventually determined) will cast in relief our own species-specific biological and cognitive endowments.

CHIMPANZEE LANGUAGE CAPACITY

People have always been fascinated by the possibility that animals that look like us might be able to think and talk like us. The most obvious candidate for a hidden human in animal form has been the chimpanzee, and earlier in this century several attempts were made to raise chimps like children (Hayes & Hayes, 1951; Kellogg & Kellogg, 1933; Kohts, 1935). Although the animals demonstrated impressive cognitive development and a degree of speech comprehension, they never learned to speak (due to lack of the requisite articulatory apparatus and motor control, as discussed above). Unfortunately, since language was equated with speech, their comprehension of spoken language was never systematically tested. But the desire to have a conversation with a chimp remained. Research demonstrated that chimps invent and use tools spontaneously, in the wild (Van Lawick-Goodall, 1971) and in the laboratory (Köhler, 1927); that they have a degree of symbolic capacity (Wolfe, 1936); that they go through stages of the development of sensory-motor intelligence similar to human children (Chevalier-Skolnikoff, 1977). They obviously use their hands well. In 1966 Allen and Beatrice Gardner took the obvious next step: they set out to teach manual sign language to a chimpanzee (Gardner & Gardner, 1974). Their success has stimulated a series of projects, teaching sign language and other language-like manual-visual systems to higher apes. David Premack has taught chimpanzees a symbolic system in which plastic chips of various shapes and colors are arranged in sequence to express a number of logical operations and proposition types, and Duane Rumbaugh and his colleagues have taught a chimpanzee an artificial language using a large keyboard of visual symbols which must be chosen in specified orders to obtain goods and services.[1] I will not summarize these many detailed and intriguing studies here, but I will raise several general questions of what can be learned about the human language capacity from such cross-species comparisons.

Descartes was wrong about the qualitative distinctiveness of the human mind. Chimpanzees, when carefully trained, are at least the equal "of the most stupid children." We do not yet know the limits of the intellectual and symbolic capacities of our neighboring primate species. While it is clear that they cannot be trained to become human beings (Kafka, 1917, notwithstanding!), it is not clear when, how, or where the border will be drawn. Although ultimately limited by the intelligence of the chimpanzee, the placement of the border is also determined by the ingenuity and perseverance of the human experimenters who attempt to trace that boundary. And so I will avoid categorical statements of the sort: "Chimpanzees cannot do X." We will look at some of the things chimpanzees CAN do, and speculate a bit about what they may not be able to do.

At best, primate language studies show which aspects of language are NOT based on uniquely human capacities. But this negative finding is primarily of interest to anthropocentric scholars who have some nonscientific investment in what Descartes called the nature of the human "soul." The study of language learning, in any species, is a means of discovering the cognitive capacities of that species. The chimpanzee studies leave us with the same questions as the study of human language capacity: what are the biological foundations of this capacity, what are the means of its acquisition, and what are the cognitive bases of its use? However, since the training conditions of nonhuman animals can be more systematically varied than in the case of human children, and since they can be subjected to more detailed neurophysiological study, we may eventually be able to discover something of the general experiential and physical bases of those aspects of language capacity which we may share with other species. At present, however, I would conclude that the chimp studies have taught us a good deal about the intelligence and abilities of chimps, but they have taught us little or nothing about the nature of human language and its psychological bases. Nevertheless, the challenge of arguing about the chimps' accomplishments has considerably sharpened our notions of what

1. A readable exposition of much of this research is provided in a book, *Apes, Men, and Language,* by Linden (1976). Popular reports of the Premack project are provided by Premack and Premack (1972) and A. Premack (1976); a detailed volume is provided by D. Premack (1976). A brief report of the Rumbaugh project is given by Rumbaugh and Gill (1976); details are in a volume edited by Rumbaugh (1977). Patterson (1977) has successfully extended sign language research to gorillas, and has begun studying auditory comprehension in a gorilla as well. Fouts and his colleagues (Linden, 1976, p. 121) are also studying English comprehension in chimpanzees. For simplicity of exposition, the discussion in this section deals with the most widely studied species—chimpanzee—though the findings are applicable to gorillas and perhaps other higher primates as well.

is involved in human psycholinguistics (just as arguments about computers and artificial intelligence have refined the thinking of psychologists and linguists). A good test of your grasp of psycholinguistic issues would be to read some of the chimp studies and ask yourself in what ways human language acquisition and language use differ from the descriptions of the animals' achievements.

The various chimp studies have several facts in common, regardless of the type of language used or training procedures followed. (1) The animals were all able to acquire symbols (gestures, arbitrary visual forms) representing objects, actions, and relations, using the symbols both in production and comprehension. (2) They were able to extend the meanings of these symbols to new referents. (3) With some difficulty, they were able to produce and interpret combinations of symbols. None of these abilities reaches a very high level in human terms—we will not lose our position at the top of the Animal Kingdom—but the achievements are striking in relation to centuries-old claims about the absolute uniqueness of man's symbolic capacity. From an evolutionary point of view this result is not surprising. Certainly our cognitive and linguistic abilities arose from an already existing biological matrix. Eventually psycholinguistic research should be able to define the primitive core of language capacity from which fully adult, human language behavior develops. For the present, however, a brief look at symbolic behavior in trained chimpanzees will give you some idea of what may have been at least the lower limit of language capacity in our prehuman ancestors.

The Acquisition of Symbols

None of the animals studied has had any difficulty in learning to use the symbols provided by humans to designate objects, events, and relations. If a human being can train an animal to use a symbol system, there must be a close relationship between the basic "world views" of the two species, independent of language. The concepts referred to by the symbols must already be accessible to the animal in order for it to consistently apply the symbols to new situations. As David Premack has repeatedly pointed out (e.g., Premack & Premack, 1972, p. 95): "To a large extent teaching language to an animal is simply mapping out the conceptual structures the animal already possesses."

By studying the range of instances to which a symbol is applied, we can discover something about the animal's underlying, nonlinguistic organization of the world. For example, Washoe—the chimp who learned American Sign Language from the Gardners—learned to sign *flower* in connection with real flowers in a garden. She extended the sign to new flowers and to pictures of flowers, indicating a general grasp of the concept, as well as an ability to recognize its schematized and two-dimensional representation. She also signed *flower* when encountering distinctive smells, such as mentholated ointment and tobacco, indicating that her concept included a component of scent as well as a visual representation. Washoe learned to sign *open* when requesting that a door be opened, and she extended the use of this sign to request the opening of various kinds of containers, and to have water faucets turned on. That is to say, she took *open* to have a GENERAL meaning of making accessible something which is in some sort of closed container. She not only used the symbols communicatively, but would sign to herself while looking through picture books and magazines, signing *drink* on encountering an ad for vermouth, and *tiger* when seeing a picture of a cat. All of these meaning extensions are similar to those observed in human children and indicate similar cognitive organization in ape and human.

The symbolic system can also be used productively. For example, Lucy, a chimpanzee learning sign language from Roger Fouts, invented the name *drinkfruit* for watermelon. As Linden (1974, pp. 108–09) points out, this name "is about as close to watermelon as any analyst might be expected to get, if the analyst's most specific term for fluids was *drink* and its most specific term for melons was *fruit* . . . and we might suppose that she came upon *drinkfruit* by an analysis of its attributes similar to that which produced our own word."

The chimps have learned more than just symbol-referent relations, because the same object can be referred to by different signs, depending on the communication situation. This is demonstrated most clearly in Washoe's response to questions. For example, a person will point to Washoe's bed and ask *What that?* Washoe responds *bed.* When asked *Whose?* in relation to the same object, she signs *mine;* and in response to *What color?* she answers *red.* Thus she is able to take different attitudes towards an object, depending on the general category called to mind by linguistic means. The symbols are used meaningfully—one might almost say thoughtfully—and cannot be dismissed as rote learning or conditioned responses.

The chimpanzees learning artificial languages show similar understanding of the symbolic nature of the system. For example, Lana, working on her computer keyboard, asked for an orange by punching the keys for *apple which-is orange-colored.* Sarah, working with Premack's plastic chips, could even learn the meanings of new symbols through the use of already known symbols. For example, she knew the symbols and meanings of *chocolate* and *color,* but did not have a symbol for the color brown. She was taught, through symbols, *Brown color of chocolate.* Later, when given the instruction *Take brown,* she was able to select a brown disc from among discs of various colors. In discussing this achievement of learning through symbols, Anne Premack notes (1976, p. 89):

> The ability to think of things not immediately present is called displacement and is considered a capacity unique to man. But Sarah was apparently able to think of chocolate (she was fond of it), even though chocolate was not immediately present. To do this, she must have been able to form a mental image of some chocolate, compare the color in her image with that of the brown disc, and match the two colors.

Clearly, all of these examples show a productive and meaningful use of symbols.

Gardner and Gardner (1971) have attempted to classify Washoe's sign combinations in terms used by Roger Brown for the semantic description of two-word utterances in children, as shown in Table 5-1. It is clear that such a comparison is feasible. Therefore whatever arguments we have made about the cognitive bases of early language in sensory-motor intelli-

TABLE 5-1
Parallel Descriptive Schemes for the Earliest Combinations of Children and Washoe[1]

Brown's (1970) Scheme for Children		Gardners' Scheme for Washoe	
Types	Examples	Types	Examples
Attributive: Ad + N	big train, red book	Object-attribute[2]	drink red, comb black
		Agent-attribute	Washoe sorry, Naomi good
Possessive: N + N	Adam checker, mommy lunch	Agent-object	clothes Mrs. G., you hat
		Object-attribute[2]	baby mine, clothes yours
N + V	walk street, go store	Action-location	go in, look out
		Action-object[3]	go flower, pants tickle[4]
Locative		Object-location	baby down, in hat[5]
N + N	sweater chair, book table		
		(not applicable)	
Agent-action: N + V	Adam put, Eve read	Agent-action	Roger tickle, you drink
Action-object: V + N	put book, hit ball	Action-object[3]	tickle Washoe, open blanket
Agent-object: N + N	mommy sock, mommy lunch	(not applicable)	
		Appeal-action	please tickle, hug hurry
(not applicable)		Appeal-object	gimme flower, more fruit

[1] Table from Gardner and Gardner (1971, p. 174).
[2,3] Indicate types classified two ways in Brown's scheme and only one way in Gardners' scheme.
[4] Answer to the question, "Where tickle?"
[5] Answer to the question, "Where brush?"

gence must be applicable to chimps as well as to humans. Given the fact that chimps do pass through the same stages of sensory-motor development as human children, this claim is not surprising. What is surprising is the chimpanzee's ability to symbolically represent the concepts it has developed. However, finding this symbolic capacity in a closely related and highly complex species in no way explains the basis of that capacity. We need to know vastly more about the neurology of the two species, and the potentials and limits of various training procedures.

Combining Symbols

Table 5-1 shows that a chimp can produce combinations of symbols, as well as single symbols. The chimps learning artificial language systems (Premack's plastic forms and Rumbaugh's symbols on computer keys) also learned the meanings of individual symbols and combinations. Having accepted that chimpanzees have symbolic capacity, the battle lines for human uniqueness versus primate continuity have been drawn in regard to these combinations. Is there any evidence for grammar, or is grammar our special domain on this planet? The question hinges, of course, on what you regard as evidence for grammar, and thus on your definition of grammar. Let us consider two issues: ordering of elements in combinations, and resultant meanings of combinations.

Order of Elements Because the chimp trainers are all speakers of English, in which word order is an essential aspect of grammar, much attention has been paid to the issue of order of symbols in chimp language performance. Gardner and Gardner followed fixed word order in their signing to Washoe, but accepted all orders from her in her signing. By and large, Washoe did not adhere to fixed orders in her own signing. Premack and Rumbaugh explicitly trained their animals to produce elements in given orders, and their animals eventually succeeded in adhering to these orders. It is possible to train chimps to produce a series of ordered actions, but this ability is clearly more accessible to human children than to chimps. Goldin-Meadow's deaf children spontaneously invented regular orders, whereas chimps have to be carefully trained to do the same.

In Washoe's early combinations, the same signs would often be used in different orders—for example, *sweet drink gimme* and *gimme sweet drink; you food me, food you me,* and *you me food. You* and *me* are simple pointing gestures at the other participant and the self, and there is some evidence that Washoe preferred to point to the human helper first, then moving her hand to herself, the recipient of the requested food or service. This is certainly an order rule, but since Washoe did not announce her own intentions to do something for someone else, we cannot tell if she would have reversed the order from *me* to *you.* However, even for human children, the existence of ordered pairs of words does not yet indicate a full grasp of grammar. Braine (1976) has demonstrated that many of children's early two-word utterances are fairly specific formulae. For example, a child may have a number of two-word utterances with *see* in first position *(see doggie, see truck,* etc.) and others with *want* in first position *(want cookie, want ride,* etc.). One cannot conclude, however, that the child has a general class of verbs, or a general verb-object rule. At this stage the child probably has a collection of separate and limited formulae, perhaps linked to particular words (e.g., that *see* comes first, that *want* comes first) or small, nongrammatical classes of words (e.g., that names of people and animals are mentioned first in an utterance). At most, the evidence on chimp signing indicates that some such limited-scope formulae occasionally occur—but with much less frequency and regularity than in child speech.

The important aspect of grammar, however, is its use in signalling meanings which go beyond the separate meanings of the words in the utterance. Utterances such as Washoe's *gimme flower* need no grammatical rules for their interpretation. Given the meanings of the two words, only one interpretation is possible, and it would be the same for *flower gimme* as well. Other utterances, even if regularly ordered, cannot be interpreted without context. Does *drink red* mean 'drink something red' or 'the drink is red'? Does *you hat* mean 'you have a hat' or 'you give me a hat' or 'you are doing something to a hat'?

The same questions can be raised in regard to human and chimp early signing or speaking. The evidence for grammar comes with a regular tendency to treat categories of words in the same fashion. Such evidence requires analysis of positional regularities of words in a large corpus of spontaneous production, and this stage is reached only after an early stage of separate positional formulae in children. Material of this sort has not yet been published for chimps, and so the question of ordered regularities based on category membership of individual elements remains open. Lana, the chimp who has learned to operate a symbolic keyboard, has learned to order symbols in a limited system. For example, the machine will only deliver rewards if the keys are punched in the following order of symbols: *please machine give* followed by a key naming something that can be given, or *please machine make* followed by the name of a desired event. When Lana was given the first part of the *please machine give* "sentence," she pushed keys for *M&M, juice,* or *water,* and not keys for other rewards, like seeing a *movie* or *music,* according to the rules of the system she was learning. Again, these could be limited-scope formulae. But this sort of performance suggests that, with detailed training, chimps can probably learn to order symbols on the basis of their category membership.

Better evidence for grammatical capacity would come from comprehension studies, such as those carried out with human children. Unfortunately, such systematic study of chimp comprehension has, to my knowledge, not yet been reported. Linden (1974, p. 103) notes informally that Lucy, the signing chimp studied by Roger Fouts, can appropriately understand the difference between *Roger tickle Lucy* (she waits to be tickled) and *Lucy tickle Roger* (she tickles Roger), but we do not know the extent of nonlinguistic cues for this performance, nor its generality to other kinds of situations and sentences. Chimpanzees and gorillas also show some comprehension of spoken English, and their grammatical abilities could be tested in response to both sign and speech. When such work is systematically done, we will know a good deal more about the grammatical capacities of these animals. For now, we must wait; and each of us will have our own prediction to make.

Meanings of Combinations   Grammar is not just a matter of producing words in particular regular orders. The orders must have significance beyond the meanings of the separate words. If Lucy correctly understands the two sentences about tickling, she also knows that the order of pointing—from person to chimp or from chimp to person—mirrors the order of action. This rule is graphically evident in action: it is a sort of pantomime. But it is a rudimentary order rule which systematically relates the meanings of the three words to an underlying proposition. The situation in human language is more complex—because it is general across the whole language, rather than isolated instances, and because it cannot be based on a visual analogue of acting out a scene. When we say, for example, that a language has subject-verb-object order, we indicate a much more complex underlying knowledge than Lucy's knowledge of the direction of pointing. We mean that, for all kinds of verb-noun combinations, the noun before the verb is the subject of the sentence and the one following is the object. Words have category membership, and the order of the categories has meaning of its own.

David and Anne Premack's chimp, Sarah, has succeeded in learning something of this sort, but with laborious training. Her "sentences" are visually present to her, in that the experimenter arrays a vertical sequence of plastic forms on a magnetic board in front of her. Sarah has as much time as she needs to scan the stimulus and figure out what to do with a limited collection of referent objects available to her. She is thus relieved of the burdens placed on rapid temporal processing by a normal language system, auditory or visual. She may take as long as a minute to figure out a symbolic instruction, indicating that this sort of task is much more of a difficult problem-solving situation than is normal comprehension of speech or sign in humans. Perhaps it is in rapid temporal processing of grammatical information that we will find our species-specific skills. Sarah's training was carried out step-by-step, rather than the spontaneous acquisition of sign in communication which occurred in the studies of Washoe and Lucy and other signing chimps. She was given a simple instruction with a minimal number of objects and was trained with explicit reward. Consider one example of comprehension which goes beyond the meanings of the individual symbols.

At some point in training Sarah was able to understand the instruction *Sarah banana pail insert*. Given several different fruits and containers, she would put the banana in the pail. She then succeeded in comprehending two such instructions: *Sarah banana pail insert Sarah cracker dish insert*. And finally she could perform in response to a reduced sentence: *Sarah banana pail cracker dish insert*. This performance requires that she know that *insert* refers to both containers in the utterance (*pail* and *dish*), and that the object mentioned before the container is the one to be inserted. She did not try to put the banana, the pail, and the cracker into the dish, indicating that she was able to break this utterance into phrases. She could even understand more complex compound sentences, with conjoining, as: *Sarah insert apple cracker dish cracker pail*, putting an apple and a cracker into the dish, and another cracker into the pail. This is one of many sorts of complex concepts which Sarah was able to learn in the symbolic medium. (She could make use of logical connectives like *and*

and *or;* she could comprehend and produce statements about *same* and *different;* she could understand *if . . . then;* and more.) Clearly, chimpanzees can learn to interpret structured aspects of symbolic utterances as having significance beyond the meanings of the separate words. The tasks are difficult for the animals, and we do not yet know where their ability will find its limits. David Premack concludes (1976, p. 317):

> The ape's relative incapacity for syntax may reflect the absence of an inherited syntactic competence or simply a weaker theory-constructing capacity in general. Finding the evidence that can decide between these alternatives is not likely to be easy.

The Use of Symbols

Sarah was trained to use symbols in artificial tasks of object manipulation and, with considerable reinforcement—and considerable resistance—she managed to do so. Lana and the signing chimps use their communication systems for pragmatic ends—mainly to receive goods and services from the human world. They do answer questions, and they do play with the symbolic systems on their own. But they do not seem to use their budding symbolic capacity for cognitive ends. Perhaps our special human adaptation lies not so much in our symbolic capacity, but in the connection of that capacity to higher order cognition and our human quest to develop and expand our understanding. That is to say, a special thing about human language is that it is intimately interconnected with cognition. It may also be in this interconnection that we will find the bases of our more complex syntactic capacities. That is, syntax may have evolved to serve the demands of thought.

The pragmatic limitations of chimp communication have been cogently summarized by Rumbaugh and Gill (1976, p. 574):

> Lana's persistence in conversation has been strictly pragmatic—once the desired incentive has been achieved, the conversation ENDS!! It should be noted also that Lana has never initiated conversations to "broaden her horizons," if you will. She has never asked for the names of things unless they held some food or drink that she apparently wanted; she has never "discussed" spontaneously the attributes of things in her world nor really ever capitalized upon conversation to extend her access to information about things. It might be that these limitations are artifacts of her training to date; perhaps she will do so someday, but at this time we are doubtful if chimpanzees will ever be noted for their exploiting linguistic-type skills to request additional information that might enhance their broad understanding of their world and how things in it work. We believe that this is an important point that might reliably differentiate language utilization by the child from the ape—perhaps the ape will use its language-type skills to the most pragmatic ends (as to obtain things), whereas the child readily goes beyond that use of language to learn about the nature of things, how they work; in short, the nature of its everyday world.

Rate of Development

In spite of the achievements of trained apes, human beings do have a special biologically-based language capacity. It is reflected—to review—in our vocal production apparatus and the specialized muscles and brain centers which control the rapid and integrated use of that apparatus for the purposes of speaking. It is reflected in our capacities to rapidly analyze and integrate structured auditory input and to relate that input to both grammatical and semantic structures. These capacities are, to be sure, an elaboration of capacities present in our ancestors, and present, to some degree, in apes. Their specialization in the vocal-auditory channel may be uniquely ours. Their degree of complexity and interrelations with higher mental processes are certainly uniquely ours. Something in our evolution selected for the combination of analytic intelligence and vocal-auditory communication. One can build many intriguing science fiction stories, involving such factors as warfare, kinship systems, diet, religion, etc. etc. Each of us can think of evolutionary stories of this sort, and many of them are beginning to be codified as semi-scientific sagas (see, for example, papers from a conference, *Origins and Evolution of Language and Speech* [Harnad, Steklis, and Lancaster, 1976]).

This evolutionary story—whatever it may have been—left permanent structural effects on our bodies and brains. In biological terms, one of the most striking effects is on RATE OF DEVELOPMENT. As Lenneberg has pointed out (1967, p. 174), man is a "fetalized" version of the general course of primate development. That is, we are born at a relatively earlier developmental period. At birth, the human brain is only 24 percent of the adult weight, while the chimpanzee brain at birth is already 60 percent of its eventual weight. Subsequent rate of human brain growth is much faster than chimp growth. Chimp and man differ more in rate of development than in overall genetic structure. We do not yet understand much about the relations between structure and rate of development, but it is clear that humans learn about language and the physical world during a period of development characterized by rapid growth of a relatively immature brain. Indeed, this precocious experience may even affect the resulting structure of the human brain. Something about this interaction of early experience, rate of growth, and inherent structure makes it very easy for human children to acquire—even invent—language, while apes can only approach the rudiments of these accomplishments with strenuous efforts of both animal and trainer. As Elizabeth Bates has put it (1977, p. 13):

> It is as though our nearest primate neighbors are at some brink in the development of tool use, imitation, and symbolization. Pushed across that brink, they can develop something like the symbolic communication of a very young human child. The difference is that our children rush across that brink with far less assistance.

6

The consistency of human behavior, such as it is, is due entirely to the fact that men have formulated their desires, and subsequently rationalized them, in terms of words. The verbal formulation of a desire will cause a man to go on pressing forward towards his goal, even when the desire itself lies dormant. Similarly, the rationalization of his desire in terms of some theological or philosophical system will convince him that he does well to persevere in this way. . . . From the psychological point of view, a theology or a philosophy may be defined as a device for permitting men to perform in cold blood and continuously actions which, otherwise, they could accomplish only by fits and starts and when the impulse was strong and hot within them. . . .

For evil, then, as well as for good, words make us the human beings we actually are. Deprived of language we should be as dogs or monkeys. Possessing language, we are men and women able to persevere in crime no less than in heroic virtue, capable of intellectual achievements beyond the scope of any animal, but at the same time capable of systematic silliness and stupidity such as no dumb beast could ever dream of.

—Aldous Huxley
(in Black, 1962, pp. 4–5)

LANGUAGE AND COGNITION

Human culture, social behavior, and thinking could not exist as we know them in the absence of language. But although no one would deny the central role of language in human life, to define the nature of that role has been a persistent and difficult problem since the beginnings of philosophy. Although language pervades mental life, it does not constitute the whole of psychological states and processes. There are images and emotions, intentions and abstractions, memories of sounds and smells and feelings, and much more. Throughout this book you have encountered examples of ideas independent of linguistic expression—aphasic separations of words and meanings, abstract structures underlying utterances, prelinguistic cognition in early childhood, and the like. Yet a dominant position in the history of psychology has been to equate language and thought. In this chapter we consider the claim that language and thought are inseparable. In the process of modifying this claim, it will become clear that human cognition is influenced by language, but it is not formed by language. Rather, language is one of many factors which play a role in "making us the human beings we actually are." In the first sections of the chapter the discussion revolves around the role of language in thinking, remembering, learning, and developing. Having delimited the extent to which language may shape human thought and action, we conclude with an old and puzzling question: Do people who speak different languages think in different ways?

LANGUAGE, SPEECH, AND THOUGHT

Twentieth-century psychology has attempted to be "scientific." This has generally meant that it is the obligation of psychologists to limit themselves to tangible phenomena—behavior that can be measured, recorded, materially manipulated. Until recently, terms like "stimulus" and "response" were preferred to notions such as "mind," "thought," "idea," and "mental representation." More recently it has become clear that regularities in measurable and observable behavior can be accounted for by postulating internal structures and processes; but in the early days of American behaviorism, such theorizing was held to a minimum. Accordingly, it was far more acceptable to talk about "speech" than to make claims about "thought." An extreme position was formulated in 1913 by John B. Watson, the father of American behaviorist psychology: ". . . according to my view, thought processes are really motor habits in the larynx." What Watson, and his followers, meant was that thought and speech are one and the same thing, thus making thought directly available to scientific study in the form of measurement of movements of the speech musculature.

A less extreme position has a rich history in Russian psychology. One of the earliest scientific positions taken on this problem was voiced in 1863 by Ivan M. Sechenov, the father of Russian physiology and mentor of Pavlov (p. 498):

> When a child thinks he invariably talks at the same time. Thought in five-year-olds is mediated through words or whispers, surely through movements of the tongue and lips, which is also very frequently (perhaps always, but in different degrees) true of the thinking of adults.

The Russian position, then, is that language and thought are closely linked in childhood, but that, in the course of development, adult thinking becomes free of language in some ways—at least free of overt or covert SPEECH RESPONSES. This position was most significantly elaborated by the great Soviet psychologist of the 1930s, L. S. Vygotsky. In his major work, *Thought and Language* (1962), first published in the USSR after his untimely death in 1934, Vygotsky developed the notion that in both phylogeny and ontogeny there are strains of nonverbal thought (e.g., "tool thought" involved in the solution of instrumental problems) and nonintellectual speech (e.g., emotional cries). He attempted to trace the interacting development of these two strains until the point in human development at which speech can serve thought and thought can be revealed in speech.

In the chapter on child language you have encountered related arguments about the ways in which cognitive development precedes and shapes linguistic development. This position—presenting a clear opposition to the behaviorist tradition—is based on the extensive work on cognitive development carried out over the past fifty years in Geneva by Jean Piaget and his colleagues. According to Piaget's school, cognitive development proceeds on its own, generally being followed by linguistic development, or finding reflection in the child's language. The child's intellect grows through interaction with things and people in the environment. To the extent that language is involved in these interactions, it may amplify or facilitate development in some cases, but it does not in itself bring about cognitive growth.

We will return to questions of mental development. But first we must assess the position of the centrality of language, in order to better understand the role which language may play in cognition.

Thought Without Speech

To begin with, we must be careful to remember the distinction between LANGUAGE and SPEECH made at the beginning of the book. Speech is a tangible, physical process resulting in the production of speech sounds, while language is an intangible system of meanings and linguistic structures. Thus Watson's position does not deal with LANGUAGE and thought at all; rather, he equates SPEECH and thought. Cognitive psychologists, like Vygotsky and Piaget, are concerned with speech and thought to the extent that speech is involved in communication of knowledge between people. But, more essentially, they are concerned with LANGUAGE and thought, that is, with the relations of inner linguistic and cognitive structures. To them, this inner use of language need not always be reflected in the articulatory movements of the vocal apparatus.

Many arguments have been raised against the strong Watsonian hypothesis (see, for example, Osgood, 1953). The most obvious criticism seems to come from the implication that a man deprived of contact with his speech musculature would lose the ability to think. If this were the case, it would be difficult to account for aphasic disturbances in which the patient can no longer speak, but can comprehend speech and otherwise behave fairly normally, indicating intact thought processes disconnected from the ability to produce articulate speech.

The *reductio ad absurdum* that thought is impossible without speech movements in the mouth has also been tested experimentally (Smith,

Brown, Toman, & Goodman, 1947). Intravenous injection of a form of the drug curare brings about temporary muscle paralysis—to the extent that oxygen and artificial respiration are required. E. M. Smith volunteered to be a subject in a difficult experiment in order to determine the effects of this drug. Although he could make no gestural or vocal responses under the influence of curare, he reported that he had been "clear as a bell," being able to accurately recall what was said and done to him during the period of paralysis. Thus it is dramatically clear that thought is possible without access to "motor habits in the larynx"—that is, without speech.

However, we can go beyond the behaviorist aversion to inner states and ask whether thought is possible without INNER SPEECH—that is, without some internal linguistic activity, even if not overtly or covertly articulated. There are many mental processes which seem to be prelinguistic or nonlinguistic. Perhaps the most familiar from everyday life is the unpleasant phenomenon of groping for a word or struggling to find the best way to express oneself. This is a momentary example in normal life of the more permanent disconnection between intentions and utterances observed in some kinds of aphasia, as discussed in Chapter 5. No one has described this better than the great psychologist William James in his famous and still highly readable textbook, *Psychology: Briefer Course* (1892, pp. 163-64):

> Suppose we try to recall a forgotten name. The state of our consciousness is peculiar. There is a gap therein; but no mere gap. It is a gap that is intensely active. A sort of wraith of the name is in it, beckoning us in a given direction, making us at moments tingle with the sense of our closeness, and then letting us sink back without the longed-for term. If wrong names are proposed to us, this singularly definite gap acts immediately so as to negate them. They do not fit into its mould. And the gap of one word does not feel like the gap of another, all empty of content as both might seem necessarily to be when described as gaps. When I vainly try to recall the name of Spalding, my consciousness is far removed from what it is when I vainly try to recall the name of Bowles. There are innumerable consciousnesses of WANT, no one of which taken in itself has a name, but all different from each other. . . . The rhythm of a lost word may be there without a sound to clothe it; or the evanescent sense of something which is the initial vowel or consonant may mock us fitfully, without growing more distinct. Every one must know the tantalizing effect of the blank rhythm of some forgotten verse, restlessly dancing in one's mind, and striving to be filled out with words.
>
> . . . And has the reader never asked himself what kind of a mental fact is his INTENTION OF SAYING A THING before he has said it? It is an entirely definite intention, distinct from all other intentions, an absolutely distinct state of consciousness, therefore; and yet how much of it consists of definite sensorial images, either of words or of things? Hardly anything! Linger, and the words and things come into the mind; the anticipatory intention, the divination is there no more. But as the words that replace it arrive, it welcomes them successively and calls them right if they agree with it, it rejects them and calls them wrong if they do not. The intention TO-SAY-SO-AND-SO is the only name

it can receive. One may admit that a good third of our psychic life consists in these rapid premonitory perspective views of schemes of thought not yet articulate.

These "schemes of thought not yet articulate" are not simply unconscious sentences waiting for expression. As we have seen in the earlier cross-linguistic comparison of the various ways of saying 'daddy gave me a ball', a sentence is not a direct mapping of a thought. And, if you think back on the many ways in which one can ask someone to 'heat the coffee', the choice of words reflects subtleties of communicative intent. If thought were no more than inner speech, why would we ever have to grope for words or carefully choose the means of expression? This problem was clearly discussed by Vygotsky (1962, pp. 149-50):

> The flow of thought is not accompanied by a simultaneous unfolding of speech. The two processes are not identical, and there is no rigid correspondence between the units of thought and speech. This is especially obvious when a thought process miscarries—when, as Dostoevski puts it, a thought "will not enter words." Thought has its own structure, and the transition from it to speech is no easy matter. . . . Thought, unlike speech, does not consist of separate units. When I wish to communicate the thought that today I saw a barefoot boy in a blue shirt running down the street, I do not see every item separately. . . I conceive of all this in one thought, but I put it into separate words. A speaker often takes several minutes to disclose one thought. In his mind the whole thought is present at once, but in speech it has to be developed successively. A thought may be compared to a cloud shedding a shower of words.

Further evidence of the independence of much of thought from verbal formulation comes from the statements of scientists, mathematicians, artists, and composers about their creative thought. A little book by Brewster Ghiselin, *The Creative Process* (1955), is full of rich examples of an initial period of "incubation" of an idea or problem, followed by a sudden resolution, after which the creator is faced with the tremendous difficulty of putting the result of his thinking into an expressive medium. The introspections of Albert Einstein in this regard are especially illuminating (in Ghiselin, 1955, p. 43):

> The words of the language, as they are written or spoken, do not seem to play any role in my mechanism of thought. The psychical entities which seem to serve as elements in thought are certain signs and more or less clear images which can be "voluntarily" reproduced and combined.
> There is, of course, a certain connection between those elements and relevant logical concepts. It is also clear that the desire to arrive at logically connected concepts is the emotional basis of this rather vague play with the above mentioned elements. But taken from a psychological viewpoint, this combinatory play seems to be the essential feature in productive thought—before there is any connection with logical

construction in words or other kinds of signs which can be communicated to others.

The above mentioned elements are, in my case, of visual and some of muscular type. Conventional words or other signs have to be sought for laboriously only in a secondary stage, when the mentioned associative play is sufficiently established and can be reproduced at will. . . . In a stage when words intervene at all, they are, in my case, purely auditive, but they interfere only in a secondary stage as already mentioned.

We would not expect Beethoven to have "talked out" the idea of a symphony to himself. His sketchbooks are full of themes and attempts at various harmonies, transitions, and orchestrations—but there are hardly any words written in them. Yet no one would say that Beethoven had not "thought out" the structure and content of his compositions. Picasso's planning of *Guernica* is reflected in numerous drawings, and not in a journal full of words. Clearly, there is more to thought than speech—either overt or covert. Speech is one of many tools of thought, but it is not thought itself.

In seeking the relations between language and cognition, then, we must ask two more differentiated questions. (1) If we view language as one of many forms of MENTAL REPRESENTATION, we must explore the various forms and ask how they are interrelated. This is essentially a structural question. There are various ways in which one can describe the structure of knowledge. The history of philosophy is a chronicle of attempts to reduce all of knowledge to linguistic structures, or to reduce linguistic structures to something else, or to posit various kinds of coexisting and interacting mental entities. This history continues in cognitive psychology. (2) If we view language as one of the TOOLS OF THOUGHT, we must examine the ways in which use of that "tool" influences cognitive processes and their development. This is essentially a question of use. In what sorts of mental activities does the use of language play a significant role? Does that role vary with the age of the individual? Does it vary with the specific language or dialect involved?

LANGUAGE AND MENTAL REPRESENTATION

Let us step back from the broad issue of "thought" and consider questions of "mental representation." In order for the processes of thought to be accomplished—reasoning, planning, problem solving, and the like—it is necessary that knowledge be coded and stored in some form. First let us consider the forms that seem most evident to consciousness: words and images. It is these forms that initially attracted the attention of philosophers and psychologists. The use of words and sentences as the medium of thought is so obvious as not to need technical description. But the role of imagery has been controversial—perhaps because people seem to differ greatly in the degree to which they experience mental imagery. Let us consider this problem, and then turn to more abstract levels of representation.

Imagery

Language is one of many ways in which we can represent knowledge to ourselves. Some knowledge seems uniquely suited to linguistic representation. How, for example, could we represent to ourselves a philosophical theory or an historical event without being able to talk about it? However, Einstein spoke of visual and muscular images in his thinking, Beethoven would certainly have spoken of auditory images, and Picasso of visual images. The mental image, or internal image, has recently regained respectability in cognitive psychology (e.g., Kosslyn, 1975; Paivio, 1971; Shepard & Chipman, 1971), and it has a long history in philosophy.

There is much current debate about what mental images are like and what they are used for, and whether they are basic or are derived from more elementary processes (Kosslyn & Pomerantz, 1977; Pylyshyn, 1973; Rosch & Lloyd, 1978). But clearly, thinking with the use of imagery does take place—and it is different from thinking in words. The great physicist, P. W. Bridgman, was much concerned with this question, and discussed it in his book, *The Nature of Physical Theory*, in 1936 (p. 25):

> Perhaps one of the best examples of . . . non-verbal thought is afforded by what we do when we analyze the action of a machine or sketch on paper the design for a piece of apparatus. What I do in designing an apparatus is to reproduce in imagination what my activities would be in watching the performance of the complete apparatus, and I know that for me such an experience is almost entirely motor in character. I see one part pushing another and have a tactile feeling for the forces and kinetic appreciation of the resulting motion, all without consciously getting on the verbal level. If I analyze what happens I think that I instinctively recognize that a certain kind of push or pull will be followed by a certain kind of motion, because I remember past situations which aroused in me the same reactions and I know what happened in those cases.

The psychologist Jerome Bruner (Bruner, Olver, & Greenfield, 1966) has pointed out that such "enactive representation" underlies motor skills generally (e.g., tying knots, using tools, dancing). Children learn much about the world through active manipulation, and there is a good deal of evidence that enactive representation, or muscular imagery, is an early means for representing objects. Even as adults we may make an arm-swinging motion when asking for a hammer, suggesting that motor patterns continue to play a role in the ways in which we conceive of objects and events.

Other kinds of life tasks rely on VISUAL imagery. Bruner points out that if you learn your way from home to work by remembering a series of left and right turns, you will have difficulty in finding yourself if you get lost, for you have no overall representation of the route. If you have a map (or a mental map) of the route, you can scan it back and forth and find your place and your way. This sort of visual representation, freed from particular action patterns, allows for greater flexibility, since it is not sequentially ordered and can be scanned in various directions. Visual imagery is the prime mode of representation in such tasks as facial recognition, color matching, interior decorating, graphic arts, and the like, where neither motor nor verbal representation are of much use.

However, on a more abstract level, are there common structures which underlie mental representation of various sorts of knowledge and abilities? We are AWARE of words and images, but below the level of conscious awareness there must be structures which are both more abstract and more general than the moment-to-moment contents of consciousness—what William James called "schemes of thought not yet articulate." We cannot know directly what such structures are like, nor whether the various forms of conscious experience all share a common underlying structure. Ever since the modern rise of interest in the unconscious, stemming in large part from the thinking of Freud, numerous attempts have been made to describe unconscious structures. In psycholinguistics this question is discussed in the framework of "semantic memory"—that is, the way in which knowledge is stored in long-term or permanent memory. (See Foss & Hakes, 1978, pp. 136-67, for an overview.) The issue began in terms of representing the structures of sentences and word meanings, and it has become extended to general questions of the structure of knowledge. Let us briefly examine several current attempts to describe "the contents of the mind" in structural terms—that is, in a form which is removed from pictures or words in the mind. We will consider two major approaches: one based on PROPOSITIONS as elementary units of thought, and one based on analysis of ELEMENTS OF MEANING (referred to as features, attributes, or components) as the basic building blocks of concepts. (These approaches are not mutually exclusive.)

Propositions

You have already encountered propositional models in the discussion of generative semantics and its application to child language. There have been many recent cognitive models which take the proposition to be the basic form in which knowledge is represented (e.g., Anderson & Bower, 1973; Fredriksen, 1972; Kintsch, 1974; Norman & Rumelhart, 1975). What these models all have in common is characterized by our familiar example of 'daddy gave me a ball'—namely, a network of interrelated concepts which is both more abstract and more general than any particular linguistic expression in words and sentences, or the image of any particular event. The underlying representation—drawn on paper in various diagrammatic ways—corresponds to something like: 'human male adult progenitor actor in past caused spherical object to move from self to human offspring recipient'.

The psychological reality of such representations is far from being resolved. Furthermore, as we have seen, such a level of representation corresponds neither to the full knowledge of the event (in that many aspects of the event do not appear in this schematic summary) nor to the precise encoding of that event in any particular language. Propositions, like images, may well be PART of mental representation, but they do not exhaustively portray the contents of the mind.

In addition, such models assume that concepts can be analyzed into semantic components or features, like 'human', 'male', and the like. It is probably not possible to analyze all concepts into sets of features, and there is also evidence that the mind does not work in such rigorously logical fashion. Let us examine some of the problems which arise when we attempt to analyze concepts or words into sets of defining "features" or "components" of meaning.

Features and Prototypes

Clearly, much of meaning can be described in terms of underlying features or attributes. Humans and mammals and fish and birds are all 'animate'; women and ewes and goddesses and mermaids are all 'female'; and so forth. However, not all meanings can be "decomposed" into such features. What, for example, are the features that distinguish red from green, or beautiful from ugly, or acquaintance from friend?

Even in cases where features are available for analysis, they may not apply in an all-or-none fashion, like 'male' and 'female', or 'animate' and 'inanimate'. Consider, for example, a featural description of chairs. This seems to be a class that shades off at its boundaries in all directions. When the back of a chair gets low enough, or its legs get long enough, it becomes a stool; when the seat gets wide enough, it becomes a bench, and so on.

The philosopher Ludwig Wittgenstein proposed that we do not organize our concepts into neat tables of intersecting features, but that we store knowledge in a less systematic way—a way that relies on partial similarities and overlapping features and dimensions. The best way in which to convey his insight is to quote his famous discussion of the meaning of *game* (1945, sections 66–67)[1]:

> Consider for example the proceedings that we call "games." I mean board-games, card-games, ball-games, Olympic games, and so on. What is common to them all?—Don't say: "There MUST be something common, or they would not be called 'games' "—but LOOK AND SEE whether there is anything common to all.—For if you look at them you will not see something that is common to ALL, but similarities, relationships, and a whole series of them at that. To repeat: don't think, but look!—Look for example at board-games, with their multifarious relationships. Now pass to card-games; here you find many correspondences with the first group, but many common features drop out, and others appear. When we pass next to ball-games, much that is common is retained, but much is lost.—Are they all 'amusing'? Compare chess with noughts and crosses. Or is there always winning and losing, or competition between players? Think of patience. In ball-games there is winning and losing; but when a child throws his ball at the wall and catches it again, this feature has disappeared. Look at the parts played by skill and luck; and at the difference between skill in chess and skill in tennis. Think now of games like ring-a-ring-a-roses; here is the element of amusement, but how many other characteristic features have disappeared! And we can go through the many, many

1. Wittgenstein desired readers of translations of his work always to have the German original at hand. Following his wishes, the original can be found in the Appendix to this book.

other groups of games in the same way; can see how similarities crop up and disappear.

And the result of this examination is: we see a complicated network of similarities overlapping and criss-crossing: sometimes overall similarities, sometimes similarities of detail.

I can think of no better expression to characterize these similarities than "family resemblances"; for the various resemblances between members of a family: build, features, colour of eyes, gait, temperament, etc., etc. overlap and criss-cross in the same way.—And I shall say: 'games' form a family.

A cognitive psychologist, Eleanor Rosch, has extended these notions in a series of theoretical and empirical studies of what she calls PROTOTYPES (Rosch, 1973, 1975; Rosch & Mervis, 1975; Rosch, Mervis, Gray, Johnson, & Boyes-Braem, 1976). Underlying the family resemblance approach is a notion of overlapping features—one member may have the nose and eye color, another the eye color and chin, and so forth—but no member has ALL of the features. Rosch went on to argue—and demonstrate—that not only are concepts generally structured in this manner, but each category has a "core," or "prototypical best exemplar," which has most attributes in common with other members of the category. For example, a robin or a sparrow is a good example of a bird—a prototypical bird, if you will. Ostriches and penguins and kiwis are also birds, but somehow not as "birdlike" as robins and sparrows—they are too big, they don't fly, and so on. If knowledge were simply organized in terms of common features, all birds would be equal, and it would be nonsense to say things like: "Technically speaking, a penguin is a bird too, but a robin is obviously a bird." Yet Rosch found that it took subjects longer to say "true" in response to sentences like *A penguin is a bird* than *A robin is a bird*. In a series of ingenious experiments, Rosch and her coworkers have shown that many categories are organized in a "fuzzy" way around a prototypical best example, shading off at the boundaries. The prototype stands out because of such features as natural salience and familiarity—with other category members partially sharing attributes of the core members, as Wittgenstein's "family resemblances." The import of this work—too complex to summarize here—is that there is more to the mind than categories made up of neat sets of features. Models which decompose words and sentences into underlying semantic elements are imperfect depictions of our mental representations.

Language and Thought Again

Any theory of the relations between language and thought requires a clear definition of thought. The brief summary of several recent approaches to mental representation, however, demonstrates that we do not have such a definition. No one of these descriptive systems characterizes all of the forms of knowledge or mental activity. And the psychological reality of each of the systems is still in question.

Furthermore, we do not know how the various systems of mental representation—linguistic and nonlinguistic—interact. To list the various forms of representation—motor, visual, auditory, propositional, featural, prototypical—does not answer the question of the role of language in cognition. Language has access to all of these forms of representation, in that we can talk about all of them. Even though sensory images are not linguistic, and are difficult or impossible to describe in words, you can answer questions as to whether, for example, nectarines taste like peaches, or whether the sound of the cello is "dark," or whether Schumann's songs capture the feeling of Heine's verse. And even though Einstein had difficulty in finding the words for his thoughts, he eventually succeeded. We can analyze experience into propositions and features and prototypes and talk about this analysis. Is there a language of the mind, a "mentalese," which can translate between sensory images and abstract thoughts and linguistic expressions? It is clear that language is not the underlying code of thought, but what is?

Needless to say, we do not have an answer to this question. As Bever (1975, p. 77) has pointed out in a psycholinguistic symposium on language and thought: "A basic conceptual goal in discussions like the present one is that the mind must be UNIFIED at some level, that there is a common mental capacity that unifies all cognitive faculties such as reasoning (e.g., logic), mental representation (e.g., imagery), and communication (e.g., language)." It is clear that language is not the unifier (though language is the means by which we talk to ourselves and try to bring about the unification). Bever suggests several possibilities: (1) a common system of representation, to which all of the various modes of representation can be reduced at some deep level; (2) a "mentalese" which translates between the various capacities; or (3) a collection of specialized mapping systems (between images and words, between logic and grammar, and so forth).

For the present—and for the indefinite future—all we can say is that language is an integral component of thought, but neither language nor speech can be equated with thought. Let us go on to consider some particular ways in which language interacts with thought and memory, taking a respectful distance from all of the hornets roused from their philosophical nests in this first section of the chapter.

LANGUAGE AS A "TOOL OF THOUGHT"

There are obviously multifarious ways in which our possession of language influences our life as human beings. We cannot even begin to list all of these influences. Here I wish to simply consider several broad areas of mental life in which the USE of language seems to have a significant effect. Language influences the ways in which we store old information and acquire new information. Language can be used internally as a tool of thought, and interpersonally as a tool of communication. Both of these aspects of language use—internal and interpersonal—have cognitive consequences. Let us first consider some of the roles played by language in learning and memory.

Verbal Mediation and Behavior

It was the initial hope of behaviorist psychology that conditioning and problem-solving experiments using animals would provide the key to human behavior as well. However, it soon becomes obvious that, in many situations, human subjects perform in very different fashion from animals because of the use of verbal thought as a means of arriving at and holding onto solutions. Indeed, Pavlov himself came to the conclusion, late in his life, that his work on conditioned reflexes had only limited application to human behavior because of the complex role of linguistic signals in calling forth complex stored structures of past experience. In his words (1927, pp. 407 . . . 357):

> Of course a word is for man as much a real conditioned stimulus as are other stimuli common to men and animals, yet at the same time it is so all-comprehending that it allows of no quantitative or qualitative comparisons with conditioned stimuli in animals. . . . The word created a second system of signals of reality which is peculiarly ours, being the signal of signals. On the one hand, numerous speech stimuli have removed us from reality. . . . On the other, it is precisely speech which has made us human.

Accordingly, in Soviet psychology much attention was paid to ways in which language mediates between stimuli and responses (Slobin, 1966b). For example, in training an animal, one repeatedly presents stimulus configurations, waiting for the animal to discover the contingencies between stimulus and response. However, in training human subjects, one can use verbal instruction. This shifts the direction of much of research toward questions of verbal training, with the aim of discovering what sorts of verbal instructions are most effective in accelerating acquisition of correct performance on various sorts of tasks.

The availability of verbal coding also plays a role in experiments on memory. For example, a familiar paradigm in experimental psychology is the delayed response experiment. A human or animal subject watches the experimenter hide a reward—often food—and is then required to wait for a given period of time before attempting to find the reward. The crucial variable is the amount of delay which the subject can tolerate before forgetting where the reward has been hidden. For some species the longest possible delay is only a few seconds. For humans, however, the delay can be indefinitely long. (In fact, with writing and other means of symbolic representation, the delay can be extended beyond living memory, as when a hunt for lost treasure is spurred by an ancient map or written clue.)

It has been found that children who have been taught verbal descriptions of the various response alternatives in an experiment rehearse the description of the cue to responding during the delay (e.g., "the peanut is under the red cup"), and in this way they can retain the appropriate set to respond over a long period of time, and over various changes in the situation. Human children are thus able to bridge the time gap by means of verbal mediation. Much work of this sort was done in the 50s and 60s, both in the United States (e.g., as reviewed by Spiker, 1963) and in the Soviet Union (e.g., as reviewed by Slobin, 1966b). The moral of this research is that human subjects can formulate a verbal rule which they use to guide their performance in certain types of psychological experiments, and, presumably, in corresponding types of real-life situations.

Verbal Coding and Memory

The ability to code experiences verbally often influences the way in which such experiences are remembered. In fact, many memories are distorted JUST BECAUSE they are stored in verbal form—because not everything can be accurately represented in a verbal summary. Verbal memory is thus a two-edged sword.

This is clearly revealed in experiments on memory for visual aspects of stimuli—e.g., form or color. Many such experiments have shown that memory of visual images can be distorted to better conform with their verbal labels (e.g., Glanzer & Clark, 1964; Lantz & Stefflre, 1964). The classic experiment in this field is a study performed in 1932 by Carmichael, Hogan, and Walter, called "An Experimental Study of the Effect of Language on the Representation of Visually Perceived Form" (see also Herman, Lawless, & Marshall, 1957). These experimenters presented subjects with a set of twelve ambiguous figures, such as O-O, which could be seen as either eyeglasses or dumbbells. The subjects were told that they would first see 12 figures, which they would later have to reproduce as accurately as possible. Each figure was named as it was presented—e.g., in one case the above figure was named *eyeglasses* and in the other, *dumbbell*. The result was that subjects tended to reproduce the ambiguous figures to better conform with their verbal labels. For example, the figure was reproduced something like O⌒O by the first group of subjects, and something like C⌒O by the second. In a task of this sort it is apparently easier for subjects to store 12 verbal labels and produce images to match these labels at a later time than it is for them to store the 12 images themselves.

Memory of real-life events, of course, is also subject to the distortions imposed by verbal encoding. This is especially evident in the case of rumor, where it is clear that verbal memory for events has changed with time, under the influence of stereotypes and expectations. This phenomenon can be reproduced in the laboratory in experiments in which a verbal description or a story is passed on from person to person, similar to the old game of "telephone." (See, for example, *Remembering* by Bartlett [1932] and *The Psychology of Rumor* by Allport and Postman [1947].) What kinds of changes take place in memory of stories or events? For one thing, there is LEVELLING: many events drop out, the story becomes much shorter and schematic. But at the same time there is SHARPENING: some details achieve a peculiar sort of salience, and are repeated time after time in retelling. And finally there is ASSIMILATION to some schemata, or stereotypes, or expectations. To a certain extent, we remember events the way we want to; memories are often changed to match our prejudices or desires—to become more plausible or acceptable to us.

This phenomenon of schematization in memory is what George Miller referred to as RECODING in his important article on memory, "The Magical Number Seven, Plus or Minus Two" (1956). In that article Miller came to the conclusion that one can hold no more than 7 ± 2 "chunks" of information in immediate memory, and he discusses the cognitive economy which comes about by lumping many things together into one chunk, so to speak. Thus, for example, it may be as easy to remember a list of seven random letters as seven random words, though the seven words contain many more letters than the list of random letters. I suspect that one way of "chunking" in memory is to recode a long experience into a short description—maybe even one word—in the hope that at some future time the details can be regenerated from the memory of their brief verbal description or tag.

Why is this sort of schematization in memory necessary? A moment's thought will make the answer obvious. If you want to recall what happened yesterday, for example, and if your memory were not of this sort, you would have to relive the entire day in memory, at the same rate at which you originally lived it. Obviously, you could make no progress this way. It would take you a whole day just to remember the previous day! So it is clear that we MUST reduce our memories to the point where we can deal with a summary of some sort. Exactly how this sort of recoding is done is still pretty much of a mystery. (For some intriguing neurological suggestions see Penfield & Roberts, 1959.)

One result of this inevitable verbal recoding of life experiences is that our personal memories become rather like stories, unwittingly shaped to fit into patterns of personal needs and cultural expectations as to what a life of a given sort should be like. This has been most clearly discussed in the psychoanalytic literature, where the role of autobiographical memory—especially memory for childhood experiences—is of central importance. It is worth taking a detour through this area for an intriguing view of the role of language in memory. (For recent research on autobiographical memory, see Linton, 1975.)

Language and Childhood Amnesia

Memory presents us with two major kinds of problems—storage and retrieval. Let us skip over the problem of storage—assuming that experience has been somehow coded in fairly permanent form—and pose the problem of retrieval. How do you get back to stored material when you need it? The problem is a familiar one when trying to recall earlier experiences. Generally some verbal formulation will help you search your memory, but this convenient device seems to be of no great aid in the search for one's memories of very early childhood. Most people can't remember much of anything that happened to them before the age of two or three. Why should such memories be so elusive?

Freud believed that memories of early childhood are actually present in the adult unconscious, but inaccessible to conscious recall because they are laden with repressed matters of infantile sexuality. Could it just be "repression" which hides early memory from us, or might there be other, more cognitive reasons? Piaget (1946) has also examined such problems, and the issue has been discussed with great insight by the psychologist Ernest Schachtel (1959). The cognitive approach to the problem reveals interesting aspects of the role played by language in memory.

Schachtel raises important objections to Freud. He points out that the Freudian explanation of repression of memories connected with infantile sexuality fails to explain why ALL memories of early childhood are so inaccessible to adult recall. Furthermore, one generally cannot bring such memories to awareness even through psychoanalysis or other means of memory stimulation.

He goes on to argue (1959, p. 284) that early autobiographical memory may be impossible for strictly cognitive reasons, because:

> The categories (or schemata) for adult memory are not suitable receptacles for early childhood experiences and therefore not fit to preserve these experiences and enable their recall. The functional capacity of the conscious, adult memory is usually limited to those types of experience which the adult consciously makes and is capable of making.

What he means to say is that the child's way of perceiving the world is so different from that of the adult that the two worlds are almost mutually incomprehensible. Consider how difficult it is to imagine what a young child is really thinking and feeling—much less an infant. One reason for the difference, of course, is simply the cognitive development which takes place in the process of growing up. Another reason is tied with the fact that adults TALK about their experiences and memories and, as we have already noted, tend to code and store their experiences linguistically. That is to say, you can get back to an adult memory by reconstructing it from a verbal description or "tag"; such verbal tags are not available for very early experiences. Schachtel points out that when you ask an adult to recount his life experiences to you, he follows certain standard "signposts" of his culture, relating such facts as education, marriage, jobs, trips, and so on. These memories are schematic and generally do not have the vividness or force of living experience. Living and telling are two different modes, and only the skilled writer or storyteller can breathe life into a retrospective account. (In reports of drug experiences the point is often made that the experience cannot be conveyed verbally; but note that this is true also of everyday experiences.)

Before returning to the problem of childhood amnesia, it is worth examining the effect of verbal retelling of life experience. Sartre, in his novel *Nausea* (1959, pp. 56-58), lucidly expresses the dilemma posed by these two modes of living or remembering—the experiential versus the symbolic or "told":

> This is what I thought: for the most banal event to become an adventure, you must (and this is enough) begin to recount it. This is what fools people: a man is always a teller of tales, he lives surrounded by his stories and the stories of others, he sees everything that happens to him through them; and he tries to live his own life as if he were telling a story.
>
> But you have to choose: live or tell. For example, when I was in Hamburg, with that Erna girl I didn't trust and who was afraid of me, I led a funny sort of life. But I was in the middle of it, I didn't think about it. And then one evening, in a little café in San Pauli, she left me to go to the ladies' room. I stayed alone, there was a phonograph playing "Blue Skies." I began to tell myself what had happened since I landed. . . . Then I felt violently that I was having an adventure. But Erna came back and sat down beside me, she wound her arms around my neck and I hated her without knowing why. I understand now: one had to begin living again and the adventure was fading out.
>
> Nothing happens while you live. The scenery changes, people come in and go out, that's all. There are no beginnings. Days are

tacked on to days without rhyme or reason, an interminable, monotonous addition. . . .

That's living. But everything changes when you tell about life; it's a change no one notices: the proof is that people talk about true stories. As if there could possibly be true stories; things happen one way and we tell about them in the opposite sense. You seem to start at the beginning: "It was a fine autumn evening in 1922. I was a notary's clerk in Marommes." And in reality you have started at the end. It was there, invisible and present, it is the one which gives to words the pomp and value of a beginning. "I was out walking, I had left the town without realizing it, I was thinking about my money troubles." This sentence, taken simply for what it is, means that the man was absorbed, morose, a hundred leagues from an adventure, exactly in the mood to let things happen without noticing them. But the end is there, transforming everything. For us, the man is already the hero of the story. His moroseness, his money troubles are much more precious than ours, they are all gilded by the light of future passions. And the story goes on in the reverse: instants have stopped piling themselves up in a lighthearted way one on top of the other, they are snapped up by the end of the story which draws them and each one of them in turn, draws out the preceding instant: "It was night, the street was deserted." The phrase is cast out negligently, it seems superfluous; but we do not let ourselves be caught and we put it aside: this is a piece of information whose value we shall subsequently appreciate. And we feel that the hero has lived all the details of this night like annunciations, promises, or even that he lived only those that were promises, blind and deaf to all that did not herald adventure. We forget that the future was not yet there; the man was walking in a night without forethought, a night which offered him a choice of dull rich prizes, and he did not make his choice.

I wanted the moments of my life to follow and order themselves like those of a life remembered. You might as well try and catch time by the tail.

We can bring this whole compelling train of thought back to the problem of childhood amnesia. In this regard, Schachtel makes two major points: (1) The child has no schemata, no internal interpretive framework, for the preservation of his very earliest memories. (2) Those schemata which he learns later in childhood are not appropriate for the interpretation or recoding of his early experience.

How can we imagine what the world looks like to an infant before he has developed concepts such as object permanence or conservation of quantity? What does life seem like before the development of the symbolic capacity? As he grows bigger, objects change in relative size for the child, and, at the same time, they are being labelled, organized, grouped, and regrouped into new categories on the basis of the language he is learning.

There is also another important way in which childhood experience differs from adult experience. Schachtel suggests that at first the child relies most heavily on the PROXIMITY SENSES (smell, taste, touch), and only later do the DISTANCE SENSES (sight, hearing) become the dominant ones. We have an inadequate vocabulary for expressing sensations of the proximity senses. Furthermore, such sensations are often taboo and seem to arouse more intense pleasure and disgust than sensations of the distance receptors. The child learns a well-developed vocabulary to deal with experiences of sight and sound, but these do not help him record his early experiences in a manner which is available to retrieval.

So it would seem that most of the child's early memories are connected with stimuli no longer available to him—stimuli of the proximity senses, stimuli falling into categories different from the ones learned later in life, and stimuli seen from a different vantage point from that used by the adult. No wonder Proust found it necessary to assume certain body postures, or find certain odors, and so on, in order to revive early memories in his "recherche du temps perdu"—in his "remembrance of times past."

To summarize Schachtel's argument in a sentence, then: One's memory of early childhood experiences may be not so much willfully repressed as simply inaccessible to recall, though not forgotten.

We have, however, a variety of ways of representing experiences to ourselves; language is only one—though a very useful one in many cases. It is depressing that our earliest experiences are generally irretrievable without special means. But what about our earliest actual memories—memories which consist of visual images and sensations, but which are accessible by means of a linkage to some verbal cue? I'm afraid that even here—with graphic memories of our own experiences—we can never be sure how much the image has been affected by the verbal encoding. As a most extreme example of the interaction of different means of representation in memory, consider the following reminiscence of Jean Piaget (1946: in 1962b, pp. 187–88):

> There is also the question of memories which depend on other people. For instance, one of my first memories would date, if it were true, from my second year. I can still see, most clearly, the following scene, in which I believed until I was about fifteen. I was sitting in my pram, which my nurse was pushing in the Champs Elysées, when a man tried to kidnap me. I was held in by the strap fastened round me while my nurse bravely tried to stand between me and the thief. She received various scratches, and I can still see vaguely those on her face. Then a crowd gathered, a policeman with a short cloak and a white baton came up, and the man took to his heels. I can still see the whole scene, and can even place it near the tube station. When I was about fifteen, my parents received a letter from my former nurse saying that she had been converted to the Salvation Army. She wanted to confess her past faults, and in particular to return the watch she had been given as a reward on this occasion. She had made up the whole story, faking the scratches. I therefore must have heard, as a child, the account of this story, which my parents believed, and projected it into the past in the form of a visual memory, which was a memory of a memory, but false. Many real memories are doubtless of the same order.

Under conditions such as these, it is very hard indeed to ever fully carry out the ancient advice, "Know thyself!" It is rather like reading the newspapers—you have to take on faith that there is some correspondence between the events and their reporting—and you know how hazardous that can be.

LANGUAGE AS A TOOL IN COGNITIVE DEVELOPMENT

The Use of Language in Childhood

After the period of early experience discussed by psychoanalysts, language comes to play an ever greater role in the child's thinking and communication. The conclusion of Chapter 4 was that language develops in roughly similar fashion in all cultures, and that it seems more often to reflect than to guide cognitive growth. However, social groups differ in the opportunities they provide children for linguistic communication. Are there developmental consequences of the USE of language in childhood? This question is of considerable practical import, since much of early education is planned in terms of notions of the role of language in development. Much of the thinking behind so-called "compensatory education" programs for lower-class minority children in the United States is based on the notions that "cultural deprivation" (which really means culture different from that of the middle-class majority) results in language deficit, and that deficient language retards or blocks full cognitive development. Psycholinguistics has an important social role to play in demonstrating that all of the links in this argument are faulty. We have already argued that all children learn language equally well, according to universal patterns of development, so that there is no such thing as a "language deficit" in child development.

But what if the deficit is in communicative skills? Social environments certainly do differ in regard to how well they match the school environment. Clearly, children who have acquired the motivations, habits, values—and form of speaking—used in the school system will (at least at first) perform better in that system than children who come from social backgrounds different from those on which the education system of a given society is based. I would not argue that children do not—eventually—need to master the linguistic code of the dominant society. But the pedagogical emphasis on the role of language as a tool of cognitive development is, I think, misplaced. In fact, linguistic communication plays a very specialized role in cognitive development—perhaps both facilitating AND retarding various aspects of the process. The mismatch between home environment and school which has been observed in various social groups in America and other countries is not based on relative mastery of language, but on the uses to which language is put. A revealing case study will help to clarify this argument.

An anthropologist and a clinical psychologist, Marida Hollos and Philip Cowan (Hollos & Cowan, 1973), carried out a detailed study of the cognitive development of children in several different social settings. Consider the first learning environment, which they describe in the following terms (pp. 632–33):

> Children spend most of their time in solitary play or in observation of others. Since there are few commercial toys and games, solitary play involves manipulation or observation of objects that occur natu-

rally in the environment. . . . Most frequent interaction takes place with the mother; the father spends much of the day away from the house. . . . The amount of verbal interaction between mother and child is limited. Mothers do not prompt or encourage children to talk, ask questions, or suggest activities. There are no periods of storytelling or discussions. . . . Interaction and communication between adult members of the family is limited to mealtimes and evenings. The major part of the evening is devoted to watching television.

This sounds like the sort of "culturally deprived" situation which has been described for lower-class Blacks in the slums of our big cities. It is, however, a description of life on isolated Norwegian farms—a setting which has an aura of "wholesomeness" far removed from the depressing standard image of such places as Harlem. Hollos and Cowan studied the development of these isolated farm children in comparison with children of families of similar size and educational background in a small village and in a medium-sized town in Norway. The village and town children spend much of their time freely playing with other children and encountering many different adults in a variety of social settings—homes, shops, on the street, and so forth. These children return in the evenings to more talkative family situations than do the isolated farm children. The language development is similar in the three settings—farm, village, and town—but the village and town children have many more opportunities for verbal interaction.

How would you expect these settings to influence cognitive development? Your answer depends on your view of the relations between language and thought in development. A theory which stresses the role of verbal interaction and contact with the viewpoints of other people would predict more advanced development in the village and town children. A theory which minimizes the role of language in cognitive development would predict no important differences between the three groups. In fact, the actual results are more differentiated and more interesting than either of these simplified theories would lead one to expect.

The children were given a number of different tests of cognitive ability. Some of the tests dealt with notions of logical classification and physical qualities. For example, in one task the child is asked to classify objects on the basis of both form and color at the same time (e.g., to pick an object to complete an array of colored shapes such that the object is both green and a star). In another task (Piaget's "conservation" task), the child is shown two glasses of water filled to the same level. Then one of the glasses is poured into a tall, thin beaker, with resulting rise in water level, and the child is asked to say if there is now more, less, or the same amount of water as in the unpoured glass. The entire collection of tasks tapped the child's ability to think logically and to make judgments about physical properties of objects and their relations.

Another collection of tasks dealt with the child's ability to take a viewpoint other than his own. In one of these tasks, he must retell a story to someone who has not heard it before, and he is scored for accuracy of communication and ability to "coordinate one's viewpoint as a speaker with that of the listener." In another task, the child is required to picture what a three-dimensional display of toy buildings would look like from other vantage points.

Hollos and Cowan found that the isolated farm children were relatively advanced on the first set of cognitive tasks—those requiring logical thinking with respect to physical objects and their classificatory features; and that the village and town children were relatively more advanced on the second set of tasks—those requiring an ability to take the role of the other.

We are left, then, with a more complex and differentiated picture of the roles played by language and verbal interaction in early cognitive development. Apparently it is mainly through nonverbal manipulation of objects and close observation of physical changes that one acquires the first set of cognitive abilities more efficiently; and it is through a good deal of verbal interaction with different sorts of others that one develops the second set of cognitive abilities. Both sorts of abilities are important for schooling and necessary for development into maturity. And, indeed, all of the Norwegian children eventually did reach acceptable levels of development on both sets of abilities. The important difference is in terms of relative RATES of development for the different abilities.

This conclusion has important implications for schooling, and we will return to this issue again later in the chapter. Because the effect of the verbal environment has a differentiated effect on cognitive development, the role of verbal training as a preparation for schooling must be looked at in a more differentiated light. The problem is neither one of teaching the child to speak, nor teaching him to think, but finding the particular abilities which are in need of stimulation. Clearly, the appropriate means of stimulation will not always be verbal. In fact, in a book on social environment and cognitive development, Hollos (1974, pp. 144–45) points out some of the possible dangers of an overly verbal approach to child development:

> Children who devote the major portion of their time to social interaction and games learn to relate to others and to communicate but have relatively less time and opportunity to concentrate on physical relations and to manipulate and observe things in the physical environment. Similarly, assuming that normal children have a certain capacity for learning at a given age and that the human mind is an active agent, it is possible that if the available energy is channeled towards social relations and verbal skills there is less capacity available to seek and act on physical concepts and thereby develop in that area of cognition.

This viewpoint can be found in one of the very earliest philosophical treatises on the nature of language, Plato's dialogue *Cratylus*. Socrates concludes his consideration of the relations between words and things by saying: "But we may admit so much, that the knowledge of things is not to be derived from names. No, things must be studied and investigated in themselves."

The Role of Linguistic Communication in Childhood

Linguistic interaction is obviously a major means by which the child acquires the knowledge and values of his society. In addition, as the Hollos and Cowan study has shown, linguistic interaction contributes to the ability to "take the role of the other." The role of communication in cognitive development has a long history in psychology, going back to work on child speech carried out in the 1920s and 1930s by Piaget, in Switzerland, and Vygotsky, in the Soviet Union. Vygotsky formulated the basic problem as one of investigating "how a function, arising in communication and at first divided between two people, can restructure all of the activity of the child and gradually change into the complicated mediated functional system which characterizes the structure of his mental processes" (in Luria, 1959, p. 524). The impetus for Vygotsky's work was Piaget's first book, *The Language and Thought of the Child* (1923). In this work Piaget distinguished between "egocentric" and "socialized" speech, and portrayed development as a transition from one to the other. In egocentric speech (Piaget, 1923: in 1955, p. 32), the child

> does not bother to know to whom he is speaking nor whether he is being listened to. He talks either for himself or for the pleasure of associating anyone who happens to be there with the activity of the moment. This talk is egocentric . . . chiefly because he does not attempt to place himself at the point of view of his hearer. . . . The child asks for no more than apparent interest, though he has the illusion . . . of being heard and understood.

Egocentric speech, for Piaget, is eventually replaced by socialized speech, which takes account of the point of view of the listener and makes true dialogue possible. Piaget was concerned mainly with the development of thought in the child and assigned no special functions to egocentric speech, attributing it to early "verbal incontinence."

Vygotsky, on the other hand, stressed that all speech is social in origin and sought to discover the functions served by early overt speech in the life of the child.[2] He opposed both Piaget's notion of the eventual atrophy of egocentric "outer speech" and Watson's position that this speech, under the pressure not to talk out loud, was simply internalized to become subvocal speech, and thus the equivalent of thought. Rather, he attempted to show that early egocentric speech splits from communicative speech and is a transition stage between full-fledged speech out loud and silent thought. In the process, egocentric speech becomes more and more abbreviated and idiosyncratic, eventually becoming inner speech, or verbal thought, qualitatively different from outer speech. In a series of ingenious experiments, Vygotsky and his co-workers in Moscow set out to show that the egocentric speech of the young child serves a useful function in his mental development, and that he does try and in fact wants to communicate with others, though at first he cannot well differentiate "speech for oneself" from "speech for others."

In one series of experiments they sought to demonstrate that the spontaneous speech of children performs a practical function, not only accompanying activity, but serving to orient it. For example, a child whose

---

2. Vygotsky's seminal ideas about the sociocultural bases of cognition have recently been translated and edited by Michael Cole, Vera John-Steiner, Sylvia Scribner, and Ellen Souberman in a posthumous collection entitled *Mind in society: The development of higher psychological processes* (Vygotsky, 1978).

crayon broke while he was drawing said the word *broken* out loud and then went on to draw a broken car. They also found that spontaneous speech increased markedly when a child was faced with problem situations, and in situations where frustrations were introduced. In other experiments, spontaneous speech seemed to be used to orient and guide the child's activity. Such findings led Vygotsky to propose that the use of speech in such situations facilitates the understanding of the problem, and that speech, even in early years, serves an adaptive planning function in the life of the child.

In other experiments, Vygotsky demonstrated that the child's speech is communicative in its aim. For example, when a child was placed in a group of deaf-and-dumb children, or children speaking a foreign language, or even in a very noisy environment, his own spontaneous speech dropped to almost nothing.

Finally, Vygotsky found that egocentric speech becomes less and less intelligible from three to seven years of age, finally disappearing on an overt level, thus supporting his notion that egocentric speech is on its way to becoming inner speech. He concluded (1962, p. 19. . .133):

> We consider that the total development runs as follows: The primary function of speech, in both children and adults, is communication, social contact. The earliest speech of the child is therefore essentially social. . . . At a certain age the social speech of the child is quite sharply divided into egocentric and communicative speech.
>
> Our experimental results indicate that the function of egocentric speech is similar to that of inner speech: It does not merely accompany the child's activity; it serves mental orientation, conscious understanding; it helps in overcoming difficulties; it is speech for oneself, intimately and usefully connected with the child's thinking. . . . In the end, it becomes inner speech.

These experimental findings and conclusions have received significant support in this country in the work of Kohlberg, Yaeger, and Hjertholm (1968), and others. And Piaget himself, who has long outlived Vygotsky, has clearly expressed similar views on the role of communication with others in aiding cognitive development. This is especially clear in his reply to the 1962 English translation of Vygotsky's *Thought and Language*—unfortunately Piaget's first reading of Vygotsky's great work of 1934. In his reply, Piaget essentially agrees with the outlines of Vygotsky's notion of the role of inner speech, and goes on to discuss the role of communication (1962*a*, pp. 3–8):

> I have used the term egocentrism to designate the initial inability to decenter, to shift the cognitive perspective. . . . Cognitive egocentrism . . . stems from a lack of differentiation between one's own point of view and the other possible ones, and not at all from an individualism that precedes relations with others. . . .
>
> . . . [Vygotsky] proposed a new hypothesis: that egocentric speech is the point of departure for the development of inner speech, which is found at a later stage of development, and that this interiorized language can serve both autistic ends and logical thinking. I find myself in complete agreement with these hypotheses.

. . . In egocentric speech the child speaks according to himself. [This is] the only valid meaning of egocentrism: the lack of decentering, of the ability to shift mental perspective, in social relationships as well as in others. Moreover, I think that it is precisely cooperation with others (on the cognitive plane) that teaches us to speak according to others and not simply from our own point of view.

This last point is especially important: Piaget sees this inability to "decenter" as a general cognitive phenomenon, from which the child frees himself, in part, through communication with others (though not necessarily ONLY linguistic communication). He implies that the ability to communicate adequately is closely bound up with cognitive development in general. (For recent discussion of the relationship between cognitive processes and the development of communication skills, see Shatz, 1978.)

Cognitive Development Without Linguistic Communication

While emphasizing the role of linguistic communication in "decentering," we have minimized the role of language in the development of logical reasoning. However, it may well be that language is still an important facilitator of cognitive development. With linguistic representation, the child can transcend immediate space and time—he can represent various outcomes to himself, he can speed up and reverse processes mentally, he can dissociate thought from action and take a more reflective view of the phenomena around him. However, it may also be that these capacities of reflection and representation are part of our general human endowment, existing without language. Piagetian research suggests that cognitive development cannot be significantly speeded up by special language training; and psycholinguistic research suggests that new concepts most often emerge before the child has mastered the relevant linguistic means of expressing those concepts. Language, rather than bringing about cognitive advances, seems to follow behind mental development, reflecting the level of reasoning and knowledge attained by the child.

The only way to pull these issues apart is to study cognitive development in the absence of language. There is only one appropriate group of children for such investigation—namely, deaf children who have learned neither speech nor sign language. Unfortunately, it was long the policy in the United States to deprive deaf children of sign language in an attempt to bring them to lip-read and speak English. Thus, except in the case of deaf children of deaf parents, most deaf children have, until recently, spent their early years under conditions of severe language deprivation. This situation has created a "natural experiment" in which one can study cognitive development in the absence of language.

Hans Furth and his co-workers at the Catholic University in Washington, D.C., carried out detailed investigations of cognitive development in such children. The central question is whether the possession and use of a structured linguistic system (either spoken or signed) is an essential determiner of the stages of cognitive development observed by Piaget and others, or whether language just provides experiences which help make this development possible. If the latter is more nearly true, then maybe the experience of living itself, in the absence of language, will also move a child forward in cognitive development.

In a book entitled *Thinking Without Language: Psychological Implications of Deafness* (1966), Furth reports a large number of studies of non-signing deaf children, pointing to the striking conclusion that they are not drastically different from hearing children in intellectual performance. The course of cognitive development in both cases follows the same basic stages, though in some instances the rate of development may be slower for the deaf. It is quite likely, though, that this occasional slowness may be due not so much to specific lack of language as to general lack of experience, given the sort of environment in which many deaf children are raised. In Furth's studies of deaf and hearing adults, he finds no significant differences in basic cognitive abilities, though most of his deaf subjects could barely read and write or speak English.

As the title of Furth's book suggests, perhaps language is not as important as many have thought. He concludes (1964, p. 160):

> By generalizing the results of the studies summarized above and applying them to a theoretical position on the influence of language on intellective development, the following is suggested: (*a*) Language does not influence intellectual development in any direct, general, or decisive way. (*b*) The influence of language may be indirect or specific and may accelerate intellectual development: by providing the opportunity for additional experience through giving information and exchange of ideas and by furnishing ready symbols (words) and linguistic habits in specific situations.
>
> From this position it should follow that persons deficient in linguistic experience or skill (*a*) are not permanently or generally retarded in intellectual ability, but (*b*) may be temporarily retarded during their developmental phase because of lack of sufficient general experience and (*c*) they may be retarded on certain specific tasks in which available word symbols or linguistic habits facilitate solution.

Furth's points *b* and *c* raise two important issues. Temporary retardation is attributed to the communicative use of language, rather than the particular structure or content of language. This point echoes the conclusions of Vygotsky and Piaget on the role of communication. As Furth puts it: ". . . deaf children are bound to be deficient in many ordinary experiences and occasions which motivate other children to ask questions, reason, and organize mentally. . . . this experiential deficiency is directly related to linguistic deficiency, or more accurately, to the prevailing lack of ordinary communication."

The other point is more complex, and needs much more detailed research. This is the claim that certain tasks are facilitated by the knowledge of language. We do not yet know how to characterize the domain of such tasks. Piaget suggests that the complex logic of formal operations, which generally emerges in adolescence, requires the presence of linguistic skills. But he is also careful to emphasize that language is a NECESSARY, but not a SUFFICIENT condition for this stage of cognitive development. Various nonlinguistic developmental factors must also be considered. (For a valuable discussion of language and cognitive development, see Cromer, 1974.)

At present we can only come to the weak conclusion that language and communication play an important role in some aspects of cognitive development. One cannot claim that there are linguistic causes or linguistic prerequisites for most of the development of mental structures in the child. At least this is true in terms of the sorts of operations of logic and judgment described by Piaget. Nor does language provide the underlying structures of propositional thinking and concept formation. The use of language in communication certainly aids the child both in gaining knowledge and learning to take other perspectives on his own thinking. No one would deny that much of the content of the mind, for children and adults as well, is made up of linguistic representations. Language may make us knowledgeable and communicative people, but it does not make us into thinking people. Indeed, the fact that tiny children are already thinking people is what makes language acquisition possible.

Language and Schooling

In discussing the studies of Norwegian children, I suggested that education must be geared to the particular sorts of abilities which need to be developed in a given child or group of children. Verbal experience is only one kind of experience which children need in order to develop skills or gain knowledge. Cultures vary in the use of verbal and nonverbal means of training, and cross-cultural investigation can give us a clearer idea of the extent to which verbal skills are necessary in different domains of learning. Yet, universally, school requires children to use language in new ways. In school, both oral and written language are used in contexts which differ from everyday language use—contexts which often are purely linguistic, without the support of things to see and manipulate. The acquisition of context-free uses of language is one of the most important results of schooling. However, we must be careful to distinguish between this special ability—that is, the ability to verbalize in educated ways—and the ability to think clearly and logically. Unfortunately, much of education is designed and evaluated in terms of the former ability, and not the latter. Recent cross-cultural studies of language and thought (e.g., Cole & Scribner, 1974) have drawn a significant distinction between knowing how to do something and knowing how to talk about it. And sociolinguistic studies (e.g., Labov, 1970) have shown that the language or dialect in which one expresses oneself does not determine one's level of thinking. Let us examine the roles of culture and dialect in education, with the practical intent of eventually modifying pedagogical practice to better suit psycholinguistic and cognitive realities.

The Role of Culture   In our culture we are used to learning skills by verbal instruction. We even buy books on how to play tennis or draw or exercise, relying solely on context-free, noninteractive language to advance knowledge and ability. But in many cultures—certainly in most preliterate cultures—skills are learned by observation, with little or no verbal instruction. And this was even true in Western society until the Industrial Revolution.

The fact that fairly complex skills can be learned on an observational basis is of theoretical importance to our earlier discussions of language and thought, indicating another separation between the two. A graphic example—fascinating in its own right—helps to make this point. The following is a description of how Mayan Indians in Cantel, Guatemala, are trained to operate factory machinery in a traditional nonverbal fashion (Nash, 1967, pp. 35–37):

New workers in the factory are trained by other Canteleños, in a manner similar to learning situations in the home and throughout childhood. A man or woman is hired as an assistant on some machine. . . . For five or six weeks the newly hired worker performs menial tasks such as bringing material to the machine or taking finished goods off of it, but most of the time is spent in observing the operations of the person running the machine. I have spent hours watching an employee learning a job. In one case a girl was learning to tend a loom. She would take her place at the side of the loom operator in the morning, bringing the cones of dyed cotton. Standing by the machine she watched the operator go through the motions of running the loom. She neither asked questions nor was given advice. When the machine snagged or stopped she would look carefully to see what the operator did to get it back into motion. When a table cloth was woven, she removed it from the loom. This constituted her daily routine for nearly six weeks and at the end of this time she announced that she was ready to run a loom. Her foreman told me that at no time during her learning and apprentice period had she touched a machine or practiced operating. When she said she was ready, the machine she had been observing for six weeks was turned over to her and she operated it, not quite as rapidly as the girl who had just left it, but with skill and assurance. What went on in the "training" period? The apprentice was applying the way of learning she had been taught in Cantel. She observes and internally rehearses the set of operations until she feels able to perform. She will not try her hand until she feels competent, for to fumble and make mistakes is a cause for *vergüenza*—public shame. She does not ask questions because that would annoy the person teaching her, and they might also think she is stupid. After sufficient observation the apprentice arrives at the point where she feels that she can carry on the necessary physical operations. I have observed this method of learning among the home weavers with their young apprentices, among the young boys who learn to drive cars, and even in the case of a man who was learning to sing but never sang a note until after a five or six hour session of just listening. In this way the recruit is inducted into his new job and its new skills easily and according to customary training patterns.

This method of learning no doubt has severe limitations and may not function when the learning is symbolic or of purely mental operations, but it works in teaching the simple tasks of running cotton textile machines. Management reports six weeks as about the upper limit of anyone learning to run a loom or a spinning machine. I am told that operating the more complex jacquard requires more learning time, and the factory looks for the *listos,* the bright ones, among its working forces to train as operators. But for other operations the illiterate farmer or housewife, a stranger to machinery, is converted into a reasonably proficient factory hand in six weeks.

The learning process is slightly modified when a Cantelense learns to be a caporal, machine shop worker, or assistant in the electrical shop. Here the technical staff gives verbal instruction and explains the principles and operations of the machine or instrument. The technical staff complains that Cantelenses do not practice and often make costly mistakes when they think they can operate one of the more complex machines. In the more skilled jobs, the complaint is that Cantelenses are often "indifferent and unenthusiastic" when they learn. This complaint of the foreign technical staff is a recognition of the Cantelense desire to appear calm and dignified, even when a neophyte may be eager to learn new skills.

Factory training, where results are rapidly achieved, contrasts with the training situation in the school. Teachers say it is difficult to get performance, and Cantelenses say that too much school work or thinking makes the head *caliente,* hot, and leads to minor illness.

All of our earlier claims about language and cognitive development are reflected in this description. Much of learning is accomplished by observation, aided by enactive and visual imagery, with little or no use of language. Yet some kinds of learning do require a verbal component (though we do not know what sort of verbalization is required for the more "technical" tasks).

The passage introduces another set of variables, which we have not considered: cultural values, reflected in such factors as motivation and socially desirable behavior. The problem facing a teacher of Cantelense children is not one of teaching them to speak properly or to think properly, but rather of encouraging them to apply the skills of language and thought which they already possess to the strange context and goals of the school situation. In many studies, the effect of schooling is not so much the instillation of new cognitive abilities, but a certain flexibility—a willingness to try to apply existing abilities to new, nontraditional problems. In an insightful review of the role of cultural differences in psychological processes, Cole and Bruner (1971) present this point as a general guideline for teachers. First they survey investigations of various SITUATIONAL effects on performance cross-culturally. For example, although measurement skills are generally superior among educated subjects, Gay and Cole (1967) found that Liberian rice farmers were more accurate in making estimates of volume than were Yale sophomores—when the task involved estimation of the number of cups of rice in various bowls. Here the content of the task played a significant role. In other studies, the motivational context is significant. For example, scores on formal tests of intelligence and verbal ability can be raised in settings of rapport and informality, when children are more at ease than in formal testing situations. Summarizing such effects of task content and motivation, Cole and Bruner conclude (1971, p. 874):

... when we systematically study the situational determinants of performance, we are led to conclude that cultural differences reside more in differences in the situations to which different cultural groups apply their skills than to differences in the skills possessed by the groups in question.

The resulting pedagogical advice is that: ". . . the teacher should stop laboring under the impression that he must create new intellectual structures and start concentrating on how to get the child to TRANSFER skills he already possesses to the task at hand." This means that the goal of teaching culturally different groups of children (or children from one's own culture) is not to change HOW they talk—that is, not to change the dialect or language—but rather to change WHAT they talk about.

Cole and Scribner (1974, pp. 118-21) discuss a study of classificatory behavior in Liberia, showing the effect of schooling on verbalization. Both nonliterate adults and ten- to fourteen-year-old school children were quite similar in sorting twenty-five familiar objects into categories of hunting implements, foods, cooking utensils, clothes, and sewing things; and could re-sort the objects into more abstract, superordinate categories (e.g., classifying food and utensils together as household things). This sort of abstract thinking apparently develops in the absence of formal schooling. Where the groups differed, however, was in their ability to verbalize the basis for their groupings. The high-school children gave category labels ("these are clothes") or mentioned a common attribute ("you can hunt with these"). But most of the illiterate adults could only give arbitrary reasons for their groupings, such as "I like them this way" or "my sense told me to do it this way." Surveying a number of studies of the effects of education on cognitive tasks, Cole and Scribner conclude (1974, p. 122):

> . . . the one unambiguous finding in the studies to date is that schooling (and only schooling) contributes to the way in which people describe and explain their own mental operations. This last fact suggests an important distinction that should be made in future research—that is, a differentiation between what people DO and what people SAY they do.

This conclusion should not lead you to believe, of course, that schooling has no effect other than getting people to talk about what they know. The very use of context-free language is an important skill in itself, and is crucial for adapting to the constant innovations in the technological and social orders which all people must face in our times. Furthermore, Cole and Scribner also note a general motivational effect of schooling—a sense of possibility of alternative solutions, related to the flexibility and transfer of skills which we discussed earlier. In regard to categorization, for example, they state that (1974, p. 122):

> attendance at school apparently encourages an approach to classification tasks that incorporates a search for a rule—for a principle that can generate the answers. At the same time, schooling seems to promote an awareness of the fact that alternative rules are possible—one might call this a formal approach to the task in which the individual searches for and selects from the several possibilities a rule of solution.

In this sense, school experience provides an intense kind of linguistic interaction of the sort discussed by Vygotsky and Piaget—an interaction which encourages decentration and taking the role of the other.

Note that we have said nothing about the roles of particular speech styles—dialects of languages—except to mention in passing that the goals of early education should be more involved with such issues as motivation, transfer of skills, and the cognitive use of language—rather than to be concerned with restructuring the particular linguistic code spoken by the child. Because so much of American educational practice is concerned with trying to get children of all ethnic backgrounds to speak "standard English," this issue deserves special attention from a psycholinguistic point of view.

The Role of Dialect   In introducing the topic of language as a tool in cognitive development, I referred to the politics and policies of "compensatory education" and the notion of "cultural deprivation." Aside from the political and social goals of American education—which we cannot approach from a psycholinguistic point of view—there are theoretical assumptions to which we can respond. We have already said enough to cast serious doubt on the idea—common to much educational practice—that language is the source of mental development. And we have also questioned the assumption that cultural differences are reflected in general deficits in mental abilities. Yet it remains the goal of much of early education in the United States to try to get young Black and Puerto Rican and Chicano and Asian (and even deaf) children to speak Standard Middle-Class American English (generally referred to by teachers as "correct English"). It is certainly the case, in contemporary America, that one's chances of social and economic progress are enhanced if one speaks the dominant dialect. At some age—though not necessarily in the first years of school—it makes pedagogical sense to train students in the use of this valuable skill. In many European countries, where the home dialect is markedly different from the public language, the acquisition of the standard dialect is accomplished without becoming a serious social issue. However, for reasons familiar to every American reader, some nonstandard dialects in our country (when spoken by nonwhites), are associated with mental differences as well as linguistic differences. Yet, psycholinguistically, there is no basis for relating a particular dialect or language to special success in normal mental development. Because this issue has been most sharply raised in relation to Black English, it is worth examining this particular dialect of English in discussing relations between language and thought in development. As you can expect from the general position taken in this book, everything we have said about the nature and development of language, and its relation to cognition, is as true for speakers of Black English as it is for speakers of any other language or dialect.

In linguistic terms, Black and Standard English are minor variants of the same English language. In developmental terms, the acquisition of the two dialects follows very similar patterns in the preschool years. For example, studies we have carried out at Berkeley of Black children in the Oakland ghetto show no serious differences in the basic pattern of language development outlined in Chapter 4. This is true even though the Oakland children spend most of their time learning language from the older siblings and playmates who watch over them during much of the day. (This situation is extremely widespread among the cultures of the world, and seems to have no effect on the basic rate of language acquisition [Slobin, 1975].) Table 6-1, for example, shows utterances from the Oakland sample and Roger Brown's sample of Harvard children. Note that the two dialects are especially close at the preschool period in their use of negatives, auxiliaries,

TABLE 6-1
Preschool Negative Utterances in Children
Learning Black and Standard English[1]

Oakland Ghetto Children	Harvard Children
That's not no bathroom.	It wasn't no chicken.
I'm not doing nothing.	I wasn't doing nothing.
I don't get no whipping.	I don't want no milk.
Nobody wasn't scared.	But nobody wasn't gonna know it.
Why bears can't talk?	Why I can't put them on?
But Renée or nobody wouldn't peel me no kinda orange.	Nobody won't recognize me.
Why she won't sit up?	Why we didn't? Why it's not working?
Nobody wouldn't help me.	No one didn't took it.
I don't have no suitcase.	It don't have no wings.
Never I don't get no whipping.	I never won't get it.

[1] The Oakland examples are drawn from unpublished data of Claudia Mitchell-Kernan and the Harvard examples from unpublished data of Roger Brown.

and question forms. The dialects diverge at a later stage in childhood, but at the preschool level they are roughly equivalent on functional and grammatical grounds. (Where the dialects differ, of course, is in their social consequences in the contemporary American social system.)

Even for adult speakers, the differences between the dialects are superficial in linguistic terms, as it has been pointed out most clearly by the linguist William Labov in many publications (e.g., Labov, 1972). For example, Black English is often criticized by school teachers for an apparent lack of the verb *to be*. Labov (1969) has shown, however, that this special verb does occur in many places in Black English, and that its occurrence follows regular linguistic rules. In Standard English we can often contract *to be* to a simple *'s* in the present tense (e.g., *He's busy* rather than *He is busy*). Wherever Standard English can contract, Black English can omit the verb (e.g., *He busy*). But this is not simply a matter of omission of an important part of English grammar, as you can see in Table 6-2. Because wherever it is impossible to contract *to be* in Standard English, it is impossible to delete *to be* in Black English. That is to say, where a form of *to be* is needed to carry out special grammatical functions—like marking emphasis, questions, imperatives, and so forth—it appears in both dialects. For example, in both dialects the same form is needed to carry stress (e.g., *He IS busy*), and it comes to the surface in full form in Black English as well as in Standard English. Thus a more subtle linguistic analysis shows that *to be* is, in fact, present in both dialects. The only difference is a relatively superficial one—namely, that wherever Standard English can contract, Black English can delete *is* and *are,* and wherever Standard English cannot contract these forms, they cannot be deleted in Black English.

Given differences as subtle and superficial as these, it would be hard to argue that Black English, as a version of English, should have any consequences for cognitive development. And given the reasoning presented above about the roles of language and verbal interaction in cognitive devel-

TABLE 6-2
Examples of *be* in Two Dialects of American English[1]

DELETION OF *be*	CONTRACTION OF *be*
Black English	*Standard English*
She the first one.	She's the first one.
But he wild.	But he's wild.
You out the game.	You're out of the game.
We on tape.	We're on tape.
He always complainin'.	He's always complaining.
He gon' try to get up.	He's gonna try to get up.

NON-DELETION OF be

I was small.	I was small.
I'm tired.	I'm tired.
It's a real light yellow color.	It's a real light yellow color.
Wha's a virgin?	What's a virgin?
You got to be good.	You've got to be good.
Be cool, brothers!	Be cool, brothers!
He *is* a expert.	He *is* an expert.
Is he dead?	Is he dead?
Are you down?	Are you down?
Is that a shock or is it not?	Is that a shock or is it not?
I don't care what you are.	I don't care what you are.
Do you see where that person is?	Do you see where that person is?

[1] After Labov (1969). The Black English examples are drawn from Labov (with some abbreviation), and the Standard English equivalents have been supplied for the purposes of this comparative table.

opment, it would be hard to argue that training little Black (or Chicano or Puerto Rican or Asian) children to speak Standard English should be one of the first goals for preschool or early education. Eventually these children will have to come to terms with the standard dialect as a tool for practical social and economic purposes in our society. But our current understanding of developmental psychology and psycholinguistics would suggest that this aspect of education can best be postponed to the later school years.

In addition to arguments about dialect, however, some educators have argued that poor Black children hear and use little language, and do not even speak a fully developed form of child language. This, of course, goes counter to everything we know about language development. The most decisive answer to this misconception has been given by Labov (1970, pp. 153-54):

> The concept of verbal deprivation has no basis in social reality. In fact, Negro children in the urban ghettos receive a great deal of verbal stimulation . . . and participate fully in a highly verbal culture. They have the same basic vocabulary, possess the same capacity for conceptual learning, and use the same logic as anyone else who learns to speak and understand English.

In support of the last point—the independence of logical thinking from the dialect one speaks—Labov (1970) has presented an elegant and forceful analysis of "the logic of nonstandard English." He contrasts a discourse by a fifteen-year-old Black gang member, in fully colloquial Black English, with an interview in Standard English with an upper-middle-class, college-educated Black. Carrying out a careful logical analysis of the two discourses, Labov finds that the gang member has produced a logically argued, complex set of interdependent propositions, concisely presented, with ingenuity and a quick wit. By contrast, the educated discourse sounds intelligent and reasonable, but it turns out to be verbose, repetitive, and illogical. Labov says, in relation to the educated speaker, that he sounds intelligent because we credit speakers who use certain stylistic devices with education, thereby assuming them to be intelligent. But he warns that speaking Standard English is no more a guarantee of logical thinking than is speaking Black English a guarantee of the opposite. He ends with a caveat to educators (1970, p. 171):

All too often, standard English is represented by a style that is simultaneously overparticular and vague. The accumulating flow of words buries rather than strikes the target. It is this verbosity which is most easily taught and most easily learned, so that words take the place of thoughts, and nothing can be found behind them. . . . When we have discovered how much of middle-class style is a matter of fashion and how much actually helps us express ideas clearly, we will have done ourselves a great service. We will then be in a position to say what standard grammatical rules must be taught to nonstandard speakers in the early grades.

This final point—the independence of logic from particular dialects of a language—brings us to the final section of this chapter. Labov's argument may be based on the fact that he is dealing with two dialects of the same language. Is there any way in which the particular language one speaks shapes or determines one's thinking?

LINGUISTIC RELATIVITY AND DETERMINISM

The notion that different languages influence thinking in different ways has been present since the beginning of philosophy. In American social science this hypothesis of LINGUISTIC RELATIVITY AND DETERMINISM has come to bear the name of the "Whorfian hypothesis," after the linguist Benjamin Lee Whorf who devoted great attention to the problem (Whorf, 1956). Let us begin with an early statement of the problem by Edward Sapir, the great linguist who was Whorf's teacher (in Mandelbaum, 1958, p. 162):

Human beings do not live in the objective world alone, nor alone in the world of social activity as ordinarily understood, but are very much at the mercy of the particular language which has become the medium of expression for their society. It is quite an illusion to imagine that one adjusts to reality essentially without the use of language and that language is merely an incidental means of solving specific problems of communication or reflection. The fact of the matter is that the "real world" is to a large extent unconsciously built up on the language habits of the group. . . . We see and hear and otherwise experience very largely as we do because the language habits of our community predispose certain choices of interpretation.

The statement raises several important points. Sapir holds that ALL of experience is influenced by the particular language one speaks. (We are not told what aspects of language are relevant.) The strength of this influence is not clear: earlier he says we are "at the mercy of language"; later he simply says that "the language habits . . . predispose certain choices of interpretation." The earlier statement is quite strong, while the later, weaker, statement can be accommodated to the arguments developed earlier in this chapter. It is also clear from the statement that different languages are held to have different effects on thought and experience. Sapir's statement thus advances the notions of LINGUISTIC DETERMINISM (language can determine cognition) and LINGUISTIC RELATIVITY (the determinism is relative to the particular language spoken), in both a strong and weak version. These notions must be examined more carefully.

First of all, why should one even expect there to be language-specific effects on cognition—that is, what sort of evidence impels one to postulate linguistic relativity? Students are often struck by the apparent strangeness of foreign languages, especially when the language is not closely related to the native language. People begin to think about linguistic relativity when they compare languages and discover how different the categories of experience embodied in various languages can be. Categories can be represented in various ways by language: (1) by individual words in the lexicon (*house, white,* etc.), (2) also by parts of words which perform grammatical functions (*house* vs. *houses* vs. *house's; white* vs. *whiter* vs. *whiten* vs. *whiteness;* etc.), and (3) also by a variety of grammatical processes (e.g., word order as used to distinguish subject and object in English: *The man hit the ball* vs. *The ball hit the man*). As you will see shortly, languages differ greatly both in the categories they express and the particular linguistic means used for the representation of given categories. These differences go deeper than the well-known fact that most words have no completely perfect translation equivalent from one language to another, for you will note from the above English examples that categories can be expressed both LEXICALLY and GRAMMATICALLY. We'll go into this distinction in more detail in a moment. But first let me point out why we have to specify what sorts of differences between languages we want to deal with in trying to connect linguistic with nonlinguistic phenomena.

The specification of differences is the first of three problems which must be considered in trying to relate these two sorts of phenomena. The first question asks: (1) WHAT KINDS OF LINGUISTIC FACTS ARE BEING REFERRED TO? Are we concerned with whether a language has a term for a specific concept, or whether a concept is embodied in an obligatory grammatical distinction, and so on.

Of course, there is a necessary second question: (2) WITH WHAT KINDS OF PHENOMENA IS A CONNECTION BEING MADE? For example, do we want to relate the linguistic facts we have discovered with facts of sense perception, or memory, or cultural behavior, or what? Whorf was most interested in relating both the lexicon and the grammar—especially the grammar—to the total *Weltanschauung,* the total world view of a culture. His was the most pervasive sort of equation proposed, and so his approach is sometimes called the "language-Weltanschauung hypothesis."

And finally we must also ask: (3) WHAT IS THE NATURE OF THE CONNECTION? Is it a causal relation—and, if so, which is the causal factor, the linguistic or the nonlinguistic? Most of the provocative theorizing on this matter assumes that the language in some way determines other behaviors, rather than the other way around. And there are two broad types of theories here, frequently referred to as the "strong" and the "weak" versions of the Whorf hypothesis. The strong form—often espoused by Whorf himself—holds that the language DETERMINES thought and behavior patterns; that the language is a sort of mold for thought and philosophy. The weak form—usually held today in one way or another—merely asserts that certain aspects of language can predispose people to think or act in one way rather than another, but that there is no rigid determinism: One is not fully a prisoner of one's language; it is just a guide to thought and other sorts of behavior.

Thus we have a two-way classification, in which one looks either to the lexicon or the grammar, and posits either a strong or a weak relation between an aspect of language and aspects of thought or action. There are accordingly at least four forms of the linguistic relativity and determinism hypothesis, fitting into the four cells of the following table:

LINGUISTIC VARIABLES

	Lexical	Grammatical
Strong		
Weak		

FORM OF DETERMINISM

I think there are also other confusions in regard to the causal question. Clearly the case must be different for the history of a CULTURE and the history of an INDIVIDUAL. As Sapir pointed out so well in 1912, cultural phenomena must, in very early times, have determined certain linguistic forms; but culture changes much more quickly than language, and so many archaisms, from a cultural-determinism point of view, are found in every language. In this sense, then, the language, and not the cultural behavior, is seen as the dependent variable. But this is an historical question. As far as any individual is concerned, each person is born into an existing cultural and linguistic community, and both cultural and linguistic forms influence cognitive development.

Finally, Sapir also points out another sort of causal relation—one in which both the linguistic forms and the cultural forms are determined by a third factor, for example, the topography of the geographical area in which a society dwells. He speaks (1912) of the Paiute Indians, who live in the desert and are faced with the need of finding water. Their language allows them to describe topological features in great detail. Here is a case where environment determines both the linguistic and the cultural concern with the topology of the terrain.

It is important to bear these three questions in mind: the nature of the linguistic evidence, the nature of the behavioral evidence, and the causal nature of the connection. Most of the early philosophers and linguists concerned with linguistic relativity and determinism failed to spell out the second and third questions carefully, and they often spoke as if a linguistic difference necessarily implied a cognitive difference, without presenting further evidence. Only a few psychological experiments have tried to relate SPECIFIC linguistic differences to SPECIFIC sorts of behavior—and even when a relation IS found, it is not clear just what the causal nature of the relation is. (See Brown, 1976, and Rosch, 1974, for further discussion.)

The Lexical Level

Let us now take up these questions in more detail. First of all, what sorts of evidence have brought people to talk about linguistic relativity at all? We can begin with the lexical level—the matter of what words are found in a given language, and what they refer to. (This discussion follows, in part, Fishman's "systematization of the Whorfian hypothesis" [1960].)

When you compare two languages, you may find that one of them has a word for which there is no one-word equivalent at all in the other language. For example, there is no one-word English equivalent for the German *Gemütlichkeit*. (But note that this does not prevent us from learning what the German term means, and borrowing it for use in English. We have thousands of words which we have borrowed from other languages whenever necessary. I think it could only be argued, in this regard, that the Germans may be more sensitive to the attribute of *Gemütlichkeit*—but this would be a very difficult sort of nonlinguistic behavior to measure. Note also that when new concepts arise, we invent new words to refer to them: *hippie, de-escalation,* and on and on.)

Languages also differ in providing superordinate terms to name various categories. For example, English has the superordinates *animal, bird, insect,* and *creature*, which some languages lack; but, on the other hand, we don't have a superordinate term for 'fruit and nuts', while the Chinese do. (This sort of evidence can only be used in regard to the weak form of the hypothesis; we can certainly conceive of grouping fruit and nuts together—though we may not ordinarily do so; and we can use the productive aspects of our language to form an expression such as *fruit and nuts* when a single word is lacking.) Similarly, the Arabs were said to have many terms for various breeds of horses, but no superordinate term for horses in general; the Aztecs had one word for snow, ice, and cold, where we have several and the Eskimos have even more; and so on, ad infinitum. Such evidence was adduced by the volumes by German philologists of the nineteenth century, and served as grist for the mills of those philosophers and social theorists who wanted to show that other peoples thought in distinctly different ways (generally inferior) from "modern Europeans."

Languages also differ lexically in the ways in which they divide various semantic domains. For many years, one of the most popular areas of investigation in this regard was that of color. Languages differ in the number of color terms they have, and how they divide up the color continuum. A great deal of research (summarized by Brown, 1976) indicated that colors which are easily named—that is, colors which are highly CODABLE—are well retained in various memory and recognition tasks. The initial conclusion was that codability influences memory. Ironically, this research ended up making a clearly anti-Whorfian point (Berlin & Kay, 1969; Heider, 1972; Heider & Olivier, 1972; Rosch, 1973). For it turns out that regardless of how many color terms a language has, and regardless of the boundaries between the various color terms, there is a physiologically determined collection of FOCAL, or PROTOTYPICAL colors. For example, consider the following three languages: (1) Language A has only three color terms, *white, black,* and *red.* (2) Language B has these three, as well as a color term for *blue,* which also names various shades which we would consider *greenish-blue* or *greenish.* (3) Language C is English. It turns out that speakers of all three languages agree on what is the best example of *blue.* Even speakers of Language A, which has no term for *blue,* will find it easier to learn a word for *blue* if it represents what speakers of Languages B and C (and presumably everyone else in the world) considers *a really good, basic blue,* than if they are trained to associate a new word with an off-blue color. (This is the work of Eleanor Rosch, 1973.) The color space turns out to be one semantic domain in which there are universal natural categories, or prototypes, independent of language or culture.

If this finding were limited to color, it could be dismissed as a special feature of the physiology of color perception. However, Rosch (Rosch et al., 1976) has gone on to demonstrate that many categories have universal natural prototypes. For example, she worked with the Dani, a stone-age group in New Guinea who had no terms for geometric forms (and who correspond to speakers of Language A, above). She taught them names for circle, square, and equilateral triangle—for one group of subjects using what we consider good forms; for another, using distorted forms (which had gaps or curves where straight lines are normal). The task was easier for those subjects learning names for the good forms, suggesting that these forms have some natural reality even if they are not named or encountered. Furthermore, following her work on prototypes, Rosch found that even those subjects who eventually learned to name the distorted forms, considered the good forms to be the best examples of these categories.

In further work (Rosch et al., 1976), Rosch goes on to show that there is a universality to the way in which many semantic domains are structured for purposes of naming. Even if languages differ in the number and kinds of distinctions they make, there are basic principles of category formation. To the extent that the content and form of categories are universally determined by psychological factors, of course, one cannot expect to find either linguistic relativity or linguistic determinism. (See Rosch & Lloyd, 1978, for recent papers on cognition and categorization.)

Still, languages do differ in how they divide some semantic domains. Two issues must be raised: (1) the nature of codability, and (2) the effects of codability. In regard to the first point, consider Whorf's (1956) frequently-cited example of the richness of Eskimo vocabulary for snow. Note that in all such cases it is the presence or absence of a SINGLE word which is offered as evidence for linguistic relativity and determinism. But remember that every language makes it possible to COMBINE words productively; indeed, Whorf could not have explained the Eskimo distinctions without recourse to the English means of forming phrases and sentences. Little American children can freely use phrases to describe different kinds of snow—*good packing, too mushy for a snowman,* and so on. At issue here is the relative ease with which a concept can be encoded in a given language. To speak of ease of codability, however, clearly returns us to the weak form of the Whorfian hypothesis: in some languages it may be EASIER for speakers to think or talk about certain things because their language makes it easy for them to do so.

This brings us to the second issue: the effect of codability. The problem throughout is one of clearly demonstrating the influence of codability on some other behavior. Let me give you another example here that is frequently cited: In some languages certain words have additional shades or ranges of meaning than their cognates or best equivalents in other languages. In French one term, *conscience,* is used for the two English terms, *conscience* and *consciousness.* On the one hand, this means that French speakers do not have as easily available to them a distinction that we have. On the other hand, it means that they have more easily available to them a partial identity of these two terms which is very difficult for us to fully appreciate. Some people think it possible to demonstrate that this linguistic identity has led to a greater conceptual fusion for French thinkers between the concepts of 'conscience' and 'consciousness' than has been true for English or German thinkers.

Lexical differences between languages can be characterized in terms of the three sorts of differences just considered: missing terms, missing superordinates, and different divisions of domains. The major issue here seems to hinge on the relative codability of concepts. Although it is a debatable point, I would tend to believe that any concept can somehow be encoded in any language, though with ease in some, and by complex circumlocutions in others. Thus, in regard to the lexical level, I would favor the weak form of the Whorfian hypothesis. This form draws an important distinction between HABITUAL and POTENTIAL behavior. For example, although all people can potentially discriminate a huge number of colors, most people use but a few habitual color terms in everyday speech. While it may be true that, with some effort, one could say anything in any language, we tend to say things which can be fairly conveniently encoded, and we frequently assimilate experience to the categories of the linguistic code. Thus a list of frequently-occurring words in a given language community will give you a good preliminary index of what is probably of special importance to the members of that group. Other things can, of course, be conveyed by more complex utterances, but this is not economical for important discriminations.

The Grammatical Level

Now what about the GRAMMATICAL level? Here I think the question of determinism becomes quite intriguing, because there is a variety of obligatory classifications embodied in grammar, to which we do not usually attend and which do not even become obvious until you begin to compare languages. One of the most striking examples comes from Sapir (in Mandelbaum, 1958, pp. 157–59), and is well worth quoting in full. In reading it, bear in mind Vygotsky's example of expressing in words the single fact of a barefoot boy in a blue shirt running down the street, and the problem of a child learning to say 'daddy gave me a ball'.

The natural or, at any rate, the naïve thing is to assume that when we wish to communicate a certain idea or impression, we make something like a rough and rapid inventory of the objective elements and relations involved in it, that such an inventory or analysis is quite inevitable, and that our linguistic task consists merely of the finding of the particular words and groupings of words that correspond to the terms of the objective analysis. Thus, when we observe an object of the type that we call a "stone" moving through space towards the earth, we involuntarily analyze the phenomenon into two concrete notions, that of a stone and that of an act of falling, and, relating these two notions to each other by certain formal methods proper to English, we declare that "the stone falls." We assume, naïvely enough, that this is about the only analysis that can properly be made. And yet, if we look into the ways that other languages take to express this very simple kind of impression, we soon realize how much may be added to, subtracted from, or rearranged in our own form of expression without materially altering our report of the physical fact.

In German and in French we are compelled to assign "stone" to a gender category—perhaps the Freudians can tell us why this object is masculine in the one language, feminine in the other; in Chippewa we cannot express ourselves without bringing in the apparently irrelevant fact that a stone is an inanimate object. If we find gender beside the point, the Russians may wonder why we consider it necessary to specify in every case whether a stone, or any other object for that matter, is conceived in a definite or an indefinite manner, why the difference between "the stone" and "a stone" matters. "Stone falls" is good enough for Lenin, as it was good enough for Cicero. And if we find barbarous the neglect of the distinction as to definiteness, the Kwakiutl Indian of British Columbia may sympathize with us but wonder why we do not go a step further and indicate in some way whether the stone is visible or invisible to the speaker at the moment of speaking and whether it is nearest to the speaker, the person addressed, or some third party. "That would no doubt sound fine in Kwakiutl, but we are too busy!" And yet we insist on expressing the singularity of the falling object, where the Kwakiutl Indian, differing from the Chippewa, can generalize and make a statement which would apply equally well to one or several stones. Moreover, he need not specify the time of the fall. The Chinese get on with a minimum of explicit formal statement and content themselves with a frugal "stone fall."

These differences of analysis, one may object, are merely formal; they do not invalidate the necessity of the fundamental concrete analysis of the situation into "stone" and what the stone does, which in this case is "fall." But this necessity, which we feel so strongly, is an illusion. In the Nootka language the combined impression of a stone falling is quite differently analyzed. The stone need not be specifically referred to, but a single word, a verb form, may be used which is in practice not essentially more ambiguous than our English sentence. This verb form consists of two main elements, the first indicating general movement or position of a stone or stonelike object, while the second refers to downward direction. We can get some hint of the feeling of the Nootka word if we assume the existence of an intransitive verb "to stone," referring to the position or movement of a stonelike object. Then our sentence, "The stone falls," may be reassembled into something like "it stones down." In this type of expression the thing-quality of the stone is implied in the generalized verbal element "to stone," while the specific kind of motion which is given us in experience when a stone falls is conceived as separable into a generalized notion of the movement of a class of objects and a more specific one of direction. In other words, while Nootka has no difficulty whatever in describing the fall of a stone, it has no verb that truly corresponds to our "fall."

Examples such as these make it dramatically clear why the notion has been advanced that the grammatical categories of language COVERTLY bring us to pay attention to different attributes of situations. Vygotsky may indeed have seen a barefoot boy in a blue shirt running down the street, but, as you have just seen, the translation from such a sense impression into a linguistic expression is no simple matter. Did this translation in any way affect what Vygotsky actually saw or to what he was particularly sensitive in that event? This is an exceedingly difficult question to answer. Though direct evidence is lacking, one cannot help but feel that such obligatory grammatical distinctions as those discussed by Sapir do sensitize speakers to certain aspects of the world—at least when speaking.

To me a most graphic example of this suggestion is revealed by the use of pronouns of address in various languages (see Brown, 1965, Chapter 2). Take German, for example, where one must choose between the "familiar" *du* and the "polite" *Sie*, or between the corresponding *tu* and *vous* of French, using, at the same time, the appropriate verb conjugational forms. These are obligatory grammatical distinctions: when speaking German or French you must—whenever you talk to anyone—take note of what your relationship is to him or her in terms of status and intimacy, as defined by the norms of the society. Of course, even in English you often have to think of such things—you have to decide what style of speech to use, what topics to discuss, whether to use first name or title and last name, and so on. But I think that in comparing English with French or German, for example, we have a clear demonstration of the importance of an OBLIGATORY grammatical distinction in predisposing speakers to attend to certain things. Very often in English we can get away from these problems of social relations by just saying *you*, talking generally, and never using a name. But, even more importantly, there are many situations in English when you simply never think much about the status and solidarity relations between yourself and the person to whom you are speaking. Think of the various people to whom you talk during a day—people you casually know in a course or at work, people you meet in the coffee room, people of various ages and status levels—I'm sure that most often you do not have to go through the sort of agonizing decision you would have to make in many cases if we were all

compelled to speak French, for example, and thus were CONSTANTLY RE-
QUIRED to decide which pronoun, or which verb form to use—in almost
every remark. If we suddenly all switched to French, we would find our
attention focused on many aspects of social relations which were previously
not of central concern. It is not that we never have to think of these things
when speaking English, but that in speaking French, or some other language, we would almost certainly have to pay more daily attention to such
matters.

Another sort of argument advanced on the grammatical front of the
Whorf hypothesis is the matter of the part of speech membership of a
word, and the semantic implications of such membership. For example,
'heat', in Indo-European languages, is a noun. A large number of nouns
designate concrete things. Perhaps this is why so much fruitless effort was
expended in the history of Western science in the search for a heat substance, like "phlogiston" and "caloric." Perhaps if Western scientists had
spoken a language like Hopi, where 'heat' is a verb, they may have started
out with the more appropriate kinetic theory of heat at which they finally
arrived. (But note that in spite of the language—if it WAS a determiner—
Western scientists did eventually free themselves from the notion of a heat
substance when this notion proved itself inadequate on empirical and ra-
tional grounds.)[3]

These numerous examples should give you a good idea of just how
strikingly different languages can seem—different enough to have led
many thinkers to conclude that there must be some sort of cognitive relativity to correspond to the linguistic relativity. We could go on and on
listing differences such as these, but the main point is simply that languages do seem rather different, one from the other, in the categories which
they embody—both lexically and grammatically. If you look at all of these
linguistic differences carefully, though, I think you will have to conclude
that the striking differences between languages are not so much in what
they are ABLE to express, but in what they HABITUALLY DO express and are
required to express.

The basic DIMENSIONS along which linguistically-expressed categories
vary are surely universals of human cognition. The basic FUNCTIONS are
performed by all languages—making and negating assertions, asking questions, giving commands, and so on. Certainly the basic FORM of human
language is universal. If anything, I have suggested in Chapter 3 that the
form of language in general may be determined by the nature of cognition
and the uses to which language is put. This is to turn the Whorfian hypothesis on its head and assert that thought determines language. There is
undoubtedly some truth in both versions, but the strong form of the hypothesis, although often appealing, can no longer be supported (Whorf,
1940, in Carroll, 1956, pp. 213-14):

3. In a similar vein, consider the many nouns used by psychologists—*mind, behavior,
cognition, rule,* and the many more you have encountered in this book and elsewhere. Our
vocabulary can lead us astray here as well, promoting an endless search for psychological or
physiological "entities" where we ought to seek understanding of processes and dynamics,
equilibrium and disequilibrium, and other more "verb-like" notions.

We cut nature up, organize it into concepts, and ascribe significances as we do, largely because we are parties to an agreement to organize it in this way—an agreement that holds throughout our speech community and is codified in the patterns of our language. The agreement is, of course, an implicit and unstated one, BUT ITS TERMS ARE ABSOLUTELY OBLIGATORY; we cannot talk at all except by subscribing to the organization and classification of data which the agreement decrees.

If the statement were true in the bold form, certainly deaf children could not develop in the normal fashion revealed by Furth, as discussed above; and certainly linguistic science could not have achieved the striking successes it has achieved in describing features common to all human languages. A more modest, but also more acceptable formulation is offered by the linguist Charles Hockett (1954, p. 122):

> Languages differ not so much as to what CAN be said in them, but rather as to what it is RELATIVELY EASY to say in them. The history of Western logic and science constitutes not so much the story of scholars hemmed in and misled by the nature of their specific languages, as the story of a long and fairly successful struggle AGAINST inherited linguistic limitations. Where everyday language would not serve, special subsystems (mathematics, etc.) were devised. However, even Aristotle's development of syllogistic notation carries within itself aspects of Greek language structure.
>
> The impact of an inherited linguistic pattern on activities is, in general, LEAST important in the most practical contexts and most important in such "purely verbal" goings-on as storytelling, religion, and philosophizing. As a result, some types of literature are extremely difficult to translate accurately, let alone appealingly.

An Experimental Test

So much for abstract reasoning and anecdotal examples. The issues of linguistic relativity and determinism have been extremely difficult to study by the controlled methods of scientific psychology, but let us, finally, examine at least one concrete experiment which has been performed in an attempt to relate a specific aspect of a given language to a specific sort of behavior. From the point of view of the grand sweep of the Whorf hypothesis, such a restricted experiment may seem disappointing, but the problems of studying global relationships between a linguistic system and an entire world-view are obviously beyond our grasp.

An important collection of experiments was carried out in the late 1950s in connection with the Southwest Project in Comparative Psycholinguistics (Carroll & Casagrande, 1958). A particularly interesting experiment from this Project deals with grammatical determinism in Navaho (pp. 26–27):

> It is obligatory in the Navaho language, when using verbs of *handling*, to employ a particular one of a set of verbal forms according to the shape or some other essential attribute of the object about which one

is speaking. Thus, if I ask you in Navaho to hand me an object, I must use the appropriate verb stem depending on the nature of the object. If it is a long flexible object such as a piece of string, I must say *šańléh*; if it is a long rigid object such as a stick, I must say *šańtį́įh;* if it is a flat flexible material such as paper or cloth, I must say *šańiłcóós,* and so on.

On the basis of this interesting grammatical distinction, Carroll and Casagrande proposed that (p. 27):

Navaho-speaking children would learn to discriminate the "form" attributes of objects at an earlier age than their English-speaking compeers. The finding of American and European psychologists that children tend first to distinguish objects on the basis of size and color might—at least at the level of verbal facility in dealing with these variables—be partly an artifact of the particular language they use. The hypothesis was, then, that this feature of the Navaho language would affect the relative potency or order of emergence of such concepts as color, size, shape or form, and number in the Navaho-speaking child, as compared with English-speaking Navaho children of the same age, and that Navaho-speaking children would be more inclined than the latter to perceive formal similarities between objects.

The method was an object triads test, in which the child had to pick which two objects, of three presented, "went best" together (p. 28): "For example, one of the pairs consisted of a yellow stick and a piece of blue rope of comparable size. The child was then shown a yellow rope, and the basis of his choice could be either color or the Navaho verb-form classification— since different verbal forms are used for a length of rope and a stick." Children were presented with triads such as blue rope—yellow rope—blue stick; small blue cube—medium blue cube—small blue sphere; blue stick— yellow stick—blue oblong block; and so on.

The experiment showed that (p. 30): "In both the Navaho groups [Navaho-dominant and English-dominant children] . . . the trend is toward the increasing perceptual saliency of shape or form, as compared with color, with increasing age. The curve starts lower and remains lower for English-dominant Navaho children, although it rises rather rapidly after the age of seven. Navaho children stay ahead of their English-speaking age mates, although the two curves tend to converge as age increases." In other words, children who speak only Navaho group on the basis of form or shape at an earlier age than those who speak English, although all of the children come from the same reservation and live under similar circumstances. It thus appears that language has some effect on cognitive development in this case.

The picture becomes more complicated, however, when English-speaking children off the reservation are given the same test. Here we find a very interesting phenomenon. White American children in a Boston suburb are more similar to the Navaho-dominant than to the English-dominant Indians; that is, they tend early to sort on the basis of form and shape, rather than color. On the other hand, Black slum children in Harlem are more similar to the English-dominant Indians, giving up color matching at a later age. Thus two sorts of variables must be considered: environmental characteristics and native language. Carroll and Casagrande speculate that certain aspects of the environment of the white suburban child—perhaps playing with puzzles and toys which emphasize attention to form in themselves—can bring an English-speaking child to attend to form and shape at an early age. In an environment presumably lacking such nonlinguistic means of drawing attention to form (Indian reservations and urban slums), speaking a language like Navaho can accelerate cognitive development in regard to form versus color matching. As Carroll and Casagrande put it (p. 31):

> ... we may amend our hypothesis in possibly the following form: The tendency of a child to match objects on the basis of form or material rather than size or color increases with age and may be enhanced by either of two kinds of experiences; (a) learning to speak a language like Navaho, which because of the central role played by form and material in its grammatical structure, requires the learner to make certain discriminations of form and material in the earlier stages of language learning in order to make himself understood at all; or (b) practice with toys and other objects involving the fitting of forms and shapes, and the resultant greater reinforcement received from form-matching.

One is reminded of Furth's discussion of the cognitive development of deaf children: language is but ONE of various ways of bringing a child to attend to certain attributes of the stimulus world.

Conclusion

The fate of the Sapir-Whorf hypothesis at the present time is interesting: today we are more concerned with linguistic universals and cultural universals than with linguistic and cultural relativity. Chomsky has suggested that Whorf was too much concerned with surface structures of languages, while on their deeper levels all languages are of the same universally human character. Cultural anthropologists are looking for ways in which the underlying structures of cultures are alike, and psychologists are moving out of Western culture to cross-cultural studies, in an attempt to understand general laws of human behavior and development. Perhaps in an age when our world has become so small, and the most diverse cultures so intimately interrelated in matters of war and peace, it is best that we come to an understanding of what all people have in common. But at the same time it would be dangerous to forget that different languages and cultures may indeed have important effects on what people will believe and what they will do.

. . . Words strain,
Crack and sometimes break, under the burden,
Under the tension, slip, slide, perish,
Decay with imprecision, will not stay in place,
Will not stay still. . . .

—T. S. Eliot
(1943, p. 121)

RECAPITULATION: FORM AND FUNCTION IN LANGUAGE

Rather than attempt to summarize the preceding six chapters, in this last chapter I try to bring together what you have learned by considering the FORM of language in the light of its FUNCTIONS.[1] The argument was anticipated in Chapter 3, where I proposed "that language has the form which it does because of the uses to which it is put." Within the defining contexts of biology and society, our species has developed a communicative system which reflects the resolution of various competing pressures. An examination of these forces on language serves to recapitulate major psycholinguistic themes.

Underlying the following somewhat technical discussion is a basic theme: Language does not stay put over time. Every language is constantly in the process of historical change. Language change is not a unidirectional evolutionary process towards some ideal end state, but rather a constant dynamic attempt to maintain equilibrium. A change in one part of a language system has effects on other parts. Both simplification and elaboration occur, balancing each other off again and again. Our goal in this final chapter is to understand the forces which give human language its form and which keep each language in a state of dynamic equilibrium. These forces can be understood by considering the ways in which language is used under the temporal and social constraints of communication.

When speaker and listener interact, the speaker wants to express him- or herself clearly, efficiently, effectively, and reasonably quickly. The listener, in turn, wants to quickly and efficiently retrieve a clear and informative message. These needs and constraints of speaker and listener shape the form of language. In order for a communicative system to function as a human language, it must adhere to four sorts of basic ground rules. Let us conceptualize these ground rules as imperatives to a semi-mythical beast— *Language* (with a capital L). The four charges to Language are: (1) BE CLEAR. (2) BE HUMANLY PROCESSIBLE IN ONGOING TIME. (3) BE QUICK AND EASY. (4) BE EXPRESSIVE. Language cannot fulfill all four of the charges completely, because they are partially in competition. For example, if we were perfectly clear, messages would take too long to get across; if we were fully expressive, we may not be clear; and so forth. Consider each of the "charges" to Language in turn, thinking of how they define and constrain the nature of human language.

BE CLEAR

This "charge," or constraint on the form of Language, means that surface structures must not be too different in form and organization from the semantic structures which underlie them. You encountered this principle in Chapter 4 as Operating Principle D for child language acquisition: "Underlying semantic relations should be marked overtly and clearly." You will remember that systems closer to one-to-one mappings between meaning and surface form—like the Turkish inflectional paradigm—are easier for children to learn than systems which deviate from this principle. We

---

1. This chapter is a condensed adaptation of my paper, "Language change in childhood and in history" (in J. Macnamara, Ed., *Language learning and thought*. New York: Academic Press, Inc., 1977. Pp. 185-214.).

reviewed other evidence that children strive to maintain this sort of semantic clarity or transparency, as in their simplifications and regularizations of English verb inflections and Slavic noun inflections.

In historical change, as well, there is pressure on language to move towards greater semantic transparency. For example, Old English was similar to the present-day Slavic languages in having a complex and irregular inflectional system. Presumably this caused difficulty to English children then, just as it presently causes difficulty to Russian and Yugoslav children (as discussed in Chapter 4). English gradually changed from using inflections and relatively free word order, to omitting inflections and relying on fixed word order and particles such as prepositions to indicate such things as subject and object of sentences. That is, English (and Indo-European languages generally) has moved from being a relatively SYNTHETIC language, in which grammatical inflections compactly expressed several underlying meanings, to a relatively ANALYTIC language, in which a number of separate words are strung together. You can still see the tail end of this process at work today. For example, in more archaic and literary English we say WHOM *did you give the book?*, while in more colloquial speech we say WHO *did you give the book* TO? Instead of a compact, synthetic word with an accusative case inflection, *whom,* we analyze this expression into two separate words *who* and *to.* When too many elements of meaning come to be fused in a single surface form, there is a tendency to replace that form by more analytic structures, in which underlying semantic elements are pulled apart in surface expression. (But note that in historical time, languages constantly move back and forth between the poles of compact, synthetic expression and segmented, analytic expression. This is because the charge to be clear is always in competition with the charge to be quick and easy, as we will see below.)

In general, there are universal constraints on the degree to which a language system can be compact and still be meaningful and processible. Oscillations are possible within these constraints, but the general principles of the human means of mapping meanings onto sounds exist within narrowly definable limits.

BE PROCESSIBLE

Most of Chapter 2 is devoted to examples of how Language conforms to the charge to be humanly processible in ongoing time. The first charge has to do with the mappings between sounds and their underlying meaningful structures (syntactic and semantic). This second charge has to do with the form of the surface cues which speaker and listener must use in the processes of programming and deciphering utterances. In Chapter 3 you saw that many processing strategies are interlinked, resulting in a collection of TYPES of human languages. A typology based on surface forms and their associated processing strategies shows that some theoretically possible human languages do not occur. Because Language must be processible by human beings under the time constraints of immediate memory and communicative pressures, only languages which adhere to overall processing demands are possible.

When a language moves too far from this requirement, changes occur. For example, if a verb-final language—for various reasons brought about by contact with other languages—begins to use many verb-medial constructions, speakers begin to have difficulty processing postpositions, modifiers, and auxiliaries. As you will remember from Chapter 3, the position of these elements should be consistent with the position of the verb in order for fully efficient processing. So with change in one part of a linguistic system—like the position of the verb—placement of many other elements will also change, in order to maintain processibility.

You have also seen the influence on processing constraints in the case of Russenorsk. Even this simple contact language required a general preposition and a verb marker, presumably in order to make sentences processible. Often pidgin languages must become more elaborated, as they come to to serve a wider range of communicative functions and eventually become native languages for children born of parents who speak pidgin. When a pidgin language is acquired as a native language by children, it is called a CREOLE. Creoles are marked by more elaborate surface grammar than pidgins. Because the creole has become the medium of more complex and differentiated communication, it needs more surface cues to aid processing of complex utterances. You will remember Margaret Mead's example of a court discourse in New Guinea Pidgin English. This language has now become a creole, called *Tok Pisin*, used in government, education, and everyday life by an entire speech community. The pressure for elaboration has come from the fourth charge to Language, which we have not yet considered—the charge to "be expressive." However, the means of being expressive must be consistent with the charge to be processible. Tok Pisin has evolved a means for forming relative clauses—that is, a means of embedding one sentence within another for purposes of modification. The new means clearly adheres to the charge to be processible: a particle is inserted at the beginning of a relative clause and, unless the clause coincides with the end of the sentence, also at the end of the clause. It is as if the language has provided listeners with an audible bracketing of a clause which can interrupt a sentence, thus insuring that sentence processing strategies will not be led astray. The following examples (from Sankoff & Brown, 1976) make this point clear:

Na pik IA [*ol ikilim bipo* IA] *bai ikamap olsem draipela ston.*
'And this (the) pig they had killed before would turn into a huge stone.'

Meri IA [*em i yangpela meri, draipela meri* IA] *em harim istap.*
'The girl, who was a young, big girl, was listening.'

Em wanpela America IA [*iputim naim long en*].
'It was an American who gave her her name.'

The particle, *ia* (derived from *here*), functions both as a cue to the listener's perceptual strategies and as a device for the speaker to keep track of the listener's attention. The speaker announces an interruption to provide additional information cued by *ia*. Once the additional information has been given, the end of the interruption (or subordination) is marked by another occurrence of *ia*, often with rising intonation to allow the listener to indicate assent. This bracketing use of *ia* clearly serves processing strategies, and it is striking to find that it has evolved in a creole language which was so recently a pidgin without clear means of marking subordination. (You will be reminded of discussion of the role of relative pronouns in Chapter 2, where it was shown that they facilitate sentence processing in English. We also know from psycholinguistic research with children that relative clauses are more easily processed if a relative particle is present.)

Chapter 4 also presents evidence that certain linguistic forms are more easily processed by children than others, thus facilitating certain aspects of language acquisition. Operating Principle A is a reflection of the charge to be processible: "Pay attention to the ends of words." In order for languages to be processible by child learners, linguistic markers must occur in positions which children are able to notice and remember. Thus the charge to be processible insures both that language can be used effectively by human beings, and that human children can find their way into the system.

BE QUICK AND EASY

It is not enough simply to be clear and processible—because we are often in a hurry. This third charge to Language allows for human weakness and perversity. Somehow it's hard to keep languages from getting blurry: speakers seem to "smudge" phonology wherever possible, to delete and contract surface forms, and so forth. (Think of the ways in which you REALLY pronounce such things as *would you* and *could you* in rapid speech!) There are many reasons why "cutting corners" is as much a part of human language as are the charges to be clear and processible. A principle of "least effort" (a polite term for "laziness") certainly plays some role. And there are interactive needs to get in a lot of information before the listener gets bored or takes over the conversation. There are also short-term memory constraints which make it necessary to get a message across before the listener (or speaker!) loses track of what is going on.

The charge to be quick and easy competes with the first two charges, as we have already noted. Inflectional systems get blurred and have to be replaced with new formal means which are more clear in their mapping and more processible in terms of surface marking. As children gain linguistic maturity, they speak more rapidly and more sloppily (which, paradoxically, makes them sound more grown-up). It has even been claimed that creole languages are spoken more rapidly than pidgins. The speech of native speakers of Tok Pisin is more rapid and has more reductions and contractions than the speech of fluent non-natives. This phenomenon will obviously have an influence on the form of the language, eventually "wearing away" some of the newly evolving grammatical markers and creating a pressure for the development of other markers to replace them. Language is in constant flux because of the dynamic equilibrium maintained between these competing pressures.

BE EXPRESSIVE

Finally we must attend to the basic goal of all of this linguistic work—to say something to someone. There are two ways in which Language must be expressive. It is necessary to convey basic meanings—that is, to convey propositions made up of meaningful words. This is the bare minimum of communication, needed even by the speakers of Russenorsk. We can refer to it as the charge to be expressive in the SEMANTIC sense. In addition to conveying logical propositions and referential information, however, speakers wish to communicate WELL and EFFECTIVELY. We can refer to this as the charge to be expressive in the RHETORICAL sense. That is to say, a speaker must be able to direct the listener's attention, to take account of his knowledge and expectations; the speaker must have means for surprising, impressing, playing up to, or putting down his conversational partner; he must have linguistic means of expressing relations of status and affiliation between himself and the person he is talking to. All of these rhetorical or pragmatic needs vastly increase the complexity and diversity of linguistic structures, putting strains on the charges to be clear and to be processible. Again, there is an evident competition between the charges.

Be Semantically Expressive

This aspect of expressivity is related to discussions in Chapter 4 of the course of language development. The range of notions discussed by the child is limited by his stage of cognitive development. He will seek out linguistic means of expression of those notions most readily salient or accessible to him, expanding the scope of his linguistic expression as his conceptual scope expands.

All full-fledged languages are fully expressive in the semantic sense, and in the last chapter we have given short shrift to the notion that the meanings embodied in the lexicon or grammar of a language determine the thought patterns of the speakers. The charge to be semantically expressive is a charge TO Language FROM Thought. We do not know what was expressed in primordial languages, and the languages of technologically primitive peoples today are just as rich and complex as our own. However, as pidgin languages elaborate into creoles, one can observe them taking on a greater range of both semantic and rhetorical functions. It is possible that the semantic notions which are always marked in pidgins are also those most salient to children. Study along these lines may reveal a basic semantic "core" to human cognition, and a path of growth from that core. This suggestion has been provocatively posed by Paul Kay and Gillian Sankoff (1974, p. 69):

> Given the hypothesis that there is a certain basic (and small) set of underlying semantic notions which are always grammatically marked, even in the most reduced contact vernaculars [pidgins], and that as communicative functions increase, other markers are introduced, it is possible that in the development of contact vernaculars there exists an ordering in the introduction of such additional markers. For example, prepositions may be ordered such that when a pidgin has only two, one marks genitive and the other has a generalized locative function [think of Russenorsk], with specific locatives (e.g., *in, on, under*) coming later; location may be marked earlier than time; pronominal systems may mark person and number before they mark gender or case, and so on. The general point is that certain semantic notions

which may be more psychologically salient or functionally necessary or both are grammatically marked earlier than others. Contact vernaculars at various stages of development may provide evidence for verifying such notions of universal saliency or function.

I have quoted Kay and Sankoff at length to remind you of the theme of the primacy of cognitive development in determining the course of language development, and to remind you of the theme of universality underlying apparent diversity among the world's languages. The thinking applied here to the development of pidgin and creole languages is consistent with earlier discussions of the work of Piaget and Rosch, and my own crosslinguistic work on child language. You should also be reminded of the discussion in Chapter 3 of the influence of human ways of thinking on the nature of language.

Be Rhetorically Expressive

This charge reflects the discourse constraints raised in Chapter 3, and the repeated references to pragmatic aspects of language throughout the book. It is this charge above all which makes Language as complex as it is. It is no accident that a developing language like Tok Pisin should have to find means of encoding relative clauses, while a contact vernacular like Russenorsk or a two-year-old speech system can manage without relative clauses. In order for Language to be rhetorically expressive, it must be possible to present information in a variety of ways, by focusing on one aspect or another, by guiding or checking the listener's attention, by distinguishing between what is new or old information, expected or unexpected, and so forth.

Pidgin languages and early child speech admirably fulfill the first two charges to Language—to be clear and processible. And these codes are semantically expressive within the needs of their speakers. But when a language acquires a broad range of communicative functions—either through maturity of its speakers in the case of an established language, or creole formation in the case of pidgin languages—it loses this enviable clarity. Why should communicative needs require GRAMMATICAL complexity? Apparently grammar develops—both in creoles and in children—to fulfill more communicative needs than the direct expression of propositional content. Adherence to the first two charges alone would produce a language in which the range of surface expressions for each underlying semantic configuration would be extremely limited. As such, ongoing speech would be as close to a series of underlying propositions as possible— given the time constraints on processing. But speech in the settings of mature and developed communication requires more. As Labov (1971, p. 72) has pointed out, grammar is not just a tool for expressing basic referential propositions. In his words: "Grammar is busy with emphasis, focus, down-shifting and up-grading; it is a way of organizing information and taking alternative points of view." This is true at the level of spoken discourse, and even more in literate discourse, where styles of writing exploit and extend the grammatical possibilities of a language. Everything we have said about the other charges to Language, therefore, must accommodate these rhetorical needs for richness and diversity of linguistic forms.

CONCLUSION

Consider what you know about Language and what you have learned about psycholinguistics. We cannot understand the nature of Language without attending to the complex and contradictory pressures of these four charges. Psycholinguistically, we only know a little bit about the functioning of each of these pressures. Linguistically we are only part-way toward the goal of describing individual languages and discovering general principles. Running through the charges in reverse order, consider what sort of dynamic balance is needed in order to characterize the nature of our common linguistic ability. A fully developed human language must be rhetorically flexible, semantically expressive, rapid in tempo, readily decipherable, and semantically clear. Children have the capacity to construct such languages, and the human mind has the capacity to consistently maintain and adjust Language so that it remains in consonance with all of these goals. We are a long way from knowing the limits of the capacity of scholarly minds to construct an account of this subject which Plato, speaking through Cratylus, called "perhaps the very greatest of all."

APPENDIX

Original German Version of Wittgenstein's Discussion of 'Game'[1]

66. Betrachte z.B. einmal die Vorgänge, die wir "Spiele" nennen. Ich meine Brettspiele, Kartenspiele, Ballspiele, Kampfspiele, usw. Was ist allen diesen gemeinsam?—Sag nicht: "Es MUSS ihnen etwas gemeinsam sein, sonst hiessen sie nicht 'Spiele' "—sondern SCHAU, ob ihnen allen etwas gemeinsam ist.—Denn, wenn du sie anschaust, wirst du zwar nicht etwas sehen, was ALLEN gemeinsam wäre, aber du wirst Ähnlichkeiten, Verwandtschaften, sehen, und zwar eine ganze Reihe. Wie gesagt: denk nicht, sondern schau!—Schau z.B. die Brettspiele an, mit ihren mannigfachen Verwandtschaften. Nun geh zu den Kartenspielen über: hier findest du viele Entsprechungen mit jener ersten Klasse, aber viele gemeinsame Züge verschwinden, andere treten auf. Wenn wir nun zu den Ballspielen übergehen, so bleibt manches Gemeinsame erhalten, aber vieles geht verloren.—Sind sie alle 'UNTERHALTEND'? Vergleiche Schach mit dem Mühlfahren. Oder gibt es überall ein Gewinnen und Verlieren, oder eine Konkurrenz der Spielenden? Denk an die Patiencen. In den Ballspielen gibt es Gewinnen und Verlieren; aber wenn ein Kind den Ball an die Wand wirft und wieder auffängt, so ist dieser Zug verschwunden. Schau, welche Rolle Geschick und Glück spielen. Und wie verschieden ist Geschick im Schachspiel und Geschick im Tennisspiel. Denk nun an die Reigenspiele: Hier ist das Element der Unterhaltung, aber wie viele der anderen Charakterzüge sind verschwunden! Und so können wir durch die vielen, vielen anderen Gruppen von Spielen gehen, Ähnlichkeiten auftauchen und verschwinden sehen.

Und das Ergebnis dieser Betrachtung lautet nun: Wir sehen ein kompliziertes Netz von Ähnlichkeiten, die einander übergreifen und kreuzen. Ähnlichkeiten im Grossen und Kleinen.

67. Ich kann diese Ähnlichkeiten nicht besser charakterisieren als durch das Wort "Familienähnlichkeiten"; denn so übergreifen und kreuzen sich die verschiedenen Ähnlichkeiten, die zwischen den Gliedern einer Familie bestehen: Wuchs, Gesichtszüge, Augenfarbe, Gang, Temperament, etc. etc.—Und ich werde sagen: die 'Spiele' bilden eine Familie.

---

1. From L. Wittgenstein, *Schriften*. Frankfurt am Main: Suhrkamp Verlag, 1960. Pp. 324-25.

GLOSSARY

ACCUSATIVE: the grammatical category of the direct object of a verb (e.g., as marked in English active sentences by the position following the verb: *the boy kissed* THE GIRL)

ANOMALY: an expression which does not seem to make sense (e.g., *colorless green ideas sleep furiously*)

APHASIA: speech disorder caused by brain damage

ARGUMENT: in generative semantics, the notion or notions which, in relation to a PREDICATE, constitute a PROPOSITION (e.g., in a proposition such as 'she gives milk to the cat', the predicate 'give' relates three arguments: an agent—'she', an object—'milk', and a recipient—'the cat')

CASE GRAMMAR: an approach to grammar which attempts to derive the surface structures of sentences from underlying semantic structures in the form of verbs and nouns in particular case roles to those verbs (e.g., agent, object, instrument); an early form of GENERATIVE SEMANTICS, developed by Charles Fillmore

CHAIN MODELS: a model of language in which each linguistic element is directly determined by the immediately preceding element

CLAUSE: a phrase which corresponds to an underlying proposition

COGNITION: the processes and structures of knowing, and the branch of psychology which studies knowing (including the study of perception, attention, memory, problem solving, thinking, language)

COMPETENCE: knowledge or ability which one infers to be present in a person on the basis of his or her observable behavior (PERFORMANCE)

CONSTITUENT: a structured unit of a sentence, generally replaceable by a single word performing the same function as the unit (e.g., a noun phrase, replaceable by a single noun: A PSYCHOLINGUIST FROM BERKELEY *wrote this definition*/SLOBIN *wrote this definition*)

CREOLE LANGUAGE: a language which arose as a PIDGIN but has come to be used as a native language by children; a pidgin language that has developed into a primary language of a speech community

DEEP STRUCTURE: the organization of a sentence which is closest to its underlying meaning

EMBEDDING: the insertion of one grammatical structure into another (e.g., the embedding of a relative clause between the subject and verb of a sentence: *the story* THAT HE TOLD *was amusing*)

EMPIRICISM: (1) the doctrine that knowledge is derived from sense experience (as opposed to NATIVISM) ("the empiricist doctrine"); (2) the method of gathering knowledge through processes of controlled observation and experimentation ("the empirical method")

FUNCTION WORD: a word which does not make direct reference, but rather serves to mark words grammatically or to mark grammatical relations between words. Examples of function words (sometimes also called *functors*) are articles, prepositions, conjunctions.

GENERATIVE SEMANTICS: an approach to grammar which attempts to derive the surface structures of sentences from underlying semantic structures (often in the form of PROPOSITIONS defined as PREDICATE-ARGUMENT structures)

GRAMMAR: the study of linguistic structure, traditionally embracing morphology (word formation) and syntax (sentence formation); often including additional areas of linguistic structure: semantics (meaning), pragmatics (social use), phonology (sound structure)

INFLECTION: a particle affixed to a word (e.g., prefix or suffix) encoding grammatical relations, such as number (plural *-s*), tense (past *-ed*), case (accusative inflection in various languages), etc.

LATERALIZATION: the concentration of a particular mental function in one of the two hemispheres of the brain

LEXICALIZE: to express a notion in a word

LEXICON: the vocabulary, or total stock of words of a language, or of an individual speaker

LINGUISTIC UNIVERSAL: an aspect of language thought to occur in all languages

MORPHOLOGY: the study of the meaningful parts of words and the linguistic means for forming words

MOTOR CORTEX: the portion of the cerebral cortex which controls muscular movements

NATIVISM: the doctrine that (some) knowledge is innate (inborn), and not derived from experience

PERFORMANCE: behavior which can be observed and recorded; the overt manifestation of COMPETENCE

PHONEME MONITORING: a research technique in which the listener is to indicate, as quickly as possible, the occurrence of a word beginning with a given sound. Response delay is considered to be a reflection of difficulty of speech processing at the point where the given sound occurs.

PHONOLOGY: the study of the sound systems of languages

PHRASE STRUCTURE GRAMMAR: a model of language in which constituents of sentences are derived by the successive application of formational rules

PIDGIN LANGUAGE: a simplified language which arises in the course of interaction between the speakers of two different languages; a contact vernacular

POSTPOSITION: a grammatical particle which serves the same function as a preposition, but comes after the noun which it modifies

PRAGMATICS: the branch of the study of language concerned with the social and interpersonal uses and effects of speech

PREDICATE: in generative semantics, the notion which, in relation to one or more ARGUMENTS, constitutes a PROPOSITION (e.g., the predicate 'give' relates the arguments of an agent, an object, and a recipient in a proposition such as 'she gives milk to the cat')

PROCESSING STRATEGIES: the procedures used by a listener in perceiving and interpreting linguistic messages, and the procedures used by a speaker in constructing linguistic messages to communicate his or her intentions

PROPOSITION: an underlying semantic structure consisting of a PREDICATE and its ARGUMENT(S)

RECALL: voluntary remembering of a past experience or of knowledge stored in memory

RECOGNITION: remembering of a past experience or of knowledge stored in memory by re-experiencing the original situation in whole or in part

SEMANTICS: the study of the structures of meaning underlying words and sentences

SURFACE STRUCTURE: the organization of a sentence which is closest to its spoken or written form

SYNTAX: the study of the means of putting words and parts of words together to form sentences

TRANSFORMATIONAL GRAMMAR: an approach to grammar, developed by Noam Chomsky, in which underlying, or DEEP syntactic structures are transformed into SURFACE syntactic structures of sentences. Deep structures relate to meanings and surface structures relate to sounds.

BIBLIOGRAPHY

Abrahamsen, A. A. *Child language: An interdisciplinary guide to theory and research.* Baltimore: University Park Press, 1977.

Abrams, K., & Bever, T. G. Syntactic structure modifies attention during speech perception and recognition. *Quarterly Journal of Experimental Psychology,* 1969, *21,* 280-290.

Akmajian, A., & Heny, F. *An introduction to the principles of transformational syntax.* Cambridge, Mass.: M.I.T. Press, 1975.

Allport, G. W., & Postman, L. *The psychology of rumor.* New York: Henry Holt & Co., 1947.

Anderson, J. R., & Bower, G. H. *Human associative memory.* Washington, D.C.: V. H. Winston & Sons, 1973.

Antinucci, F., & Parisi, D. Early language acquisition: A model and some data. In C. A. Ferguson & D. I. Slobin (Eds.), *Studies of child language development.* New York: Holt, Rinehart & Winston, 1973. Pp. 607-619.

Antinucci, F., & Parisi, D. Early semantic development in child language. In E. H. Lenneberg & E. Lenneberg (Eds.), *Foundations of language development: A multidisciplinary approach* (Vol. 1). New York: Academic Press, Inc., 1975. Pp. 189-202.

Augustine, Saint. *The confessions of Saint Augustine.* (E. B. Pusey, Trans.). New York: The Modern Library, 1949.

Bach, E., & Harms, R. T. *Universals in linguistic theory.* New York: Holt, Rinehart & Winston, 1968.

Bar-Adon, A., & Leopold, W. F. (Eds.). *Child language: A book of readings.* Englewood Cliffs, N.J.: Prentice-Hall, Inc., 1971.

Bartlett, F. C. *Remembering: A study in experimental and social psychology.* Cambridge: Cambridge University Press, 1932.

Bates, E. *Language and context: The acquisition of pragmatics.* New York: Academic Press, Inc., 1976.

Bates, E. *The emergence of symbols: Does ontogeny recapitulate phylogeny?* Paper delivered at Minnesota Symposium on Child Psychology, University of Minnesota, Minneapolis, 1977. [Extended version published as Bates, E., with L. Benigni, I. Bretherton, L. Camaioni, & V. Volterra. *The emergence of symbols: Cognition and communication in infancy.* New York: Academic Press, Inc., 1979.]

Bates, E., Benigni, L., Bretherton, I., Camaioni, L., & Volterra, V. From gesture to the first word: On cognitive and social prerequisites. In M. Lewis & L. Rosenblum (Eds.), *Interaction, conversation and the development of language.* New York: John Wiley & Sons, Inc., 1977. Pp. 247-307.

Bates, E., Camaioni, L., & Volterra, V. The acquisition of performatives prior to speech. *Merrill-Palmer Quarterly,* 1975, *21,* 205-226.

Behagel, O. *Deutsche Syntax: eine geschichtliche Darstellung.* Heidelberg: Carl Winter, 1923.

Bellugi-Klima, U. Linguistic mechanisms underlying child speech. In E. M. Zale (Ed.), *Proceedings of the conference on language and language behavior.* New York: Appleton-Century-Crofts, 1968.

Berko, J. The child's learning of English morphology. *Word*, 1958, *14*, 150-177. [Reprinted in S. Saporta (Ed.), *Psycholinguistics: A book of readings*. New York: Holt, Rinehart & Winston, 1961. Pp. 359-375.] [Reprinted in L. Bloom (Ed.), *Readings in language development*. New York: John Wiley & Sons, Inc., 1978. Pp. 39-59.]

Berlin, B., & Kay, P. *Basic color terms: Their universality and evolution*. Berkeley & Los Angeles: University of California Press, 1969.

Bever, T. G. The cognitive basis for linguistic structures. In J. R. Hayes (Ed.), *Cognition and the development of language*. New York: John Wiley & Sons, Inc., 1970. Pp. 279-352.

Bever, T. G. Discussion paper: Some theoretical and empirical issues that arise if we insist on distinguishing language and thought. In D. Aaronson & R. W. Rieber (Eds.), *Developmental psycholinguistics and communication disorders*. New York: New York Academy of Sciences, 1975. Pp. 76-83.

Bever, T. G., & Chiarello, R. J. Cerebral dominance in musicians and nonmusicians. *Science*, 1974, *185*, 137-139.

Black, M. (Ed.). *The importance of language*. Englewood Cliffs, N.J.: Prentice-Hall, Inc., 1962.

Bloom, L. M. *Language development: Form and function in emerging grammars*. Cambridge, Mass.: M.I.T. Press, 1970.

Bloom, L. *One word at a time: The use of single word utterances before syntax*. The Hague: Mouton Publishers, 1973.

Bloom, L. (Ed.). *Readings in language development*. New York: John Wiley & Sons, Inc., 1978.

Bloom L. M., Hood, L., & Lightbown, P. Imitation in language development: If, when and why. *Cognitive Psychology*, 1974, *6*, 380-420. [Reprinted in L. Bloom (Ed.), *Readings in language development*. New York: John Wiley & Sons, Inc., 1978. Pp. 452-488.]

Bloom, L., & Lahey, M. *Language development and language disorders*. New York: John Wiley & Sons, Inc., 1978.

Bloom, L. M., Lightbown, P., & Hood, L. Structure and variation in child language. *Monographs of the Society for Research in Child Development*, 1975, *40* (Serial No. 160).

Blount, B. G. *Acquisition of language by Luo children*. Unpublished doctoral dissertation, University of California, Berkeley, 1969. [Working Paper No. 19 (1969), Language-Behavior Research Laboratory, University of California, Berkeley.]

Blumenthal, A. L. *Language and psychology: Historical aspects of psycholinguistics*. New York: John Wiley & Sons, Inc., 1970.

Bolinger, D. L. *Aspects of language* (2nd ed.). New York: Harcourt Brace Jovanovich, Inc., 1975.

Bower, G. H. Experiments on story understanding and recall. *Quarterly Journal of Experimental Psychology*, 1976, *28*, 511-534.

Bowerman, M. *Early syntactic development: A cross-linguistic study with special reference to Finnish*. Cambridge: Cambridge University Press, 1973.

Bowerman, M. Semantic factors in the acquisition of rules for word use and sentence construction. In D. M. Morehead & A. E. Morehead (Eds.), *Normal and deficient child language*. Baltimore: University Park Press, 1976. Pp. 99-179.

Bowerman, M. Semantic and syntactic development: A review of what, when, and how in language and acquisition. In R. L. Schiefelbusch (Ed.), *Bases of language intervention*. Baltimore: University Park Press, 1978.

Bowerman, M. Cross-cultural perspectives on language development. In H. C. Triandis (Ed.), *Handbook of cross-cultural psychology* (Vol. III). Boston: Allyn & Bacon, in press.

Braine, M. D. S. The ontogeny of English phrase structure: The first phase.

Language, 1963, *39,* 1-13. [Reprinted in C. A. Ferguson & D. I. Slobin (Eds.), *Studies of child language development.* New York: Holt, Rinehart & Winston, 1973. Pp. 407-420.] [Reprinted in L. Bloom (Ed.), *Readings in language development.* New York: John Wiley & Sons, Inc., 1978. Pp. 60-73.]

Braine, M. D. S. Children's first word combinations. *Monographs of the Society for Research in Child Development,* 1976, *41* (Serial No. 164).

Bransford, J. D., Barclay, J. R., & Franks, J. J. Sentence memory: A constructive versus interpretive approach. *Cognitive Psychology,* 1972, *3,* 193-209.

Bresnan, J. A realistic transformational grammar. In M. Halle, J. Bresnan, & G. A. Miller (Eds.), *Linguistic theory and psychological reality.* Cambridge, Mass.: M.I.T. Press, 1978.

Bridgman, P. W. *The nature of physical theory.* Princeton, N.J.: Princeton University Press, 1936.

Broch, O. Russenorsk. *Archiv für slavische Philologie,* 1927, *41,* 209-262.(a)

Broch, O. Russenorsk. *Maal og mine: Norske studier,* 1927, 82-130.(b)

Broch, O. Russenorsk tekstmateriale. *Maal og mine: Norske studier,* 1930, 113-140.

Bronckart, J. P., & Sinclair, H. Time, tense, and aspect. *Cognition,* 1973, *2,* 107-130.

Brown, R. *Social psychology.* New York: The Free Press, 1965.

Brown, R. *A first language: The early stages.* Cambridge, Mass.: Harvard University Press, 1973.

Brown, R. Reference: In memorial tribute to Eric Lenneberg. *Cognition,* 1976, *4,* 125-153.

Brown, R., & Bellugi, U. Three processes in the child's acquisition of syntax. *Harvard Educational Review,* 1964, *34,* 133-151. [Reprinted in E. H. Lenneberg (Ed.), *New directions in the study of language.* Cambridge, Mass.: M.I.T. Press, 1964. Pp. 131-162.] [Reprinted in R. Brown, *Psycholinguistics.* New York: The Free Press, 1970. Pp. 75-99.]

Brown, R., Cazden, C. B., & Bellugi, U. The child's grammar from I to III. In J. P. Hill (Ed.), *Minnesota Symposia on Child Psychology* (Vol. 2). Minneapolis: University of Minnesota Press, 1969, Pp. 28-73. [Also in R. Brown, *Psycholinguistics.* New York: The Free Press, 1970. Pp. 100-154.] [Also in C. A. Ferguson & D. I. Slobin (Eds.), *Studies of child language development.* New York: Holt, Rinehart & Winston, 1973. Pp. 295-332.]

Bruner, J. S. The ontogenesis of speech acts. *Journal of Child Language,* 1975, *2,* 1-19.

Bruner, J. S., Olver, R. R., Greenfield, P. M., et al. *Studies in cognitive growth.* New York: John Wiley & Sons, Inc., 1966.

Cairns, H. S., & Cairns, C. E. *Psycholinguistics: A cognitive view of language.* New York: Holt, Rinehart & Winston, 1976.

Caplan, D. Clause boundaries and recognition latencies for words in sentences. *Perception and Psychophysics,* 1972, *12,* 73-76.

Carmichael, L., Hogan, H. P., & Walter, A. A. An experimental study of the effect of language on the reproduction of visually perceived form. *Journal of Experimental Psychology,* 1932, *15,* 73-86.

Carpenter, P. A., & Just, M. A. Integrative processes in comprehension. In D. LaBerge & S. J. Samuels (Eds.), *Basic processes in reading: Perception and comprehension.* Hillsdale, N.J.: Lawrence Erlbaum Associates, 1977.

Carroll, J. B. (Ed.). *Language, thought, and reality: Selected writings of Benjamin Lee Whorf.* Cambridge, Mass.: The Technology Press of Massachusetts Institute of Technology / New York: John Wiley & Sons, Inc., 1956.

Carroll, J. B., & Casagrande, J. B. The function of language classification. In E. E. Maccoby, T. M. Newcomb, & E. L. Hartley (Eds.), *Readings in social psychology* (3rd ed.). New York: Holt, Rinehart & Winston, 1958. Pp. 18-31.

Carroll, J. M., & Bever, T. G. Sentence comprehension: A case study in the relation of knowledge and perception. In E. C. Carterette & M. P. Friedman (Eds.), *Handbook of perception.* Vol. 7, *Language and speech.* New York: Academic Press, Inc., 1976. Pp. 209-344.

Carter, A. L. Development of the presyntactic communication system: A case study. *Journal of Child Language,* 1975, *2,* 233-250.

Chafe, W. L. Language and consciousness. *Language,* 1974, *50,* 111-133.

Chafe, W. L. Givenness, contrastiveness, definiteness, subjects, topics, and point of view. In C. N. Li (Ed.), *Subject and topic.* New York: Academic Press, Inc., 1976. Pp. 25-55.

Chapin, P. G., Smith, T. S., & Abrahamson, A. A. Two factors in perceptual segmentation of speech. *Journal of Verbal Learning and Verbal Behavior,* 1972, *11,* 164-173.

Chevalier-Skolnikoff, S. The ontogeny of primate intelligence: Implications for communicative potential. A preliminary report. In S. Harnad, H. Steklis, & J. Lancaster (Eds.), *Origins of language and speech.* New York: New York Academy of Sciences, 1976.

Chomsky, N. *Syntactic structures.* The Hague: Mouton Publishers, 1957.

Chomsky, N. A review of *Verbal Behavior,* by B. F. Skinner. *Language,* 1959, *35,* 26-58. [Reprinted in J. A. Fodor & J. J. Katz (Eds.), *The structure of language: Readings in the philosophy of language.* Englewood Cliffs, N.J.: Prentice-Hall, Inc., 1964. Pp. 547-578.] [Reprinted in L. A. Jakobovits & M. S. Miron (Eds.), *Readings in the psychology of language.* Englewood Cliffs, N.J.: Prentice-Hall, Inc., 1967. Pp. 142-171.]

Chomsky, N. *Current issues in linguistic theory.* The Hague: Mouton Publishers, 1964. [Also in J. A. Fodor & J. J. Katz (Eds.), *The structure of language: Readings in the philosophy of language.* Englewood Cliffs, N.J.: Prentice-Hall, Inc., 1964. Pp. 50-118.]

Chomsky, N. *Aspects of the theory of syntax.* Cambridge, Mass.: M.I.T. Press, 1965.

Chomsky, N. *Language and mind.* New York: Harcourt Brace Jovanovich, Inc., 1968.

Chomsky, N. Remarks on nominalization. In R. A. Jacobs & P. S. Rosenbaum (Eds.), *Readings in English transformational grammar.* Boston: Ginn & Co., 1970. Pp. 184-221.

Chomsky, N. Some empirical issues in the theory of transformational grammar. In S. Peters (Ed.), *Goals of linguistic theory.* Englewood Cliffs, N.J.: Prentice-Hall, Inc., 1972.

Chomsky, N. *Reflections on language.* New York: Pantheon Books, 1975.

Chomsky, N. *Essays on form and interpretation.* Amsterdam: Elsevier North-Holland, Inc., 1977.

Chukovsky, K. *From two to five.* Berkeley & Los Angeles: University of California Press, 1963. [Edited translation by Miriam Morton of *Ot dvuk do pyati.* Moscow: Gos. Izd-vo Detskoy Literatury, 1961.]

Clark, E. V. Non-linguistic strategies and the acquisition of word meanings. *Cognition,* 1973, *2,* 161-182.

Clark, E. V. Knowledge, context, and strategy in the acquisition of meaning. In D. P. Dato (Ed.), *Georgetown University round table on languages and linguistics 1975.* Washington, D.C.: Georgetown University Press, 1975. Pp. 77-98.

Clark, E. V. Strategies and the mapping problem in first language acquisition. In J. Macnamara (Ed.), *Language learning and thought.* New York: Academic Press, Inc., 1977. Pp. 147-168.

Clark, E. V., & Clark, H. H. Universals, relativity, and language processing. In J. H. Greenberg (Ed.), *Universals of human language.* Vol. 1, *Method and theory.* Stanford, Calif.: Stanford University Press, 1978. Pp. 225-278.

Clark, H. H., & Clark, E. V. *Psychology and language: An introduction to psycholinguistics.* New York: Harcourt Brace Jovanovich, Inc., 1977.

Clark, H. H., & Haviland, S. E. Comprehension and the given-new contract. In R. O. Freedle (Ed.), *Discourse production and comprehension.* Norwood, N.J.: Ablex Publishing, 1977. Pp. 1-40.

Cole, M., & Bruner, J. S. Cultural differences and inferences about psychological processes. *American Psychologist,* 1971, *26,* 867-876.

Cole, M., & Scribner, S. *Culture and thought: A psychological introduction.* New York: John Wiley & Sons, Inc., 1974.

Cole, P., & Morgan, J. L. (Eds.). *Syntax and semantics.* Vol. 3, *Speech acts.* New York: Seminar Press, 1975.

Cooper, W. E., & Ross, J. World order. In R. Grossman, L. San, & T. Vance (Eds.), *Papers from the parasession on functionalism.* Chicago: Chicago Linguistic Society, 1975.

Cromer, R. F. The development of language and cognition: The cognition hypothesis. In B. Foss (Ed.), *New perspectives in child development.* Harmondsworth, England: Penguin Books, 1974. Pp. 184-252.

Cromer, R. F. The cognitive hypothesis of language acquisition and its implications for child language deficiency. In D. M. Morehead & A. E. Morehead (Eds.), *Normal and deficient child language.* Baltimore: University Park Press, 1976. Pp. 283-334.

Curtiss, S. *Genie: A psycholinguistic study of a modern-day "wild child."* New York: Academic Press, Inc., 1977.

Dale, P. S. *Language development: Structure and function* (2nd ed.). New York: Holt, Rinehart & Winston, 1976.

DeCamp, D., & Hancock, I. F. (Eds.). *Pidgins and creoles: Current trends and prospects.* Washington, D.C.: Georgetown University Press, 1974.

Dennis, M., & Whitaker, H. A. Hemispheric equipotentiality and language acquisition. In S. J. Segalowitz & F. A. Gruber (Eds.), *Language development and neurological theory.* New York: Academic Press, Inc., 1977. Pp. 93-106.

Descartes, R. *Discourse on method.* 1637. [English translation by L. J. Lafleur of *Discours de la méthode.* New York: The Liberal Arts Press, 1956.]

de Villiers, J. G., & de Villiers, P. A. A cross-sectional study of the development of grammatical morphemes in child speech. *Journal of Psycholinguistic Research,* 1973, *2,* 267-278.

de Villiers, J. G., & de Villiers, P. A. *Language acquisition.* Cambridge, Mass.: Harvard University Press, 1978.

Dowty, D. On the syntax and semantics of the atomic predicate CAUSE. *Papers from the Sixth Regional Meeting of the Chicago Linguistic Society,* 1972.

Dresher, B. E., & Hornstein, N. On some supposed contributions of artificial intelligence to the scientific study of language. *Cognition,* 1976, *4,* 321-398.

Dresher, B. E., & Hornstein, N. Reply to Schank and Wilensky. *Cognition,* 1977, *5,* 147-150.

Dresher, B. E., & Hornstein, N. Reply to Winograd. *Cognition,* 1977, *5,* 377-391.

Edwards, D. Sensory-motor intelligence and semantic relations in early child grammar. *Cognition,* 1973, *2,* 395-434.

Eimas, P. D. Auditory and linguistic processing of cues for place of articulation by infants. *Perception and Psychophysics,* 1974, *16,* 513-521.

Eimas, P. D., Siqueland, E. R., Jusczyk, P., & Vigorito, J. Speech perception in infants. *Science,* 1971, *171,* 303-306. [Reprinted in L. Bloom (Ed.), *Readings in language development.* New York: John Wiley & Sons, Inc., 1978. Pp. 87-93.]

Eliot, T. S. *The complete poems and plays: 1909-1950.* New York: Harcourt Brace & Co., 1958.

El'konin, D. B. General course of development in the child of the grammatical structure of the Russian language (according to A. N. Gvozdev). In C. A. Ferguson & D. I. Slobin (Eds.), *Studies of child language development.* New York: Holt, Rinehart & Winston, 1973. Pp. 565-594. [English translation by

D. I. Slobin of pp. 34-61 of El'konin, D. B. *Razvitiye rechi v doshkol'nom vozraste*. Moscow: Izd-vo Akademii Pedagogicheskikh Nauk RSFSR, 1958.]

Entus, A. K. Hemispheric asymmetry in processing of dichotically presented speech and nonspeech stimuli by infants. In S. J. Segalowitz & F. A. Gruber (Eds.), *Language development and neurological theory*. New York: Academic Press, Inc., 1977. Pp. 64-73.

[Ervin-Tripp] Ervin, S. M. Imitation and structural change in children's language. In E. H. Lenneberg (Ed.), *New directions in the study of language*. Cambridge, Mass.: M.I.T. Press, 1964. Pp. 163-189. [Reprinted in C. A. Ferguson & D. I. Slobin (Eds.), *Studies of child language development*. New York: Holt, Rinehart & Winston, 1973. Pp. 391-406.]

Ervin-Tripp, S. M., & Mitchell-Kernan, C. (Eds.). *Child discourse*. New York: Academic Press, Inc., 1977.

Ferguson, C. A., & Slobin, D. I. (Eds.). *Studies of child language development*. New York: Holt, Rinehart and Winston, 1973.

Fillmore, C. J. The case for case. In E. Bach & R. T. Harms (Eds.), *Universals in linguistic theory*. New York: Holt, Rinehart & Winston, 1968. Pp. 1-90.

Fishman, J. A. A systematization of the Whorfian hypothesis. *Behavioral Science*, 1960, *5*, 1-29.

Fodor, J. A., & Bever, T. G. The psychological reality of linguistic segments. *Journal of Verbal Learning and Verbal Behavior*, 1965, *4*, 414-420.

Fodor, J. A., Bever, T. G., & Garrett, M. F. *The psychology of language: An introduction to psycholinguistics and generative grammar*. New York: McGraw-Hill Book Co., 1974.

Fodor, J. A., & Garrett, M. F. Some syntactic determinants of sentential complexity. *Perception and Psychophysics*, 1967, *2*, 289-296.

Fodor, J. A., Garrett, M. F., and Bever, T. G. Some syntactic determinants of sentential complexity, II: Verb structure. *Perception and Psychophysics*, 1968, *3*, 453-461.

Foss, D. J. Decision processes during sentence comprehension: Effects of lexical item difficulty and position upon decision times. *Journal of Verbal Learning and Verbal Behavior*, 1969, *8*, 457-462.

Foss, D. J. Some effects of ambiguity upon sentence comprehension. *Journal of Verbal Learning and Verbal Behavior*, 1970, *9*, 699-706.

Foss, D. J., & Hakes, D. T. *Psycholinguistics: An introduction to the psychology of language*. Englewood Cliffs, N.J.: Prentice-Hall, Inc., 1978.

Fredriksen, C. H. Effects of task induced cognitive operations on comprehension and memory processes. In R. Freedle & J. Carroll (Eds.), *Language comprehension and the acquisition of knowledge*. Washington, D.C.: Winston, 1972.

Fredriksen, C. H. Effects of context-induced processing operations on semantic information acquired from discourse. *Cognitive Psychology*, 1975, *7*, 139-166.

Fromkin, V., & Rodman, R. *An introduction to language* (2nd ed.). New York: Holt, Rinehart & Winston, 1978.

Furth, H. G. Research with the deaf: Implications for language and cognition. *Psychological Bulletin*, 1964, *62*, 145-164.

Furth, H. G. *Thinking without language: Psychological implications of deafness*. New York: The Free Press, 1966.

Gardner, B. T., & Gardner, R. A. Two-way communication with an infant chimpanzee. In A. M. Schrier & F. Stollnitz (Eds.), *Behavior of nonhuman primates* (Vol. 4). New York: Academic Press, Inc., 1971. Pp. 117-184.

Gardner, B. T., & Gardner, R. A. Comparing the early utterances of child and chimpanzee. In A. Pick (Ed.), *Minneosta Symposia on Child Psychology*. (Vol. 8). Minneapolis: University of Minnesota Press, 1974. Pp. 3-23.

Garrett, M. F. The analysis of sentence production. In G. H. Bower (Ed.), *The psychology of learning and motivation*, Vol. 9. New York: Academic Press,

Inc., 1975. Pp. 133-177.

Garrett, M. F., Bever, T. G., & Fodor, J. A. The active use of grammar in speech perception. *Perception and Psychophysics,* 1966, *1,* 30-32.

Gay, J., & Cole, M. *The new mathematics and an old culture.* New York: Holt, Rinehart & Winston, 1967.

Gazzaniga, M. S. The split brain in man. *Scientific American,* 1967, *217,* 24-29.

Gazzaniga, M. S. *The bisected brain.* New York: Appleton, 1970.

Gazzaniga, M. S., & Hillyard, S. A. Language and speech capacity of the right hemisphere. *Neuropsychologia,* 1971, *9,* 273-280.

Geschwind, N. Disconnexion syndromes in animals and man. *Brain,* 1965, *88,* 237-294, 585-644.

Geschwind, N. Language and the brain. *Scientific American,* 1972, *226,* 76-83.

Geschwind, N., & Levitsky, W. Human brain: Left-right asymmetries in temporal speech region. *Science,* 1968, *161,* 186-187.

Ghiselin, B. *The creative process.* New York: Mentor Books, 1955.

Givón, T. Serial verbs and syntactic change: Niger-Congo. In C. N. Li (Ed.), *Word order and word order change.* Austin: University of Texas Press, 1975. Pp. 47-112.

Givón, T. (Ed.). *Syntax and semantics.* Vol. 12, *Discourse and syntax.* New York: Academic Press, Inc., 1979.

Glanzer, M., & Clark, W. H. The verbal-loop hypothesis: Conventional figures. *American Journal of Psychology,* 1964, *77,* 621-626.

Goldin-Meadow, S. Structure in a manual communication system developed without a conventional language model: Language without a helping hand. In H. Whitaker & H. A. Whitaker (Eds.), *Studies in neurolinguistics* (Vol. 4). New York: Academic Press, Inc., in press.

Goldin-Meadow, S., & Feldman, H. The development of language-like communication without a language model. *Science,* 1977, *197,* 401-403.

Goodglass, H., & Geschwind, N. Language disorders (aphasia). In E. C. Carterette & M. P. Friedman (Eds.), *Handbook of perception.* Vol. 7. *Language and speech.* New York: Academic Press, Inc., 1976. Pp. 389-428.

Goodglass, H., & Kaplan, E. *The assessment of aphasia and related disorders.* Philadelphia: Lea & Febiger, 1972.

Gordon, D., & Lakoff, G. Conversational postulates. In *Papers from the Seventh Regional Meeting, Chicago Linguistic Society,* 1971. Pp. 63-84. [Reprinted in P. Cole & J. Morgan (Eds.), *Syntax and semantics.* Vol. 3, *Speech acts.* New York: Seminar Press, 1975.]

Gough, P. B. Grammatical transformations and speed of understanding. *Journal of Verbal Learning and Verbal Behavior,* 1965, *4,* 107-111.

Gough, P. B. The verification of sentences: The effects of delay of evidence and sentence length. *Journal of Verbal Learning and Verbal Behavior,* 1966, *5,* 492-496.

Greenberg, J. H. Some universals of grammar with particular reference to the order of meaningful elements. In J. H. Greenberg (Ed.), *Universals of language.* Cambridge, Mass.: M.I.T. Press, 1963. Pp. 58-90.

Greenberg, J. H. Language universals. In T. A. Sebeok (Ed.), *Current trends in linguistics* (Vol. 3). The Hague: Mouton Publishers, 1966. Pp. 61-112. [Also published separately by Mouton Publishers: Series Minor, Nr. LIX, 1966.]

Greenberg, J. H. (Ed.). *Universals of human language.* Vol. 1, *Method and theory.* Vol. 2, *Phonology.* Vol. 3, *Word structure.* Vol. 4, *Syntax.* Stanford, Calif.: Stanford University Press, 1978.

Greenberg, J. H., Osgood, C. E., & Jenkins, J. J. Memorandum concerning language universals presented to the Conference on Language Universals, Gould House, Dobbs Ferry, N.Y., April 13-15, 1961. In J. H. Greenberg (Ed.), *Universals of language* (2nd ed.). Cambridge, Mass.: M.I.T. Press, 1966. Pp. xv-xxvii.

Greenfield, P. M., & Smith, J. H. *The structure of communication in early language development.* New York: Academic Press, Inc., 1976.

Grice, H. P. William James Lectures, Harvard University, 1967. Published in part as "Logic and conversation." In P. Cole & J. L. Morgan (Eds.), *Syntax and semantics.* Vol. 3, *Speech acts.* New York: Seminar Press, 1975. Pp. 41-58.

Gvozdev, A. N. *Formirovaniye u rebenka grammaticheskogo stroya russkogo yazyka.* Moscow: Izd-vo Akademii Pedagogicheskikh Nauk RSFSR, 1949. [Reprinted in A. N. Gvozdev, *Voprosy izucheniya detskoy rechi.* Moscow: Izd-vo Akademii Pedagogicheskikh Nauk RSFSR, 1961. Pp. 149-467.]

Haggard, M. P., & Parkinson, A. M. Stimulus and task factors as determinants of ear advantages. *Quarterly Journal of Experimental Psychology,* 1971, *23,* 168-177.

Hakes, D. T. Effects of reducing complement constructions on sentence comprehension. *Journal of Verbal Learning and Verbal Behavior,* 1972, *11,* 278-286.

Hakes, D. T., & Cairns, H. S. Sentence comprehension and relative pronouns. *Perception & Psychophysics,* 1970, *8,* 5-8.

Halliday, M. A. K. *Learning how to mean: Explorations in the development of language.* London: Edward Arnold, 1975.

Harnad, S., Steklis, H., & Lancaster, J. (Eds.). *Origins of language and speech.* New York: New York Academy of Sciences, 1976.

Haviland, S. E., & Clark, H. H. What's new? Acquiring new information as a process in comprehension. *Journal of Verbal Learning and Verbal Behavior,* 1974, *13,* 512-521.

Hawkins, J. A. Word order change in relation to the logical status of linguistic universals. Unpublished paper, Department of Linguistics, UCLA, 1976.

Hayes, J. R. (Ed.). *Cognition and the development of language.* New York: John Wiley & Sons, Inc., 1970.

Hayes, K. J., & Hayes, C. Intellectual development of a home-raised chimpanzee. *Proceedings of the American Philosophical Society,* 1951, *95,* 105-109.

Heider, E. R. [Rosch, E.] Universals in color naming and memory. *Journal of Experimental Psychology,* 1972, *93,* 10-20.

Heider, E. R. [Rosch, E.], & Olivier, D. C. The structure of the color space in naming and memory for two languages. *Cognitive Psychology,* 1972, *3,* 337-354.

Herman, D. T., Lawless, R. H., & Marshall, R. W. Variables in the effect of language on the reproduction of visually perceived forms. *Perceptual and Motor Skills,* 1957, *7, Monograph Supplement 2,* 171-186. [Reprinted in S. Saporta (Ed.), *Psycholinguistics: A book of readings.* New York: Holt, Rinehart & Winston, 1961. Pp. 537-551.]

Hockett, C. F. Chinese vs. English: An exploration of the Whorfian thesis. In H. Hoijer (Ed.), *Language in culture.* Chicago: The University of Chicago Press, 1954.

Hollos, M. *Growing up in Flathill: Social environment and cognitive development.* Oslo: Universitetsforlaget, 1974.

Hollos, M., & Cowan, P. A. Social isolation and cognitive development: Logical operations and role-taking abilities in three Norwegian social settings. *Child Development,* 1973, *44,* 630-641.

Huttenlocher, J. The origins of language comprehension. In R. L. Solso (Ed.), *Theories in cognitive psychology.* Potomac, Md.: Lawrence Erlbaum Associates, 1974. Pp. 331-368.

Huxley, A. Words and their meanings. In M. Black (Ed.), *The importance of language.* Englewood Cliffs, N.J.: Prentice-Hall, Inc., 1962. Pp. 1-12.

Hymes, D. H. (Ed.). *Pidginization and creolization of languages.* Cambridge and New York: Cambridge University Press, 1971.

Jackendoff, R. S. *Semantic interpretation in generative grammar.* Cambridge, Mass.: M.I.T. Press, 1972.

Jakobson, R. Linguistic types of aphasia. In R. Jakobson, *Selected Writings II.* The Hague: Mouton Publishers, 1971.

James, W. *Psychology: Briefer course.* New York: Henry Holt & Co., 1892.

Jarvella, R. J. Syntactic processing of connected speech. *Journal of Verbal Learning and Verbal Behavior,* 1971, *10,* 409-416.

Jenkins, J. J., & Palermo, D. S. Mediation processes and the acquisition of linguistic structure. In U. Bellugi & R. Brown (Eds.), The acquisition of language. *Monographs of the Society for Research in Child Development,* 1964, *29,* (1), 141-169.

Johnson, M. K., Bransford, J. D., & Solomon, S. Memory for tacit implications of sentences. *Journal of Experimental Psychology,* 1973, *98,* 203-205.

Johnston, J. R. *The growth of propositional complexity: New data and critique.* Unpublished paper, Department of Psychology, University of California, Berkeley, 1976.

Just, M. A., & Carpenter, P. A. (Eds.). *Cognitive processes in comprehension.* Hillsdale, N.J.: Lawrence Erlbaum Associates, 1977.

Kafka, F. Ein Bericht für eine Akademie. 1917. [Reprinted in numerous anthologies and translations as *Report to an academy.*]

Kaplan, E. L. *The role of intonation in the acquisition of language.* Unpublished doctoral dissertation, Cornell University, 1969.

Kaplan, R. Augmented transition networks as psychological models of sentence comprehension. *Artificial Intelligence,* 1972, *3,* 77-100.

Kaplan, R. A general syntactic processor. In R. Rustin (Ed.), *Natural language processing.* Englewood Cliffs, N.J.: Prentice-Hall, Inc., 1973. Pp. 193-241.

Katz, J. J., & Postal, P. M. *An integrated theory of linguistic descriptions.* Cambridge, Mass.: M.I.T. Press, 1964.

Kay, P., & Sankoff, G. A language-universals approach to pidgins and creoles. In D. DeCamp & I. F. Hancock (Eds.), *Pidgins and creoles: Current trends and prospects.* Washington, D.C.: Georgetown University Press, 1974. Pp. 61-72.

Kellogg, W. N., & Kellogg, L. A. *The ape and the child.* New York: McGraw-Hill Book Co., 1933.

Kernan, K. T. *The acquisition of language by Samoan children.* Unpublished doctoral dissertation, University of California, Berkeley, 1969. [Working Paper No. 21 (1969), Language-Behavior Research Laboratory, University of California, Berkeley.]

Kimball, J. P. Seven principles of surface structure parsing in natural language. *Cognition,* 1973, *2,* 15-47.

Kimura, D. The asymmetry of the human brain. *Scientific American,* 1973, *228,* 70-78.

Kintsch, W. *The representation of meaning in memory.* Hillsdale, N.J.: Lawrence Erlbaum Associates, 1974.

Kintsch, W. *Memory and cognition.* New York: John Wiley & Son, Inc., 1977.

Kintsch, W., & van Dijk, T. A. Comment on rapelle et on résume des histoires. *Languages,* 1975, *9,* 98-116.

Kohlberg, L., Yaeger, J., & Hjertholm, E. Private speech: Four studies and a review of theories. *Child Development,* 1968, *39,* 691-736.

Köhler, W. *The mentality of apes.* New York: Harcourt, 1927.

Kohts, N. *Infant ape and human child (instincts, emotions, play, habits).* English appendix to Ladygina-Kots, N. N. *Ditya shimpanze i ditya cheloveka v ikh instinktakh, emotsiyakh, igrakh, privychkakh i vyrazitel'nykh dvizheniyakh.* Moscow: Gosudarstvennyy Darvinovskiy Muzey, 1935.

Kosslyn, S. M. Information representation in visual images. *Cognitive Psychology,* 1975, *7,* 341-370.

Kosslyn, S. M., & Pomerantz, J. R. Imagery, propositions, and the form of internal representation. *Cognitive Psychology,* 1977, *9,* 52-76.

Kuno, S. The position of relative clauses and conjunctions. *Linguistic Inquiry,* 1974, *5,* 117-136.

Labov, W. Contraction, deletion, and inherent variability of the English copula. *Language,* 1969, *45,* 715–762.

Labov, W. The logic of nonstandard English. In F. Williams (Ed.), *Language and poverty: Perspectives on a theme.* Chicago: Markham, 1970. Pp. 153–189.

Labov, W. The study of language in its social context. In J. Fishman (Ed.), *Advances in the sociology of language,* Vol. 1. The Hague: Mouton Publishers, 1971. Pp. 152–216.

Labov, W. *Language in the inner city: Studies in the Black English vernacular.* Philadelphia: University of Pennsylvania Press, 1972.

Lahey, M. (Ed.). *Readings in childhood language disorders.* New York: John Wiley & Sons, Inc., 1978.

Lakoff, G. *Irregularity in syntax.* New York: Holt, Rinehart & Winston, 1970.

Lakoff, G., & Thompson, H. Introducing cognitive grammar. In C. Cogen, H. Thompson, G. Thurgood, K. Whistler, & J. Wright (Eds.), *Proceedings of the First Annual Meeting of the Berkeley Linguistics Society.* Berkeley, Calif.: Berkeley Linguistics Society, 1975. Pp. 295–313.

Lantz, D. L., & Stefflre, V. Language and cognition revisited. *Journal of Abnormal and Social Psychology,* 1964, *69,* 472–481.

Lashley, K. S. The problem of serial order in behavior. In L. A. Jeffress (Ed.), *Cerebral mechanisms in behavior.* New York: John Wiley & Sons, Inc., 1951. Pp. 112–136. [Reprinted in S. Saporta (Ed.), *Psycholinguistics: A book of readings.* New York: Holt, Rinehart & Winston, 1961. Pp. 180–198.]

Lenneberg, E. H. Understanding language without ability to speak: A case report. *Journal of Abnormal and Social Psychology,* 1962, *65,* 419–425.

Lenneberg, E. H. *Biological foundations of language.* New York: John Wiley & Sons, Inc., 1967.

Lenneberg, E. H., & Lenneberg, E. (Eds.). *Foundations of language development: A multidisciplinary approach.* (Vols. 1 & 2). New York: Academic Press, Inc., 1975.

Leonard, L. B. *Meaning in child language: Issues in the study of early semantic development.* New York: Grune & Stratton, Inc., 1976.

Levy, J. Lateral specialization of the human brain: Behavioral manifestations and possible evolutionary basis. In J. Kiger, Jr. (Ed.), *The biology of behavior.* Corvallis, Oreg.: Oregon State University Press, 1972.

Li, C. N. (Ed.). *Subject and topic.* New York: Academic Press, Inc., 1976.

Li, C. N. (Ed.). *Mechanisms of syntactic change.* Austin: University of Texas Press, 1977.

Liberman, A. M., Cooper, F., Shankweiler, D., & Studdert-Kennedy, M. Perception of the speech code. *Psychological Review,* 1967, *74,* 431–459.

Lieberman, P., *On the origins of language: An introduction to the evolution of human speech.* New York: Macmillan, Inc., 1975.

Linden, E. *Apes, men, and language.* New York: Penguin Books, 1974.

Linton, M. Memory for real-world events. In D. A. Norman, D. E. Rumelhart, & the LNR Research Group (Eds.), *Explorations in cognition.* San Francisco: W. H. Freeman & Co., 1975. Pp. 376–404.

Luria, A. R. Razvitiye rechi v formirovaniye psikhicheskikh protsessov [Speech development in the formation of mental processes]. In *Psikhologicheskaya nauka v SSSR.* Vol. 1. Moscow: Izd-vo Akademii Pedagogicheskikh Nauk RSFSR, 1959. Pp. 516–577. [Translation in *Psychological science in the USSR* (Vol. 1). Washington, D.C.: U.S. Joint Publication Research Service No. 11466, 1961. Pp. 704–787.]

Luria, A. R. *Traumatic aphasia: Its syndromes, psychology and treatment.* The Hague: Mouton Publishers, 1970.

Macaulay, R. K. S. The myth of female superiority in language. *Journal of Child Language,* 1978, *5,* 353–74.

Macnamara, J. (Ed.). *Language learning and thought.* New York: Academic Press, Inc., 1977.

MacWhinney, B. Starting points. *Language,* 1977, *53,* 10-26.

MacWhinney, B. Processing a first language: The acquisition of morphophonology. *Monographs of the Society for Research in Child Development,* 1978, *39.*

Mandelbaum, D. B. (Ed.). *Selected writings of Edward Sapir in language, culture and personality.* Berkeley & Los Angeles: University of California Press, 1958.

Maratsos, M. P. How to get from words to sentences. In D. Aaronson & R. Rieber (Eds.), *Perspectives in psycholinguistics.* Hillsdale, N.J.: Lawrence Erlbaum Associates, in press.

Marin, O. S. M., Saffran, E. M., & Schwartz, M. F. Dissociations of language in aphasia: Implications for normal function. In S. Harnad, H. Steklis, & J. Lancaster (Eds.), *Origins and evolution of language and speech.* New York: New York Academy of Sciences, 1976.

McCawley, J. D. Prelexical syntax. In R. J. O'Brien (Ed.), *Linguistics: Developments of the sixties—Viewpoints of the seventies.* Monograph Series in Languages and Linguistics, 1971, *24,* 19-33. Washington, D.C.: Georgetown University Press.

McMahon, L. E. *Grammatical analysis as part of understanding a sentence.* Unpublished doctoral dissertation, Harvard University, 1963.

McNeill, D. Developmental psycholinguistics. In F. Smith & G. A. Miller (Eds.), *The genesis of language: A psycholinguistic approach.* Cambridge, Mass.: M.I.T. Press, 1966. Pp. 15-84.

McNeill, D. Semiotic extension. In R. L. Solso (Ed.), *Information processing and cognition: The Loyola Symposium.* Hillsdale, N.J.: Lawrence Erlbaum Associates, 1975. Pp. 351-380.

Mead, M. *Growing up in New Guinea.* New York: William Morrow, 1930.

Miller, G. A. The magical number seven, plus or minus two: Some limits on our capacity for processing information. *Psychological Review,* 1956, *63,* 81-97.

Miller, G. A. Some psychological studies of grammar. *American Psychologist,* 1962, *17,* 748-762.

Miller, G. A., Galanter, E., & Pribram, K. *Plans and the structure of behavior.* New York: Holt, Rinehart & Winston, 1960.

Miller, G. A., Heise, G., & Lichten, W. The intelligibility of speech as a function of the context of the test materials. *Journal of Experimental Psychology,* 1951, *41,* 329-335.

Molfese, D. L. Infant cerebral asymmetry. In S. J. Segalowitz & F. A. Gruber (Eds.), *Language development and neurological theory.* New York: Academic Press, Inc., 1977. Pp. 22-37.

Moore, T. E. (Ed.). *Cognitive development and the acquisition of language.* New York: Academic Press, Inc., 1973.

Morehead, D. M., & Morehead, A. E. (Eds.). *Normal and deficient child language.* Baltimore: University Park Press, 1976.

Nash, M. *Machine age Maya: The industrialization of a Guatemalan community.* Chicago: University of Chicago Press, 1967.

Nebes, R. D. Hemispheric specialization in commissurotomized man. *Psychological Bulletin,* 1974, *81,* 1-14.

Nelson, K. Structure and strategy in learning to talk. *Monographs of the Society for Research in Child Development,* 1973, *38.*

Neumann, G. Russenorwegisch und pidginenglish. *Nachrichten der Giessener Hochschulgesellschaft,* 1965, *34,* 219-234.

Newport, E. L., Gleitman, H., & Gleitman, L. R. Mother, I'd rather do it myself: Some effects and non-effects of maternal speech style. In C. E. Snow & C. A. Ferguson (Eds.), *Talking to children: Language input and acquisition.* Cambridge: Cambridge University Press, 1977. Pp. 109-150.

Norman, D. A., Rumelhart, D. E., & the LNR Research Group (Eds.). *Explorations in cognition.* San Francisco: W. H. Freeman & Co., 1975.

Ochs, E., & Schieffelin, B. B. (Eds.). *Developmental pragmatics.* New York: Academic Press, Inc., 1979.

Olson, G. M., & Clark, H. H. Research methods in psycholinguistics. In E. C. Carterette & M. P. Friedman (Eds.), *Handbook of perception.* Vol. 7, *Language and speech.* New York: Academic Press, Inc., 1976. Pp. 25–74.

Osgood, C. E. *Method and theory in experimental psychology.* New York: Oxford University Press, 1953. Part IV, pp. 601–727.

Osgood, C. E. Where do sentences come from? In D. D. Steinberg & L. A. Jakobovits (Eds.), *Semantics: An interdisciplinary reader in philosophy, linguistics, and psychology.* Cambridge: Cambridge University Press, 1971. Pp. 497–529.

Osgood, C. E., & Bock, J. K. Salience and sentencing: Some production principles. In S. Rosenberg (Ed.), *Sentence production: Development in research and theory.* Hillsdale, N.J.: Lawrence Erlbaum Associates, 1977.

Paivio, A. *Imagery and verbal processes.* New York: Holt, Rinehart & Winston, 1971.

Palermo, D. S., *Psychology of language.* Glenview, Ill.: Scott, Foresman & Co., 1978.

Papçun, G., Krashen, S., Terbeek, D., Remington, R., & Harshman, R. Is the left hemisphere specialized for speech, language, and/or something else? *Journal of the Acoustical Society of America,* 1974, *55,* 319–327.

Parisi, D., & Antinucci, F. Early language development: A second stage. In *Problèmes actuels en psycholinguistique.* Paris: Éditions du Centre National de la Recherche Scientifique, 1974. Pp. 129–143.

Parisi, D., & Antinucci, F. *Essentials of grammar.* New York: Academic Press, Inc., 1976. [Translation by E. Bates of *Elementi di grammatica.* Turin, Italy: Boringhieri, 1973.]

Patterson, F. The gestures of a gorilla: Language acquisition in another primate species. In Hamburg, J. Goodall, & McCown (Eds.), *Perspectives in human evolution* (Vol. IV). Menlo Park, Calif: Benjamin Press, 1977.

Pavlov, I. P. *Conditioned reflexes: An investigation of the physiological activity of the cerebral cortex.* London: Oxford University Press, 1927.

Penfield, W., & Rasmussen, T. *The cerebral cortex of man.* New York: Hafner, 1968.

Penfield, W., & Roberts, L. *Speech and brain mechanisms.* Princeton, N.J.: Princeton University Press, 1959.

Piaget, J. *Le langage et la pensée chez l'enfant.* Neuchâtel and Paris: Delachaux et Niestlé, 1923. [English translation by M. Gabain: *The language and thought of the child.* New York: Meridian Books, 1955.]

Piaget, J. *La formation du symbole chez l'enfant: Imitation, jeu et rêve, image et représentation.* Neuchâtel: Delachaux et Niestlé, 1946. [English translation by C. Gattegno & F. M. Hodgson: *Play, dreams, and imitation in childhood.* New York: W. W. Norton & Co., Inc., 1962.]

Piaget, J. *The child's construction of reality.* London: Routledge & Kegan Paul, 1955. [Translation of *La construction du réel chez l'enfant.* Neuchâtel: Delachaux et Niestlé, 1937.]

Piaget, J. *Comments on Vygotsky's critical remarks concerning "The Language and Thought of the Child" and "Judgment and Reasoning in the Child."* Cambridge, Mass.: M.I.T. Press, 1962.

Plato. *The collected dialogues of Plato.* (E. Hamilton & H. Cairns, Eds.) Bollingen Series LXXI. New York: Pantheon Books, 1961.

Pollack, I., & Pickett, J. M. Intelligibility of excerpts from fluent speech: Auditory vs. structural context. *Journal of Verbal Learning and Verbal Behavior,* 1964, *3,* 79–84.

Premack, A. J. *Why chimps can read.* New York: Harper & Row, 1976.

Premack, A. J., & Premack, D. Teaching language to an ape. *Scientific American,* 1972, *227,* 92–99.

Premack, D. *Intelligence in ape and man.* Hillsdale, N.J.: Lawrence Erlbaum Associates, 1976.

Pylyshyn, Z. W. What the mind's eye tells the mind's brain: A critique of mental imagery. *Psychological Bulletin,* 1973, *80,* 1-24.

Radulovic, L. *Acquisition of language: Studies of Dubrovnik children.* Unpublished doctoral dissertation, University of California, Berkeley, 1975.

Rosch, E. Natural categories. *Cognitive Psychology,* 1973, *4,* 328-350.

Rosch, E. Linguistic relativity. In A. Silverstein (Ed.), *Human communication: Theoretical explorations.* New York: Halsted Press, 1974. Pp. 95-121.

Rosch, E. Universals and cultural specifics in human categorization. In R. W. Brislin, S. Bochner, & W. J. Lonner (Eds.), *Cross cultural perspectives on learning.* New York: Halsted Press, 1975. Pp. 177-206.

Rosch, E., & Lloyd, B. B. (Eds.). *Cognition and categorization.* New York: Academic Press, Inc., 1978.

Rosch, E., & Mervis, C. B. Family resemblances: Studies in the internal structure of categories. *Cognitive Psychology,* 1975, *7,* 573-605.

Rosch, E., Mervis, C. B., Gray, W. D., Johnson, D. M., & Boyes-Braem, P. Basic objects in natural categories. *Cognitive Psychology,* 1976, *8,* 382-439.

Rosenberg, S. (Ed.). *Sentence production: Developments in research and theory.* New York: Halsted Press, 1977.

Ross, J. R. Paper presented to Berkeley Linguistic Society, University of California at Berkeley, 1975.

Rumbaugh, D. M. (Ed.). *Language learning by a chimpanzee: The Lana Project.* New York: Academic Press, Inc., 1977.

Rumbaugh, D. M., & Gill, T. V. The mastery of language-type skills by the chimpanzee *(Pan).* In S. Harnad, H. Steklis, & J. Lancaster (Eds.), *Origins and evolution of language and speech.* New York: New York Academy of Sciences, 1976. Pp. 562-578.

Rumelhart, D. E. Notes on a schema for stories. In D. G. Bobrow & A. M. Collins (Eds.), *Representation and understanding: Studies in cognitive science.* New York: Academic Press, 1975. Pp. 211-236.

Rumelhart, D. E. Understanding and summarizing brief stories. In D. LaBerge & S. J. Samuels (Eds.), *Basic processes in reading: Perception and comprehension.* Hillsdale, N.J.: Lawrence Erlbaum Associates, 1977.

Sachs, J. S. Recognition memory for syntactic and semantic aspects of connected discourse. *Perception and Psychophysics,* 1967, *2,* 437-442.

Sachs, J. S. Memory in reading and listening to discourse. *Memory and Cognition,* 1974, *2,* 95-100.

Sachs, J. S., & Truswell, L. Comprehension of two-word instructions by children in the one-word stage. *Papers and Reports on Child Language Development* (Department of Linguistics, Stanford University), 1976, *12,* 212-220.

Sankoff, G., & Brown, P. The origins of syntax in discourse: A case study of Tok Pisin relatives. *Language,* 1976, *52,* 631-666.

Sapir, E. Language and environment. *American Anthropologist,* 1912, n.s., 226-242. [Reprinted in D. G. Mandelbaum (Ed.), *Selected writings of Edward Sapir in language, culture and personality.* Berkeley and Los Angeles: University of California Press, 1958. Pp. 89-103.]

Sartre, J. P. *Nausea.* New York: New Directions Publishing Corporation, 1959. [English translation by L. Alexander of *La nausée.* Paris: Librairie Gallimard, 1938.]

Schachtel, E. G. *Metamorphosis.* New York: Basic Books, Inc., 1959. (Chap. 12: "On memory and childhood amnesia.")

Schank, R. C. Conceptual dependency: A theory of natural language understanding. *Cognitive Psychology,* 1972, *3,* 552-631.

Schank, R. C. Identification of conceptualizations underlying natural language. In R. C. Schank & K. M. Colby (Eds.), *Computer models of language and thought.* San Francisco: W. H. Freeman & Co., 1973.

Schank, R. C., & Abelson, R. P. *Scripts, plans, goals and understanding.* New York: Halsted Press, 1977.

Schank, R. C., & Wilensky, R. Response to Dresher and Hornstein. *Cognition,* 1977, *5,* 133–146.

Schiefelbusch, R. L., & Lloyd, L. L. (Eds.). *Language perspectives: Acquisition, retardation and intervention.* Baltimore: University Park Press, 1974.

Schiefelbusch, R. L. (Ed.). *Bases of language intervention.* Baltimore: University Park Press, 1978.

Schlesinger, I. M. Production of utterances and language acquisition. In D. I. Slobin (Ed.), *The ontogenesis of grammar: A theoretical symposium.* New York: Academic Press, Inc., 1971. Pp. 63–101.

Searle, J. R. *Speech acts.* Cambridge: Cambridge University Press, 1969.

Searle, J. R. A taxonomy of illocutionary acts. In K. Gunderson (Eds.), *Minnesota studies in the philosophy of language.* Minneapolis: University of Minnesota Press, 1975. Pp. 344–369.

Sechenov, I. M. Refleksy golovnogo mozga [Reflexes of the brain]. *Meditsinskiy vestnik,* 1863, *3,* 461–464, 493–512.

Segalowitz, S. J., & Gruber, F. A. (Eds.). *Language development and neurological theory.* New York: Academic Press, Inc., 1977.

Shatz, M. The relationship between cognitive processes and the development of communication skills. In B. Keasey (Ed.), *Nebraska Symposium on Motivation, 1977: Social cognitive development.* Lincoln: University of Nebraska Press, 1978.

Shepard, R. N., & Chipman, S. Second-order isomorphism of internal representations: Shapes of states. *Cognitive Psychology,* 1971, *1,* 1–17.

Sinclair, A., Jarvella, R., & Levelt, W. J. M. (Eds.). *The child's conception of language.* Berlin: Springer-Verlag, 1978.

Slobin, D. I. *Grammatical transformations in childhood and adulthood.* Unpublished doctoral dissertation, Harvard University, 1963.

Slobin, D. I. Grammatical transformations and sentence comprehension in childhood and adulthood. *Journal of Verbal Learning and Verbal Behavior,* 1966, *5,* 219–227. (a)

Slobin, D. I. Soviet psycholinguistics. In N. O'Connor (Ed.), *Present-day Russian psychology: A symposium by seven authors.* Oxford: Pergamon Press, 1966. Pp. 109–151. (b)

Slobin, D. I. The acquisition of Russian as a native language. In F. Smith & G. A. Miller (Eds.), *The genesis of language: A psycholinguistic approach.* Cambridge, Mass.: M.I.T. Press, 1966. Pp. 129–148. (c)

Slobin, D. I. (Ed.). *A field manual for cross-cultural study of the acquisition of communicative competence.* Berkeley: Language-Behavior Research Laboratory, University of California, 1967.

Slobin, D. I. Imitation and grammatical development in children. In N. S. Endler, L. R. Boulter, & H. Osser (Eds.), *Contemporary issues in developmental psychology.* New York: Holt, Rinehart and Winston, 1968. Pp. 437–443.

Slobin, D. I. Universals of grammatical development in children. In G. B. Flores d'Arcais & W. J. M. Levelt (Eds.), *Advances in psycholinguistics.* Amsterdam: North-Holland Publishing Co., 1970. Pp. 174–186.

Slobin, D. I. (Ed.). *The ontogenesis of grammar: A theoretical symposium.* New York: Academic Press, Inc., 1971.

Slobin, D. I. *Leopold's bibliography of child language.* Revised and augmented. Bloomington: Indiana University Press, 1972.

Slobin, D. I. Cognitive prerequisites for the acquisition of grammar. In C.A. Ferguson & D. I. Slobin (Eds.), *Studies of child language development.* New York: Holt, Rinehart & Winston, 1973. Pp. 175–208.

Slobin, D. I. *Psycholinguistics.* Glenview, Ill.: Scott, Foresman & Co., 1974.

Slobin, D. I. On the nature of talk to children. In E. H. Lenneberg & E.

Lenneberg (Eds.), *Foundations of language development: A multidisciplinary approach* (Vol. 1). New York: Academic Press, Inc., 1975. Pp. 283-298.

Slobin, D. I. Language change in childhood and in history. In J. Macnamara (Ed.), *Language learning and thought.* New York: Academic Press, Inc., 1977. Pp. 185-214.

Slobin, D. I. *Universal and particular in the acquisition of language.* Paper presented at workshop-conference on "Language Acquisition: State of the Art," Philadelphia, University of Pennsylvania, 1978. [To be published in proceedings edited by L. R. Gleitman & E. Wanner.]

Slobin, D. I., & Welsh, C. A. Elicited imitation as a research tool in developmental psycholinguistics. In C. A. Ferguson & D. I. Slobin (Eds.), *Studies of child language development.* New York: Holt, Rinehart & Winston, 1973. Pp. 485-497.

Smith, E. M., Brown, H. O., Toman, J. E. P., & Goodman, L. S. The lack of cerebral effects of *d*-tubocurarine. *Anesthesiology, 1947, 8,* 1-14.

Snow, C. E., & Ferguson, C. A. (Eds.). *Talking to children: Language input and acquisition.* Cambridge: Cambridge University Press, 1977.

Snyder, L. *Pragmatics in language-deficient children: Prelinguistic and early verbal performatives and presuppositions.* Unpublished doctoral dissertation, University of Colorado, 1975.

Spiker, C. C. Verbal factors in the discrimination learning of children. *Monographs of the Society for Research in Child Development, 1963, 28* (2), 53-68.

Spuhler, J. N. (Ed.). *The evolution of man's capacity for culture.* Detroit: Wayne State University Press, 1959.

Stern, W. *Zur Psychologie der Aussage.* Berlin: J. Guttentag, 1902.

Stevens, S. S. (Ed.). *Handbook of experimental psychology.* New York: John Wiley & Sons, Inc., 1951.

Stross, B. *The origin and evolution of language.* Dubuque, Iowa: William C. Brown Co., 1976.

van Dijk, T., & Kintsch, W. Cognitive psychology and discourse: Recalling and summarizing stories. In W. U. Dressler (Ed.), *Trends in text-linguistics.* New York and Berlin: De Gruyter, 1977.

Van Lawick-Goodall, J. *In the shadow of man.* Boston: Houghton Mifflin, 1971.

Vennemann, T. An explanation of drift. In C. N. Li (Ed.), *Word order and word order change.* Austin: University of Texas Press, 1975. Pp. 269-305.

Vygotsky, L. S. *Thought and language.* Cambridge, Mass.: M.I.T. Press/New York: John Wiley & Sons, Inc., 1962. [Edited translation by E. Hanfmann and G. Vakar of *Myshleniye i rech'.* Moscow: Sotsekgiz, 1934.]

Vygotsky, L. S. *Mind in society: The development of higher psychological processes.* (M. Cole, V. John-Steiner, S. Scribner, & E. Souberman, Eds.). Cambridge, Mass.: Harvard University Press, 1978.

Wada, J. A., Clarke, R., & Hamm, A. Cerebral hemispheric asymmetry in humans. *Archives of Neurology, 1975, 32,* 239-246.

Wanner, E., & Maratsos, M. An ATN approach to comprehension. In M. Halle, J. Bresnan, & G. A. Miller (Eds.), *Linguistic theory and psychological reality.* Cambridge, Mass.: M.I.T. Press, 1978.

Warren, R. M., & Warren, R. P. Auditory illusions and confusions. *Scientific American, 1970, 223,* 30-36.

Washburn, S. L. Speculations on the interrelations of the history of tools and biological evolution. In J. N. Spuhler (Ed.), *The evolution of man's capacity for culture.* Detroit: Wayne State University Press, 1959. Pp. 21-31.

Watson, J. B. Psychology as the behaviorist views it. *Psychological Review, 1913, 20,* 158-177.

Watt, W. C. On two hypotheses concerning psycholinguistics. In J. R. Hayes (Ed.), *Cognition and the development of language.* New York: John Wiley & Sons, Inc., 1970. Pp. 137-220.

Wells, G. Learning to code experience through language. *Journal of Child Language,* 1974, *1,* 243-270.

Whitaker, H. A. Neurolinguistics. In W. O. Dingwall (Ed.), *A survey of linguistic science.* College Park, Md.: Linguistics Program, University of Maryland, 1971. Pp. 137-251.

Whitaker, H., & Whitaker, H. A. *Studies in neurolinguistics.* Vol. 1 (1976), Vol. 2 (1977), Vol. 3 (1977), Vol. 4 (in press). New York: Academic Press, Inc.

Whorf, B. L. Science and linguistics. *Technology Review,* 1940, *42*(6), 227-231, 247-248. [Reprinted in Carroll, J. B. (Ed.), *Language, thought, and reality: Selected writings of Benjamin Lee Whorf.* Cambridge, Mass.: The Technology Press of Massachusetts Institute of Technology / New York: John Wiley & Sons, Inc., 1956. Pp. 207-219.]

Winograd, T. *Understanding natural language.* New York: Academic Press, Inc., 1972.

Winograd, T. A. Procedural models of language understanding. In R. C. Schank & K. M. Colby (Eds.), *Computer models of thought and language.* San Francisco: W. H. Freeman & Co., 1973. Pp. 152-186.

Winograd, T. Artificial intelligence: When will computers understand people? *Psychology Today,* 1974, *7*(12), 73-79.

Winograd, T. On some contested suppositions of generative linguistics about the scientific study of language: A response to Dresher and Hornstein's *On some supposed contributions of artificial intelligence to the scientific study of language. Cognition,* 1977, *5,* 151-179.

Witelson, S. F. Early hemisphere specialization and interhemisphere plasticity: An empirical and theoretical review. In S. J. Segalowitz & F. A. Gruber (Eds.), *Language development and neurological theory.* New York: Academic Press, Inc., 1977. Pp. 213-289.

Witelson, S. F., & Pallie, W. Left hemisphere specialization for language in the newborn: Neuroanatomical evidence of asymmetry. *Brain,* 1973, *96,* 641-646.

Wittgenstein, L. *Philosophical investigations.* Oxford: Basil Blackwell, 1953. [Translation by G. E. M. Anscombe of *Philosophische Untersuchungen,* completed in 1945. German text published by Suhrkamp Verlag, Frankfurt am Main, 1960.]

Wolfe, J. B. Effectiveness of token rewards for chimpanzees. *Comparative Psychology Monographs,* 1936, *12*(5).

Woolsey, C. N., & Settlage, P. H. Pattern of localization in the precentral motor cortex of *Macaca mulatta. Fed. Proc. Amer. Soc. exp. Biol.,* 1950, *9,* 140.

Wundt, W. *Die Sprache* (3rd ed.). Leipzig: Verlag von Wilhelm Engelmann, 1912.

Zakharova, A. V. Acquisition of forms of grammatical case by preschool children. In C. A. Ferguson & D. I. Slobin (Eds.), *Studies of child language development.* New York: Holt, Rinehart & Winston, Inc., 1973. Pp. 281-284. [Translation by G. Slobin of Usvoyeniye doshkol'nikami padezhnykh form. *Doklady Akademii Pedagogicheskikh Nauk RSFSR,* 1958, *2*(3), 81-84.]

NAME INDEX

SUBJECT INDEX